PRAISE FOR UP *All* NIGHT

"Fabulous Rhonda: full of life, full of fun, full of love. What a story! What a woman!"

— TWIGGY
Iconic Model, Designer

"Rhonda, as one Louisiana native to another, your story is as spicy as homemade gumbo and as sweet as a fresh beignet. You're living proof for women of every age and background that dreams can come true. Brava!"

— RANDY JACKSON
Musician, Record Producer,
Entrepreneur, and Original Judge
on American Idol

"This unstoppable hot mama of reinvention has a mind for moolah and a bod for Boomerpalooza butt-lifting panties! I'm sure Rhonda's book will keep me 'up all night'...as soon as I learn to read!"

— JUDY TENUTA
Grammy-Nominated Comedian

"Over all the years, I have watched Rhonda handle every situation with a great sense of humor and grace. Rhonda can always make you laugh with her quick wit. We can all glean inspiration from her personal journey."

— CHARLENE TILTON
Dallas Actress

"I met Rhonda twenty-five years ago when I booked her on her very first talk show. She made the most of that, and every moment, to get her to where she is today. This book is proof that there are no small parts in the game of life. Rhonda reminds us to live large, laugh a lot, and love what you do."

— **BARRY POZNICK**
Emmy Award Winner, President of Unscripted Television for MGM Television Group

---

"I cast Rhonda to play Kimmy Gibbler on *Full House* because I thought she was hilarious and headed for greatness. I was right."

— **JEFF FRANKLIN**
Emmy Award Winner, Creator of Full House *and* Fuller House

"Rhonda [is] a perpetual entrepreneur with a gift for building brands."

— **KAY KOPLOVITZ**
Founder of USA Network, First Female Network Television President

---

"Rhonda is gorgeously raucous. But get behind the blonde hair and the easy laugh and you'll find an intellect, a savvy, and a drive that is purposeful and singular. Rhonda came up the hard way, and she's a fearless streetfighter who can teach every young woman how to survive, thrive, and kick ass."

— **ANTHONY SULLIVAN**
OxiClean Spokesman, Author of You Get What You Pitch For

"*Up All Night* is a great read! Rhonda Shear obviously believes in following your dreams and never giving up!"

"The brass ring only comes around so many times in life, and if you don't grab on...next! My friend Rhonda Shear grabbed on and she is riding high now. We should all take a page from her playbook: grab the brass ring and hold on tight!"

"Rhonda Shear was not handed a silver spoon and a bundle of cash when she was born. She seized every opportunity that crossed her path and made the most of every single moment. She is so much more than just another Hollywood pretty face, although she certainly is a beauty. She has drive, determination, persistence, intelligence, and oodles of southern charm. Her smile can melt glaciers. Most importantly, she is generous with her heart. Rhonda has a lot to say and lessons to share that can inspire all of us to rise above the odds and be a star."

UP *All* NIGHT

From Hollywood Bombshell to Lingerie Mogul,
Life Lessons from an Accidental Feminist

www.mascotbooks.com

*Up All Night: From Hollywood Bombshell to Lingerie Mogul,
Life Lessons from an Accidental Feminist*

Cover Photography by Bryan Kasm
Hair and Makeup by Dollylocks (Alin Leslie and Caylin McDonie)

Second Edition

For more information, please contact:
Mascot Books
620 Herndon Parkway #320
Herndon, VA 20170
info@mascotbooks.com

CPSIA Code: PBANG1117B
Library of Congress Control Number: 2017911095
ISBN-13: 978-1-68401-501-6

Printed in the United States

UP ALL NIGHT

From Hollywood Bombshell to Lingerie Mogul, Life Lessons from an Accidental Feminist

RHONDA SHEAR

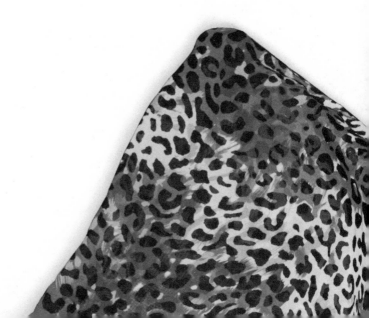

CONTENTS

To my mother, Jennie Weaker Shear, for all the life lessons, words of wisdom, and hours of dedication and sacrifice. Thank you for pushing for me to be my best and allowing me to follow my dreams.

ACKNOWLEDGMENTS

My life spans several careers and cities. These are the people who shaped my life and future:

My mom and dad, **Jennie** and **Wilbur Shear**, old school, loving, fiercely protective, adoring parents. They allowed me to follow my dreams as long as I had that "sheepskin" college diploma on the wall. I am who I am because of their strength, love, and absolute belief in me.

My dancing school teacher, **Ann Maucele** of Ann Maucele School of Dance. I wanted to be Miss Ann when I grew up. She was beautiful, graceful, classy, and strong. She encouraged me and pushed me to be my best. A strong woman who still is the matriarch of a very successful New Orleans family.

Mrs. Hamilton. A tiny forceful woman who guided me and believed in me from age fourteen on. She coordinated many local pageants, discovered me in a fabric store, and gently pushed me to follow my early dreams.

My beautiful sister, **Nona Shear Pailet**. She is sixteen years older than me and I followed her around like a puppy dog. I idolized her. She was an artist and English major and helped me with many a school project. Also, she was the encouragement behind me running for public office in New Orleans—a move that forever changed my life.

Her daughter and my niece, the gorgeous and talented **Brigitte Pailet**. She might be eleven years younger than me, but we are more sisters than aunt and niece. She has been my lifelong friend and confidante with a warm heart, and we have found ourselves in a million crazy situations.

My smart cousin, **Margo Weaker**. She is probably the reason Van and I are married. She knew him as a kid and they watched many a dance recital together. When we reunited in New Orleans, she told him, "If you let Rhonda get back on that plane to Los Angeles, the marriage won't happen." Luckily, he took her advice and we eloped two weeks later. Thank you, dear sweet cousin.

In Harvey Lembeck's comedy workshop, I met a young actor/comic named **Kenny Ellis**. I immediately identified him as the most talented guy in the class. Rubber-faced, could do an accent, and with a singing voice like an angel. I pursued him to be my scene study partner and then my first standup comedy partner. We were like Lucy and Ethel or Burns and Allen. We loved old Hollywood and snuck onto many a lot. He shaped my early years in Hollywood and I think I shaped his. I love you, Kenny.

Bobby Kelton, standup comic extraordinaire. Appearing on *The Tonight Show* with Johnny Carson twenty-one times, Bobby was a brilliant comedy writer. I became his worst nightmare when I started off as a young standup comic. He was my boyfriend and he was subjected to all my early club appearances. Also, I tried to push my way into his act constantly, like Lucy with Ricky. But he was always supportive, and we are still good friends.

Hilary Schacter changed my life completely. I was doing great in Hollywood, but had never gotten a regular part in a series until I met Hilary when he was a USA Network executive. He believed in me and hired me to be the star of *USA: Up All Night*. It was a run of almost eight years, and the show became a cult phenomenon. I also owe big thanks to producer Steve Feder and the founder/ trailblazer of USA, Kay Koplivitz, for giving me the opportunity and making me a household name for years.

A special shout-out to the men and women who made **USA: Up All Night** happen for years. They put up with me, pushed me, and challenged me. What an honor it was to work with these unbelievably talented people: **Lou Chagaris**, **Tommy Lynch**, **Kac Young**, **Marty Byk**, and **Vida Bauer**. I learned so much from each of you.

Two special souls pulled me together for years doing my makeup and hair. Besides being the most talented people in their fields they became and still are family to me: **Teri Groves** and **Walid Chaya**. Love you both.

When Van and I started Shear Enterprises, LLC, we were blessed to find the special people who came to work for us, helped us grow our company, and were loyal to a fault. We learned from them as well, and we call them true friends. Thank you **Jill Powers**, **Marie Crane**, and **Joy Ibey**.

It's hard to be on national TV in your skivvies. I've been there. I've had a loyal model and friend who has worked with my line on

HSN for more than fourteen years, never missing a show. She is ageless and the epitome of what my brand stands for. Thanks to **Regina "Gina" Marlow** for all the middle-of-the-night shows and hundreds of sleepless nights.

There are not enough words to express my thanks to the former CEO of HSN, **Mindy Grossman**. Her talent and vision are astounding, and she continues to inspire all of us with her leadership, charity work, and imagination. I thank her for believing in me and our company. She nominated me for Ernst & Young Entrepreneur of the Year, and when we took home that award, it put the Rhonda Shear brand into a completely different orbit. Mindy, when I grow up, I want to be you.

Then the most important thing a person can have in life, other than family, is true friends. I am a blessed with many. I have had friends who have been in my life from childhood until today—through the highest of highs and the lowest of lows. We have played together, been mischievous, confided in each other, partied together, and grieved together. I am so rich to have all of you in my life: **Donna Cohen Horowitz**, **Trudy Burch**, **Lisa Restivo**, **Carol Connors**, **Allegra Buffington**, and **Chuck Anderson**.

Ken Browning, my friend, advisor, and attorney. We go back many years in Hollywood. Thank you for being the spark that ignited the flame and inspired me to take a journey down memory lane to write this book. You said I should, and I did. Many thanks!

I am non-compliant by nature, something my friends know. When I decided to write a book and work with a co-writer, I interviewed quite a few...and then I decided on a man! I am the ultimate girly girl, but somehow, I knew **Tim Vandehey** would be able to tap into his inner diva. And I was right! Tim is an amazing father of two girls, a great husband, and most important for me a great writer with many bestsellers under his belt. I wanted the book to be a collaboration but to have my voice, and when I changed his beautiful writing, he never flinched. We got it done. A few great bottles of wine. Some visits to Florida. Lots of talking on the phone, emails, and texts. I thank Tim for making my dream come true. Now Van and I are friends with Tim and his beautiful family. Next, the screenplay!

Family is so important to me, and I am lucky to have a stepdaughter who has shared her smart and beautiful children with us. Being a grandparent is a blessing, and I thank **Emily Fagan** for **Kaegan**, **Kohen**, and my little dancer, **Kynslee**. I love y'all!

Finally, my incredible husband, **Van Fagan**. I'm never at a loss for words, but there would have to be a whole book thanking Van for everything he stands for and all he has done for me. We shaped each other as teens. We loved each other deeply. I never dreamed I would marry the first boy I kissed, but as an adult he has all the same qualities that made me love him as a kid. He's generous, handsome, strong, stubborn, smart, calm, always thinking things out and balancing my impulsiveness, but he's always willing to take a chance and be spontaneous. He puts up with all my shenanigans. He laughs at my jokes, listens to my hypochondriac ranting, teaches me things every day, can fix and build anything, and is still sexy as hell. Most important, he is my one and only true love and has always been supportive of me and my dreams. I love you, Daddy Dog!

PROLOGUE

*I*t might be the greatest picture I've ever taken, and I've taken a lot of pictures. In it, I have my head thrown back, eyes shining, gold gown glittering, a silver parasol cocked over one shoulder, and I'm letting loose with a full-throated N'awlins whoop that probably woke folks down in the Garden District.

Somebody took the photo during a post-midnight second line parade that sashayed down Bourbon Street in November of 2014 as I celebrated my personal "Diamond Jubilee"— my sixtieth birthday. I was surrounded by a lifetime's worth of beloved friends, every one of us surrendering to the NOLA spirit, inhibitions put in check by— ahem—generous helpings of the other kind of spirits. For those few hours, as the police cleared the way and the music played, we were the masters of the "city that care forgot."

But why is that picture my favorite? Why not something from my days as a working actress, when I could rock a bathing suit? Why not a promotional still from my nine years hosting USA: *Up All Night*, when I had the smarter-than-she-looked sex kitten act down to perfection and a nation of horny teenage boys eating out of my hand? Because while I don't really know what I was shouting (or who I was shouting at) as I strutted through the French Quarter, I like to think I was yelling, "I told you so!" to the world…

…to the New Orleans politicians who assumed I was too young

and naïve to be an effective candidate for office...

...to all the casting directors who thought I was too sexy or Jewish to be a believable TV ingénue...

...to all the comedy club owners who told me I was too pretty to be funny, including the one who told me I should "go back to law school"...

...to all the naysayers who thought I was too talentless to make a late-night B-movie comedy sketch show anything more than a curiosity...

...to everyone who assumed that I was too inexperienced to ever make it as an entrepreneur...

...to all the people who dismissed me as too ethnic, too sexy, too unmanageable—too *female*—to ever achieve my dreams. Because I had a lot of dreams.

I wanted to reign as a beauty queen, become the next Lucille Ball, and star in my own one-woman Las Vegas comedy extravaganza. I wanted to live the good life, be swept off my feet by the love of my life, and enjoy just the tiniest taste of what it was like to be a star. I wanted to help other women find better lives, create beauty, and even help to change the world. I wanted it all on my terms, which isn't asking too much, right?

But here's the thing that made that diamond jubilee as sweet as the powdered sugar on a fresh-baked beignet: *I did all of it.* I thumbed my nose at everyone who ever tried to put me in a box, tell me what I couldn't do, or impose limits on me because I'm a woman. I built a career as a working actress out of sheer chutzpah and a tireless work ethic. I scandalized the genteel New Orleans establishment by posing for *Playboy* and becoming the youngest person ever to run for office in Louisiana...and nearly winning.

I traded jokes with Robin Williams and headlined as a

comedian in Vegas. I kissed the Fonz. I got the red carpet, limo, paparazzi-shouting-my-name treatment. I reunited with my childhood sweetheart after a quarter-century apart. I started a business that turned into an empire and bought me my dream home in a tropical paradise. I've hobnobbed with George Burns and Bob Hope, Johnny Carson and Muhammad Ali, Liza Minelli and Morgan Freeman. And I've done my part to help women look, feel, and live better.

I made it. That's what that woman was shouting, the woman who was strutting down Bourbon, head held high, smiling with pure joy, blessed and lucky to be alive and in love and surrounded by people who love her back.

The Proof is in the People

My birthday bash at the Omni Royal Orleans Hotel was a gathering of a few hundred of those special people and was quite a celebration. Everybody danced to Rockin' Doopsie and the Zydeco Twisters, one of the best bands in New Orleans. My dear friend, comedian Carole Montgomery, shocked me by appearing out of nowhere and then roasting me in front of a cheering crowd, practically making me pee and cry at the same time.

I hugged childhood friends Cindy Denn, Jan Brown, Lisa Restivo, and Donna Horowitz until they couldn't breathe. I got a sash, sparkly crown, and a diamond ring big enough to cast a shadow. Wonderful comedian Ludo Vika put in an appearance. We had gorgeous go-go dancers and a show by the all-male dance troupe the 610 Stompers (in their dorky athletic shorts and red sateen jackets) that left everybody rolling in the aisles. My confidante, first comedy partner, and beloved friend of friends, the golden-voiced Kenny Ellis, took the mic and brought tears to my eyes. A camera crew from the E! reality show *New Money* recorded the entire spectacle for posterity.

Behind it all was the love of my life, my husband, business partner, and childhood sweetheart, Van Fagan. We hugged and kissed and danced the night away surrounded by music and champagne and food and laughter. It was an embarrassment of riches to be wrapped in the affection of so many accomplished people, all come down to the Crescent City to celebrate li'l old me. It was humbling, and it really got me thinking.

If you can earn people's love and remain worthy of it over the years and decades, that's proof that you must be doing something right. Somehow, in spite of Hollywood, beauty pageants, the comedy circuit, HSN, and all the rest, I feel like I've stayed the same bawdy, laugh-a-second New Orleans girl who loved giving dirty-minded old pageant judges heart attacks when I swung around at the end of a runway to reveal my curvy caboose. I think I've been able to remain true to myself and the values my mother and father taught me from beginning to end.

A Successful Woman in a Man's World

It wasn't easy. Being a young woman in entertainment, especially back in the 1970s and 1980s, meant having a lot of doors slammed in your face. Plenty of girls lost heart, gave up, and went home. But not me. My response to having one door slammed in my face was to immediately wedge another one open with my smile, smarts, and a little bit of cleavage (if necessary). Nobody taught me how to do it all, because I've never known anyone who's been a beauty queen, candidate for public office, model, actress, comedian, dancer, hostess, businesswoman, designer, philanthropist, political operator, mentor, and diva, all rolled into one.

Whew, that's a lot of hats! No wonder my neck gets tired.

But what's really amazing to me is that I've done all those things while being a woman. When I was growing up in New Orleans, and when I came to Los Angeles to launch my acting career, the entertainment world valued women mostly for our sexuality and beauty. The Hollywood Jiggle was alive and well; women were sex objects, especially in the over-the-top 1980s of big shoulder pads, big hair, and big boobs. I lost count of how many auditions—legitimate auditions at NBC, CBS, and ABC—that I had to attend in a bikini, including making a 360-degree turn so the casting people could get a look at my body from all sides. Can you imagine that today?

During my career, I definitely cultivated a sex kitten image, but I did it on my own terms. I knew exactly what I was doing: using the male-dominated system even while it thought it was using me, because that brought me closer to my goal of being a working actress. I also pushed myself to use my funny side and break away from the image of the brainless beauty queen. I wasn't afraid to look silly, act silly, or make faces—things that sexy women in the 1980s and 1990s weren't supposed to do. I've always been comfortable poking fun at myself. After all, nobody knows my many flaws better than I do.

From the beginning, I adored being funny. Comedy was my natural element. I craved experience that might one day lead to the realization of my dream: starring in my own sitcom like my idols, I Dream of Jeannie's Barbara Eden and Bewitched's Elizabeth Montgomery. They were beautiful and funny, but their characters were also smart and savvy. Trouble was, my ambition was a direct violation of the Hollywood Boys' Club bylaws, which stated that sexy girls were to be ogled, not heard. According to the prevailing wisdom, a woman couldn't be sultry and land a sharp one-liner at the same time.

But comedy was my comfort zone. I love to laugh, and making other people laugh is even better. So what if it wasn't proper for an attractive gal to stand on stage and talk about sex? If I had given the slightest damn about what was proper, I would never have spent an hour in bed with Max Von Sydow. Comedy was my first love, so I didn't listen to the people who told me it was a dead end. I hit the road and strutted my "too sexy for comedy" butt all the way up to headliner status at major venues all over America. Standup even supported Van and me when our finances fell out from beneath us just one month into our new marriage.

Take that, boys' club.

Of course, entertainment today isn't exactly a sexism-free feminist paradise, but things are better. Women like Tina Fey, Chelsea Handler, and Amy Schumer are becoming power players valued for their talent, intelligence, business-savvy, and drive instead of just their looks. The point is, women can do anything, and if you let someone tell you that you're not capable of something because of how you look, or that your looks are all you have to offer, you're selling yourself short and missing out on your true potential.

Make Your Own Rules

Instead, this book is about tapping that potential and using it to realize *every one* of your dreams. I'm proud to have lived loud and large and fearlessly, and that's something I'd like you—and every woman—to be able to do, too.

That's why I've written this. Through a lifetime of stories, characters, observations, and memories, I'll share with you the most important lesson I've ever learned: if you want a spectacular life, don't be limited by the rules that society or other people set down. Instead, make your own. Hell, I've broken every rule society sets down for women and smiled while I did it.

I learned the sex kitten game fast and then turned the tables, using my looks and sex appeal to get people's attention and then disarming them with my wit and smarts. The sheer surprise of it never failed to open doors. My ability to break out of the box Hollywood wanted to put me in is why for twenty-four years I was the epitome of a working actress. I also never stopped working, because I didn't wait around for other people to make things happen for me. I built my career myself, on my terms. I had a certain kind of life in mind, and I wasn't about to listen to anyone who told me I couldn't have it.

Along the way, I figured out something that I think a lot of women miss: being yourself means being *every version of yourself*. Every woman is a multitude; we're all complicated and multifaceted and capable of so much more than even we realize. Over the years, I've discovered a lot of different Rhondas. There's old-fashioned Rhonda, who believes in grace, dignity, manners, and romance and who's surprisingly shy when she's not standing in front of an audience of five hundred strangers. There's unfiltered, fuck-you Rhonda, who has an endless supply of delicious curse words and leaves an hourglass-shaped hole in whatever stands between her and what she wants.

There's sex kitten Rhonda, the cleavage-for-days, helium-voiced, flirty, big-haired blonde from *USA: Up All Night* who was a lot smarter than she seemed on the surface. If you believed I was really her, then I did what I set out to do. Then there's misunderstood Rhonda, the good girl trapped in a bad girl's body. I look one way but act another, and as with most women, there's a lot more hidden just beneath the surface. My mother (a nonpareil prick teaser herself) taught me the art of the flirt at an early age, and today I'm a black belt at it. I love flirting and giving people compliments. It's about making people feel good about themselves. That's using your powers for good.

All those Rhondas are me. I want this book to inspire you to be all the versions of yourself and to love each version. You're lucky enough to be living in a time when you can define who you are, transcend your appearance and age, and build the life you envision. You don't have to be "just" a wife or mother, though there's nothing wrong with either. You can be anything you dream of being, and no man has the power to tell you otherwise.

You don't have to compromise or take no for an answer. I never did, ever. I took chances, made mistakes, got myself in a few scary scrapes (and a lot of funny ones), had my heart broken, and felt the sting of rejection. All those years and pivotal moments were a part of growing up and getting me ready for the life I lead today. You think you've done silly or embarrassing things in your life? I'll show you silly and embarrassing! But I'll also show you how all that silliness can be a wonderful part of the flavor of life. I'll show you how living without fear or shame made me who I am, and introduce you to some of the generous, brilliant, unbelievably talented people who helped me perfect my Rhonda recipe.

My story is all about the American dream. It's about love, ambition, overcoming fear, and discovering strength, with a side of sexy. So if you're ready for a fun, juicy romp, pull back your sheets, slide into bed, and cozy up.

We might even stay UP...all night!

Rhonda Shear

St. Petersburg, Florida

PART One
BIG EASY YEARS

LESSON ONE
Beauty Matters

—— In which our heroine comes of age in New Orleans under the watchful eye of a sexy mom, learns to dance, gets bitten by the showbiz bug, reigns as Tarpon Rodeo Queen, becomes the would-be Lolita of a powerful politician, and discovers the power of beauty and sexuality. ——

New Orleans is the greatest show on Earth. Just ask anyone who has awakened on Bourbon Street covered in beads and with no idea how the hell they got there. Like the taste of chicory coffee, the flavor and spirit of New Orleans—the city where I was born, came of age, and met the love of my life—will never leave me. Why would I want it to? It's part of my soul.

My family was not your typical American clan. We were *yats*, a term derived from the saying, "Where ya at?", part of the patois and culture that define New Orleans. Our childhood drives around the Big Easy, for example, would have given most parents a heart attack. We would cruise down Rue du Bourbon in my father's big Oldsmobile and past the French Quarter strip clubs. The doors and windows would be wide open, displaying the girls' wares for everyone to see. Daddy would laugh and shout, "Look at the dancing girls!"

My brothers, Mel and Fred, and my sister, Nona, and I, we absolutely loved it. Go cups (the enlightened practice of giving bar patrons disposable cups to take their drinks into the street), *lagniappe* (pronounced "LAN-yap," an indigenous/Creole word meaning "a little something extra"), Mardi Gras—it was all part of our normal. The New England Puritanism that shaped so much of the rest of the country never made it down the Mississippi to the shores of Lake Pontchartrain. Instead, you have a city that's equal parts bawdy and genteel, American and Creole, Southern conservative and surprisingly moral. N'awlins is a unique blend of sweet and spicy. Take off her Mardi Gras mask and you'll find endless contradictions.

It was a marvelous, festive, magical place to grow up. The city has its own unique accent: a little Bronx, a little Boston, a little bayou. It has its signature food, gumbo, which describes the infusion of French, Acadian, Creole, African, and Native American cultures as much as the blend of onions, bell peppers, celery (often called the "holy trinity"), seafood, spices, and a good dark roux. It has its own soul: all-night bars and barkers in the French Quarter, voodoo, above-ground graveyards with moss-covered mausoleums, and jazz.

You can keep your safe, sanitized suburbs and the quiet life. New Orleans taught me and my siblings how to *live*.

Jennie and Wilbur

I guess it's not surprising that I came from such a place. What might be surprising is that despite being born into such a sensual environment, I grew up terrified of sex. I was a shy, protected girl, and my mother, Jennie Weaker Shear, was determined to keep me that way. A first-generation New Orleanian, my mom was a great beauty with a drop-dead figure who adored Betty Grable and owned a swimsuit similar to the one Grable wore in her famous "over the shoulder" pinup shot.

(Later in life, I found out that Mom had posed for a series of gorgeous semi-nude boudoir photos for my amateur photographer father. Coincidentally—or not—some of the most successful pieces in my Rhonda Shear Intimates line are a Pin-Up Panty and Bra that look a lot like what my mom wore in her pinup photos.)

Mom was raised by my widowed grandmother, the forgotten baby in a crowded household. She escaped the pressure of four overbearing older brothers by losing herself at the movies. Iconic beauties like Betty Grable, Esther Williams, and Rhonda Flemming (who I was named after) were her companions and inspiration, as one day, they would become mine. Mom ended up marrying at nineteen, in part because she dearly loved my dad, but also because she wanted to escape her brothers' constant oppression.

Mom was a lot tougher than her beauty suggested; years later, I was shocked to find out that twice she'd had to fend off rape attempts. From Grandma Fanny to Mom, the Weaker women excelled both in their looks and in the brains department.

From the time she was a young girl, beauty was everything to my mother. She would wear red lipstick like the pinup girls she admired, reapplying it even after her brothers would wipe it off. Beauty was her way of escaping the austerity of her family life. Later, when she was about fifteen, she entered a local beauty contest. She didn't even walk across the stage, but her beauty caught the eye of the judges and she won, and a lifelong lover of beauty pageants was born. But it really drove her brothers off the deep end when she eloped with a Reform Jew named Wilbur Shear.

Their meeting was like something from classic television. They were on a double date: she with my dad's cousin Carl, he with a girl no one remembers. But from the moment Wilbur saw my mother he was smitten. He was driving, and he made sure to drop her off at home last. He got her number, wooed her, sang to her, and six months later they were married.

My father was also a New Orleans native, part of a barely-visible subculture of New Orleans Jews. After he married my mother, Dad worked for the government, the weather bureau, and eventually for her family's auto parts business. But when he was fifty, he missed one week of work to have surgery, and his brother-in-law fired him. Imagine being a fifty-year-old man with four kids to feed, a middle-class lifestyle to maintain, and no job. My parents wanted all their kids to graduate from college, but that takes money.

However, I get my dogged persistence from my father. He borrowed $15,000 from a family friend and started his own truck supply company, Fleet Parts and Equipment. It thrived, and with the money from that business, Dad put all of us through college; my two brothers even ran the business alongside him for many years. Unfortunately, while my father saw some of my successes, he died of a heart attack in 1984 at the age of 69. His untimely death—and my absence when he passed—still haunts me. But while I adored my father, I was and am my mother's daughter.

Beauty Was My Religion

I was born Rhonda Honey Shear on November 12, 1954, when my mother was thirty-seven—at the time, late in life to be giving birth. I may have been born into a Jewish family, but beauty was my religion, and my mother's love of all things beautiful and feminine made her my high priestess. I was a love child, a mistake, but my mother and father couldn't have been more delighted to have a baby to dress up and pamper. And was I ever pampered, protected, and babied!

From the beginning, Mom dressed me like a doll with long, corkscrew curls and later sent me to dancing and modeling classes. I began lessons at the Ann Maucele School of Dance at the age of two. Ballet, tap, jazz, and acrobatics filled my days with twirls and my nights with dreams of footlights. With all this, from the time I got out of diapers, I was a Southern belle. Mel and Fred tried to make me a tomboy, even teaching me to throw a mean spiral with a football, but I threw it in heels and a mini-dress.

(Years later, when I auditioned to be a cheerleader in a Budweiser TV commercial, what impressed the director—and probably got me the job—was that I could throw that tight spiral.)

But my mother was really grooming me to marry a prince. For real. She wanted me to marry royalty. In the late '90s we both went on the *Maury Povich Show* for a special Mother's Day show, and she told Maury, "I want my daughter to marry Prince Charles." Maury replied, "But he's married." To the audience's delight, Mom snapped, "Eh, small detail." The crowd roared.

Mom badly wanted me to be a wealthy socialite in New York or California, someone who would only have the finest things. She never wanted me to suffer or go through what she did as a teen. Parents usually want their kids to do better in life than they did, but I wasn't comfortable with that sort of lifestyle. I've dated some incredibly wealthy men in my life, including several billionaires, but I always found that I had more in common with their security guards or domestic help than I did with them.

Shear Honesty: *It might seem like hypocrisy to live in a waterfront mansion (which I do), drive a Bentley (which I do, sometimes), and talk about relating better to working-class folks. But it's really not. There's a big difference between enjoying fine, expensive things and feeling like you're entitled to them. I love my lifestyle; it's the payoff for years of endless work and sacrifice. But none of it matters more than being a good person, being around other good people, helping others, or just sitting around drinking wine with dear friends. That's wealth. Don't lose sight of what's important: health, family, friends, laughter.*

Center of the Social Circle

When I went into the first grade, the calendar was flipping over to 1960 and change was in the air, sort of. But while things were changing all over the country, New Orleans somehow either changed more slowly or not at all. I don't know if it's the syrupy air, the French-tinged *argot*, or just Deep South stubbornness, but the Crescent City has never been quick to change. When you grow up there, you think Mardi Gras is normal. It's such a festive, anything-goes city. We would go to the French Market on Decatur Street and get coffee and beignets from all-night coffee shops with carhops. We would even do this late on a school night; when our parents said, "How about some coffee and beignets?" we would jump in the car in our PJs and head downtown at midnight.

But the center of our social life was Mom. She was funny and opinionated and sharp-tongued, qualities I definitely inherited. The kids in the neighborhood loved her because she loved hosting parties and was a terrific cook. When she fried chicken, the aroma would escape into the street, and before long every kid in the neighborhood was hovering at our back door. She loved feeding them, and they all loved Miss Jennie.

Mom also gave all the teen girls expert dating and flirting advice. To this day, my friends remind me about how my mom would sit them down in the kitchen and dispense dating wisdom. "Be just a little late when your date comes to get you. Make them wait just a little bit," she would drawl. Mom loved young people and it seemed like my friends and my siblings' friends could talk to her about anything. We always had a household full of kids and teenagers, and I think they enjoyed her company more than ours. It was cool that they had an adult they could confide in more than they could in their own parents. Everyone called my mom "Miss Jennie," and her advice was free. If she'd been born into this century, she'd have her own blog: "Miss Jennie's Views on Life and Love."

I grew up with parties, parties, and more parties. To this day, I get like a kid on Christmas Eve at the prospect of a party, even when I'm hosting it. All the kids would come to the Shear house. In part, that was so my folks could keep a watchful eye on us, but they also loved hosting. Sororities and fraternities were huge in New Orleans high schools at that time, and most of the meetings and parties, especially pool parties, wound up at our home. This is when I learned one of my first big lessons: **there is power in beauty.**

When it came to beauty and sexuality, my mother was a walking contradiction. I mean that literally. She had a drop-dead figure and knew how to dress to accentuate it. You'd see her walking down the street with her shoulders back and her head up like a movie star, and somehow, she could make a figure eight with her butt. People called it the "Jennie Walk." More than once, I saw her *literally stop traffic* with the power of her hips. Her favorite saying was, "Honey, let them look, but they can't touch." She loved the idea of being dazzling but unattainable.

By the time I was in grade school, she was teaching me what it meant to be a Southern belle: be beautiful and graceful and sexy, be a lady, never use bad language. (I violate that one all the time, but fuck it.) Flirt all you want, but don't lose your virginity 'til you're married. To Miss Jennie, beauty meant virtue. She had to look great at all times, makeup done and hair coiffed. She would cook wearing high heels and a dress like Marilyn Monroe...with a cigarette in one hand. She was a mesmerizing package.

However, Mom's near-miss with rape left her terrified that I would be sexually assaulted. She told me the facts of life at a young age so, in case someone approached me inappropriately, I would know what was going on. When I approached dating age, she warned me never to let a boy put his hand above my knee. Her constant alarms about men and their nefarious intentions made me fearful about sex for years, but they also taught me something that would prove invaluable in Hollywood: **I didn't have to spread my legs to get what I wanted. It was more effective to be alluring, seductive, and just a little bit out of reach.** Mom taught me what sexy really is, and how powerful it is.

Tiny Dancer

In the summer between sixth and seventh grades, I discovered just how powerful my sexuality could be. I got my period and started "developing." My brothers made fun of me, chanting, "Rhonda is rusting! Rhonda is rusting!" which I hated. But while I didn't fully understand what was happening, I knew my body was changing, and those changes had an immediate effect on the people around me.

In primary school, the other kids had made fun of me for my unruly, frizzy hair. But when I started middle school, I became very, very popular...especially with boys. The power of boobs and the male preoccupation with them—right, ladies? In no time, I had a figure as alluring as my mother's, which of course led some people to presume that I was a different kind of gal than I was. Nothing could have been further from the truth, but all the attention did start to give me more confidence.

I've used that experience in my work as a clothing designer. I understand that when undergarments make a woman feel better about herself, she will project confidence in her daily life and be more beautiful to herself and others.

With my new confidence, I shed some of my natural shyness and toyed with being a little flirty. This was a revelation! The more outgoing I was, the more people liked me. I had a lot of friends, but my most memorable junior high moment came during the ninth grade talent contest when I danced to the song "The Stripper." Remember, I had been in dance classes from the age of two. Mom had thought dance would give me poise and femininity, and she was right; I was the perfect little dancer. Performing was in my blood, and I worked it in that talent show!

The auditorium was the most crowded it had ever been for a talent contest. Even the teachers pushed in to see what I was going to do. I did a complicated, Bob Fosse–style jazz routine. No stripping, of course, though I think at the end I removed a glove. When I finished, the place went crazy, though I don't remember if I won or not. It didn't matter. I still get former teachers and students reaching out to me on social media, nearly fifty years later, to tell me how great my performance was. Apparently, I made an impression.

I thought that dance would be my major when I went to college and that I would move on to a career as a choreographer. That didn't happen, but dancing taught me grace and poise, how to move and understand my body—skills that are vital for physical comedy, acting, and modeling. I also trained as an acrobat and was actually a contortionist. I know...insert your own racy joke here. But I used my flexibility many times in my early years auditioning in LA. Dancing also taught me how to mug and show personality in my face, not just in my footwork.

To my delight, the old hoofer skills are still there. A few years ago, I appeared in a St. Petersburg–area *Dancing with the Stars* charity and won Best Female Dancer. The mugging didn't hurt: dancing with my feet, and flirting with my eyes. At the end of my routine, I had my group shoot cash and Mardi Gras beads onto the stage. I love showmanship!

The funny thing is that in junior high school, one of my teachers wrote in my yearbook: "Rhonda, you cannot tap dance your way through life." But all the things nobody thought I could do—being an entertainer, being in comedy, making a living as a performer—I've actually done.

I guess I get the last laugh, right, Mrs. Martin?

FOURTH WALL BREAK!

If there's a recurring theme in my life, it began here. The classic, "Rhonda, you can't do things that way" argument, no reason given. I think this is a gender-neutral thing; young guys probably hear it as much as girls. It might be because people don't really believe something can be done until someone does it, but I think it's more about envy and fear. You, the speaker, weren't able to achieve your dreams, and you're terrified that I'll achieve mine. I'm truly sorry, but don't make my dreams your collateral damage.

If You Can't Be a Princess, Be a Queen

Life and school rolled on. Integration came to my high school and I found myself instantly unpopular with some of the black girls, who didn't like the attention I was getting from the black boys. When my parents found out that several girls had threatened to beat me up, they moved me to an all-girls Catholic school, Mount Carmel.

So I entered the world of pleated skirt uniforms and nuns. Actually, the nuns were wonderful, and it was also at Mount Carmel that I met one of my lifelong best friends, Lisa Restivo. The Italian population in New Orleans is huge, and Lisa and her parents were typical New Orleans Italian. She and her family were connected with a certain Italian subculture, if you know what I mean. I went on to date a guy named Joe Marcello Jr., who was well-known down south. He turned me onto calamari and veal piccata, and we often went to La Riviera, where he always sat with his back to the wall.

Shear Honesty: *True-blue girlfriends are important, especially as you get older. Even though I had a sexy, femme fatale image in Hollywood, I always had great girlfriends like Lisa, many of whom came to my sixtieth birthday party. Today, helping women is my livelihood. Women are the best.* **Find women whom you could count on to show up at 2:00 a.m. to help you bury a body, and hold onto them with everything you've got.**

Life was becoming colorful and fun. I was dancing for the New Orleans Saints' dance team, The Mam'selles, and doing local commercials. I'd done a couple of small film roles and earned my Screen Actors Guild card, so my career seemed to be starting. I was becoming a very minor local celebrity. However, the "minor" part was about to change: Mom and I had discovered beauty pageants.

For years, I'd been aware of the beauty pageant culture that permeated New Orleans like the smells of Confederate jasmine, coffee, sweet olive, cut grass, angel's trumpet, and horse manure permeate the French Quarter. I turned sixteen in 1971, and while feminism may have been inspiring women to burn bras in other parts of the country (something I can't even *imagine* doing, dear Lord), in the Crescent City there was a flourishing subculture dedicated to celebrating the pulchritude of the young Southern belle.

It was sexist, adorable, and funny at the same time. There were beauty pageants *everywhere*, and I'm not talking about the big, prestigious competitions like Miss Louisiana or Miss New Orleans. I'm talking about tiny pageants, held mostly in parks in the sweltering humidity, like Miss New Orleans Fraternal Order of Police or Miss Ed Brauner's American Legion Post 307. I was a Queen of Endymion (a prestigious Mardi Gras Krewe) and Miss New Orleans Food Festival. There was a pageant for just about every parish (that's Louisianian for "county") like Jefferson or Baton Rouge. If you had a carnival society or a ladies' auxiliary club, you probably put on a pageant with a little picnic as an annual fundraiser.

These weren't the awful child beauty pageants we see in reality shows like *Here Comes Honey Boo-Boo*. This was all very innocent. Some of these pageant sponsors were very conservative, had been holding their pageants for decades, and took them *very* seriously. For young, pretty New Orleans girls with beautiful smiles and a flair for being on stage, pageants were a wonderful opportunity to learn poise and charm, make new friends, get our names in the paper, and make some important contacts. That's certainly what happened to me, although I had no idea how important pageants would become for my career.

It may come as a surprise that my mother didn't push me into beauty pageants. True, she loved beauty and loved being a pageant mom—shopping for the right gowns, pumps, and swimsuits—but she loved me more. She wanted me to value my mind as much as my figure. Ultimately, participating was my decision.

One day when I was fifteen years old, we were in a fabric store and ran into this woman, Mrs. Hamilton, who was maybe four-foot-nine with a shrill little voice. She happened to coordinate beauty pageants for various New Orleans organizations, and when she saw me she stopped us and said, "Your daughter needs to be in pageants," like she was reciting a law of nature.

I had never really been interested in beauty pageants. The only one I wanted to win was Miss Dance of Louisiana, because that was about dancing talent. I had no "traditional" beauty pageant skills: walking, smiling, and so on. I could do those things, of course; I was proud of my ability to walk and chew gum at the same time. But beauty pageants? They seemed empty-headed and silly, for ditzy girls who weren't as smart and quick-witted as I was. Well, Mom took care of things. She put one hand on a hip and replied, "Oh no, Rhonda's too young."

Mrs. Hamilton wasn't discouraged. "Well, take her home and feed her some peanut butter so we can fill her out a bit, especially at the top, and call me when she's sixteen," she said. Yes, there was a time when someone would want to fill out a young lady and not have her be waif-thin with a "thigh gap!" We went home, but over the next few months Mrs. Hamilton would check up on us. She would call and ask, "Is Rhonda ready yet?" It was flattering; she clearly saw something in me that I didn't see in myself.

As an aside, beauty pageants are definitely not relics of the past in New Orleans, though in keeping with the spirit of the city, they have become a lot more playful and risqué. These days, you can find a parody fundraiser pageant called Mr. Legs, which features male contestants in silly costumes and short-shorts, and the Miss Curvaceous Crustacean Beauty Pageant, which is only open to crabs. The New Orleans pageant spirit lives on.

Delightful Absurdities

When I turned sixteen, my mother told me that I could enter a pageant if I wanted to, as long as I promised to be a good sport if I didn't win. Good sportsmanship was one of the most important lessons she taught me: no matter what happens, you say hello, congratulate everybody, hug, and be gracious. **You don't need money to have class.**

I decided to give the pageant a try, although I had no idea what I was doing. I knew how to carry myself and I was in shape from my dancing, but as far as how to do the pageant walk—no clue. Somehow, I took first runner-up. That gave me a taste of glory, and at my next pageant, I won. Now I was *hooked*. I got a crown and a trophy and a banner, the teenage girl equivalent of getting a new toy. I got a write-up and photo in the *New Orleans Times-Picayune* and just like that—voila!—I was a very minor celebrity.

My father wouldn't come to my pageants because the stress was too much for his high blood pressure. My siblings resented all the attention I was getting. But my mother was in *heaven*. This was a little taste of the glamour and privilege she envisioned for me...and for herself. She wasn't a nightmare "pageant mom"; I was a natural and loved the competition and thrill of winning. Mom enjoyed her friendships with the other pageant moms and relished getting me ready for every contest.

Pageants became a lifestyle. Over the next three or four summers, I did all kinds of local pageants: Miss Banks Social and Carnival Club, Miss Pontchartrain Rodeo Queen, Miss New Orleans Power Boat Association, Miss Pelican State, Miss Fraternal Order of Police, Miss Louisiana Sportsman's Paradise, Grande Isle Tarpon Rodeo Queen, Miss Jefferson Parish, and many more.

In most of them, I either won or placed, and each title came with "royal duties" that I was expected to fulfill in the next year. For example, when I was the Tarpon Rodeo Queen, I had to fish. Would you believe I caught a huge bonito? It still hangs on my wall with a plaque reading, "To the Fishingest Queen Ever."

Pageant life was full of delightful absurdities. I won Miss Louisiana in 1974 and the president of Guatemala invited me to choose the queen of the Anacafe Coffee Festival. This was a big deal: I had my own escort and cars, was formally presented, and felt very important for a nineteen-year-old. But I had never flown and was terrified, so I talked the festival into letting me bring my sister, Nona, and Lisa Restivo as my escorts. Shockingly, from the time we landed in Guatemala, I never saw them; they were being escorted around by a pair of charming, persistent Latin men.

It was a memorable trip. Nona was cold one night and thought it would warm her hotel room if she left the hot water running all evening. Naturally, she used up all the hot water for the entire hotel. The next morning, hundreds of guests—including pageant contestants—took freezing showers. I committed my own faux pas at a dinner reception at the presidential palace. We all dined on gourmet food, and when the band started playing, I jumped up to dance. My horrified chaperone hustled me off dance floor; it was against protocol for anyone to dance before the President.

Who knew? Live and learn.

A First Taste of Feminism

Pageant life led me to modeling classes, where I learned to express myself in a way that's nothing like the "resting bitch face" you see on today's models. This was the South, so it was all about charm and seduction. There was a way to walk, take off your jacket, place your foot, and spin around. I had a signature walk in each pageant, but my mainstay was what became known as the "Rhonda Walk," which my mother, master of the traffic-stopping "Jennie Walk," helped me perfect.

In those days, the beauty pageants were *just* beauty pageants; there were no ridiculous questions about world peace or talent competitions. These were about which young lady was the most poised, the most charming, the most graceful...and let's be honest, had the best butt. Well, I had a great rear end. In fact, to this day one of my signature sayings is:

Behind every great woman is a great behind.

However, I hated knowing that when I walked downstage toward the judges (who were almost always older men) and then turned to walk upstage, they were leering and ogling my ass. I still hate making exits from a room, which is probably why I designed shapewear to enhance and smooth the derriere. Even though I was still too young and inexperienced back then to understand true sexism, this moment still made me feel like a piece of meat.

FOURTH WALL BREAK!

So how did I really feel when I was strutting my stuff in front of all those judges at all those pageants? I was a little shy, a little embarrassed, and a little empowered to know all eyes were upon me. I was sixteen, and it was new and exciting. Sexism wasn't ingrained into our Deep South heads. It was 1970 and girls down South were more conservative than girls from the coasts. But it was an out-of-body experience. I felt like I was in the audience looking at myself.

However, I was never all-in as a pageant girl. I couldn't completely get into the mindset, and I couldn't in acting, either. Perhaps that is why I chose comedy. In acting class, they asked you to become a tree or an ice cream cone, but I never could feel it. It just seemed silly to me, so I was always a little guarded, never getting completely into a role. It was safer to make fun of myself before someone else did.

However, even as a teenager, I was starting to understand something—not just about the power of sexuality, but the power of taking control of a situation with charm and confidence. I included something in the Rhonda Walk that I called the "cock and tilt." When I walked down toward the judges and then turned to go back upstage, I would cock and then tilt my head toward them, meet their eyes, and flash a dazzling smile. This made them feel too self-conscious to take their eyes off my eyes to look down at my butt. It worked just about every time.

In fact, it worked so well—and I won so often—that the other girls started emulating me, although it was never catty. I wasn't really competing with them, but with myself. The showbiz bug had bitten me, and I was starting to see pageants as a steppingstone to bigger and better things.

Shear Honesty: *I really always have been my worst critic and fiercest competition. I've competed with my fears, my insecurities, and my ambition to be, well, everything—creative, famous, secure, humble, goofy, gorgeous. I guess you could say I'm my own best friend and worst enemy. It's a good thing I found a man who accepts and loves every version of me. Not everyone is so lucky.* **Understand your inner critic and let it drive you to be better, not beat you down.**

My parents loved it all, because if I won I my picture would be in the *Times-Picayune*. We would run out at late at night and pick up several copies, and my dad would be bursting his buttons with pride. Every weekend, he and mom would cart me off to another pageant, sometimes traveling as far as Baton Rouge or Monroe. It was an amazing time. Dad may not have attended the actual competition, but he drove us all over the state. Those are some of my best memories of my father.

I was learning how to be poised and to speak in front of people and hold their attention, and organizations started asking me to host or speak at their events. Some weekends when I wasn't competing in a pageant, I would haul off to the local American Legion post to smile and wave and award someone a plaque or certificate. I was doing a lot of things that a typical seventeen-year-old girl wouldn't have done, and it gave me a lot of confidence.

The funny thing is that even though some people might have seen it as objectifying young women and boiling them down to their beauty and charisma, pageant life was really my first taste of feminism. I never saw the pageants as sexist. They were celebrating us as young women, not exploiting us. The atmosphere was sweet, wholesome, and respectful, and in doing pageants, I learned so much about competition and myself.

This time in my life marked the beginning of a pattern that I first fell into unintentionally, and later followed very consciously:

1. Walk with my eyes wide open into a system or situation that wanted to use me for my looks and sex appeal, remaining fully aware of the rules and the opportunities;

2. Play the game, but at the same time extract every advantage from the experience while never, ever letting things cross over into exploitation;

3. Subtly (or not so subtly) change the system by doing things I wasn't supposed to do or flat-out playing by a new set of rules.

This began in the world of pageants. I knew that to most pageant organizers, I was just one more in a long line of girls valued more for our Southern charm and beauty than our intelligence or talent. But in playing to that stereotype, I also got the opportunity to turn the tables and learn skills that really paid dividends later in life. I also learned that as long as I played the game, I could tilt the playing field in my favor—flashing my pearly whites to get the judges' eyes on my face and off my ass, for example. I might not have the power—yet—to change the way society saw pretty women, but I could sure as hell use it to my advantage...even while it *thought* it was using me.

The Governor and Me

I don't think there's a story that better illustrates the power a pretty woman can exert in this world than my bizarre and funny experience as the obsessive crush of Governor Edwin Edwards. It's an example of something I think all women can learn: men are always going to be men. The straight ones will always look at a beautiful woman and do whatever it takes to get into her pants. It doesn't matter how old they are. Why be surprised or offended by it? **Sexuality and beauty are currency. Rather than pretend they're not, use them.**

It was 1971 and I was sixteen years old, the winner of many beauty crowns. My junior-senior prom was held at the Rivergate Convention Center (now Harrah's New Orleans), and Governor Edwards was down the hall at another event. New Orleans loves backroom politics, and some of you might remember Governor Edwards because of the 2001 racketeering conviction that sent him to prison for ten years. If not, you may remember him because he ran for governor again in 2014 at the age of 87 and lost. But I remember dear Edwin primarily for relentlessly hitting on me when I was a teenager.

As my prom was drawing to a close, I walked out to get some air. Edwin spotted me, came over, put his arm around my waist, and said, "You are beautiful. I have to meet you." He was forty-two at the time, but devastatingly handsome. One of his henchmen came over and got my phone number, and I gave it to him because it was cool to have the governor ask for your number. Even at sixteen, I enjoyed my power. Evil laugh.

Then the governor of Louisiana started calling me at home. Maybe you're thinking that's creepy (and I guess it is), but I thought it was flattering and funny as hell. I would put my parents on the extension when Edwin called me, and they would listen in. He should have been running the state but instead, he was calling a teenage girl to fill her head with sweet nothings. It was Louisiana politics at its finest.

It turned out that our governor *really* had a thing for young girls; he had built a *literal* reputation as the father of the state. He would send me roses under the name "Bandido" and tell me that I was breaking his heart because I wouldn't meet him anywhere. Well, of course I wouldn't meet him! I was underage! One of the most ridiculous episodes came when he was on a trip in Florida. He called me and said he was writing my name in the sand and watching the waves wash it away, symbolizing how I was treating him. Hilarious.

Then Edwin did something I could never have predicted: after I won an important local pageant, he asked me to speak in front of the Louisiana Senate and House of Representatives. Now, I'm sure he did it because he thought that this would be what finally got me into his bed, but so what? At seventeen years old, I stood in front of the state legislature—the only woman in the room with close to 400 men—and gave a sincere speech about youth involvement in government. When I closed, I said, "I'd like to thank Governor Edwards for my being here today and making this possible."

At that, everyone in the room, knowing well Edwin's reputation as an unrepentant chaser of young girls, broke out laughing—and then gave me a standing ovation. Edwards was standing next to my parents at the back of the chambers, pointing and shouting, "These are her parents!" while trying to convince everyone in the room that he hadn't actually slept with me (though he'd certainly done his level best). It was almost surreal.

But that laugh and that standing ovation...they were like a drug! For that moment, as a girl a year away from voting age, I had all those powerful men in the palm of my hand. I knew right then and there that I wanted to make people laugh and command a stage. That led me to comedy, and I'm a comedian before I'm anything else.

FOURTH WALL BREAK!

Wait a second. Did innocent, seventeen-year-old me really know what I was saying when I thanked the governor and brought down the house? Yes and no. I think in the back of my mind, I knew I was going to get some sort of reaction from the all-male House of Representatives. I didn't necessarily expect thunderous applause, laughter, and a standing ovation. It was a moment of commanding an audience that I never forgot. They may have thought I was another innocent victim of the governor's advances, but I felt power standing in front of that group all by myself. That was a defining moment when I knew I would have a career speaking, acting, or even being in front of a jury as a lawyer.

That didn't end my adventures with the handsome Governor Edwards, either. Later, he tried to convince me that if I went to college at Louisiana State University in Baton Rouge and not Loyola in New Orleans, he would make me Queen of the Campus. That sounded great, but he was part of the package. No thanks. I stayed home and went to Loyola. I was learning how to play the game with men.

Many years later, while I was starring on *USA: Up All Night*, I did a soda commercial with Edwin. On camera, I did this cuddly thing against him, which was a play on his reputation for liking the ladies. After the cameras stopped rolling, he forgot that he was still wearing a live microphone, leaned over to me, and whispered, "I should have banged you when I coulda."

Everyone on the set heard him; I just smiled. *Who said you coulda?*

Bitten by the Bug

Lecherous old men notwithstanding, by the time I was eighteen, the showbiz bug had bitten me hard enough to draw blood. My dancing school friend Trudy Burch and I would choreograph dance routines and perform a USO-style show for the guys and gals at Kessler Air Force Base in Biloxi. My parents loved chauffeuring us around; my dad was working less and enjoying seeing an entirely different side of life.

I had started attending Loyola University to get a degree in communications with an eye on becoming a television reporter (and even thought about law school), but now I started dreaming about going out to Hollywood and trying to build a career as an actress. Not to gloss over Loyola: I loved the school and the Jesuits who ran it. The Dean of the University, Father James Carter, was one of my biggest fans when I made the move to Los Angeles. He even visited me there at the famous Polo Lounge of the Beverly Hills Hotel. Brother Alexis was my theater professor, and when I had an important *Happy Days* audition that involved kissing Ron Howard, I called him to coach me the night before. It might seem funny, asking a priest how to handle a kissing scene, but he was great.

I wasn't ready to move to LA yet, but I kept doing everything and anything to feed my showbiz addiction. For instance, I had dreamed of becoming a Saints cheerleader, but the year I decided to try out, the Saints changed the rules to let only high school-age boys and girls cheer. I was devastated. But the front office manager for the Saints was a lovely man named Harry Holmes. My father wrote him a letter stating how I had waited years for this opportunity and asking the Saints to make an exception. Mr. Holmes wrote a beautiful letter back expressing his regret, saying that he knew I would have been great for the team and asking me to meet with him at the Saints headquarters.

When I showed up, Mr. Holmes didn't make me a cheerleader, but instead offered me the newly-created position of assistant halftime entertainment director. It wasn't a paying gig, except for the two season tickets in the end zone, which wasn't so bad when I witnessed Tom Dempsey kick a 63-yard, record-breaking field goal for the Saints. I thought it was going to hit me in the head! Still, I was thrilled! I helped coordinate the bands, color guard, and singers on and off the field for pre-game, halftime, and post-game festivities. I was in heaven. I became friendly with the entertainment director, Barra Bircher. He was patient with me, and I learned all about organization, planning, and attending to every detail.

I'd applied for a job as eye candy and wound up with one that was all about brains and leadership. That was progress. I would hold the position all through college.

Shear Honesty: *You will learn from every job, and you won't know what you'll learn until you try. So what if you don't know what you're doing? No one taught me how to do the things I did in life, because no one in my life had ever done anything like them before. The good news is, there won't be anyone to tell you you're doing them wrong, either!* **When in doubt, say yes (unless the question is being asked by a perverted state official nearly three times your age).**

I was also a featured dancer on *The John Pela Show*, a weekend dance show formerly called *Saturday Hop* and hosted by—you guessed it—John Pela. Remember *American Bandstand*? That was *The John Pela Show*, only on a smaller local scale. The other featured dancers and I would dance on little platforms while the other kids shimmied and shook around us to songs like "Superstition," "Crocodile Rock," and "Love Train." This was during the same time that Don Cornelius of *Soul Train* was a sensation.

I can still remember what it was like to walk into the studios of WWL, our local CBS television station, on Saturday mornings: the smell of the studio's electrical wiring and cold metal, the sight of the cameras, the fascinating things the director did with green screen and graphics. And I'm not the only one with fond memories; when I'm in New Orleans I still run into people who recognize me and cry, "You were a John Pela dancer!" It was so much fun. Everyone was very young and innocent in their miniskirts, bell bottoms, and go-go boots.

I was also the "Shape Spa girl," the spokeswoman for the local Shape Spa chain of health clubs. I did television commercials and print ads wearing colorful workout leotards and reciting the tagline, "It's great to be in shape!" People who know me from those days still shout that line back to me, which never fails to make me giggle. Ironically, I never worked out at Shape Spa, but apart from giving me valuable TV experience, the job showed me the power of the catchphrase. When I got *USA: Up All Night* years later, one of the first things I did was come up with an unforgettable catchphrase of my own.

The Quest for Miss America

Even as Hollywood loomed larger and larger in my mind, I still did pageants. What was the downside? They were fun and were an opportunity to make terrific contacts and good friends. But like Dr. King, my mother had a dream: that I would win Miss America. Today, when women run for president, beauty pageants are seen as throwbacks, but back then Miss America was the crown of crowns, and my mother was determined that I would win it.

Around 1972 I started entering statewide pageants. At the time, there were three different Miss Louisiana titles: Miss Louisiana-America (which qualified the titleholder to compete for Miss America); Miss Louisiana-USA (which qualified the titleholder to compete for Miss USA); and Miss Louisiana-International (which qualified the titleholder to compete for Miss World and Miss International).

Don't try to make any sense out of it; I couldn't. Basically, the three pageants were like ABC, NBC, and CBS, putting out what was really the same product with a few superficial differences in the packaging. But all of them were a big deal. They celebrated the feminine ideal back in those days; you couldn't wear any padding in your bra and minimal makeup was allowed. Now every contestant has a boob job, nose job, and professional makeup designed to bring out her "natural beauty." Uh-huh.

To qualify for the statewide titles, you first had to win a pageant that led to the state level, such as Miss Jefferson Parish. If you won that title, you could compete for Miss Louisiana. If you won *that* title, then you were off to Miss America. I made it past all those local and parish pageants and actually held all three Miss Louisiana titles. But the first time I competed in the Miss Louisiana

International pageant, while I made the top five, I didn't win.

It was 1974. The pageant was in New Orleans and Henry Kissinger, of all people, was one of the judges. The next level was Miss World, so I knew that when it came time for the contestants to answer questions, we might face some tough ones. I studied my ass off and got all sorts of coaching on governments and the United Nations and the like, and when the big night came I answered my question just fine. Then, all of a sudden, I couldn't shut up! I babbled on and on and finally, after sticking my foot and most of my lower leg down my throat, I turned to the audience and actually said, "Let's give a round of applause to our judges!"

Really, Rhonda? Go ahead and cringe; I still do when I think about it. I looked like a first-class ass kisser and the applause was strained and embarrassed. I didn't win that pageant and I'm sure my bout of verbal diarrhea cost me the crown.

Later in 1974, I became Miss Louisiana-World and went on to compete in Miss World-USA. Dick Clark hosted and I made the top seven, but my height of five-foot-four may have kept me from going all the way. It was either that or that my natural breast size, while perky, was not as big as the winner's. Finally, in 1975, I went on to win Miss Louisiana, which led to the Miss USA pageant, a franchise that Donald Trump owned for years. But I didn't win that title, either, and my Miss America hopes were shattered.

In the end, I won more than fifty beauty pageants, collected a shit-ton of tiaras, met a lot of amazing people, learned how to command a stage, and got a master class in poise, charm, and the power of sexuality. But that wasn't the end of my life as a beauty queen. My mother had one more chance for her baby to win Miss America. But you'll have to wait for the Hollywood portion of our story for that.

⤚ ON THE WAY TO TODAY ⤙

What did our intrepid heroine take away from these adventures? Well...

- ☐ *Behind every great woman is a great behind.*

- ☐ *Sex and beauty matter. Smarts and hard work matter more.*

- ☐ *You don't need money to have class. In fact, class and money often move in opposite directions.*

- ☐ *Always say yes to any opportunity that doesn't involve taking your clothes off, unless it's Playboy (see next chapter).*

- ☐ *Listen to your mother.*

- ☐ *Learning to speak well, behave with charm, and display poise in any situation will never steer you wrong.*

- ☐ *There will always, always be people who tell you that what you want to do can't be done. The only power their words have is the power you give them.*

- ☐ *Never underestimate the attraction of an older man to a (much) younger woman.*

- ☐ *Learning to be organized and detailed, get things done, and lead others is at least as important as what you'll learn in books.*

LESSON TWO
Everybody Needs Allies

—— In which our heroine becomes embroiled in a controversy, learns the power of maintaining long-term relationships, bleaches her nether regions, embraces her sexy, and finds out that if you can see them, they can definitely see you. ——

We're going to jump around in time a little in this book, because I learned different lessons at different periods in my life that I've used to get where I am today. So we need to spend a little time talking about one of the most important forces for good in my life, *Playboy*.

I can hear your eyes rolling from here. *Playboy's* an irrelevant relic of a pre-feminist time, right? Didn't Hugh Hefner set the women's movement back a generation by collecting hot wives one-fourth his age as fast as he could pop Viagra tablets? Maybe. Maybe not. But you won't hear any criticism from me, because for forty years *Playboy* has been great for Rhonda Shear, from when I lost a beauty crown due to a phony scandal, all the way up to its current role in my company.

To me, Hef will always be an icon. He changed the way we saw the female body. *Playboy* was never degrading like *Penthouse* or *Hustler*.

Hef believed in putting women on pedestals, but also in featuring cutting-edge interviews and great journalism. He was a trailblazer. The magazine never portrayed women in compromising poses; even the suggestion of bondage or exploitation was taboo. In my "Rhonda Is Up All Night" layout, I had gorgeous jewelry handcuffs hanging off my wrists for the picture that portrayed me as a judge in a night court...and a *Playboy* graphic artist Photoshopped them out of the final image.

If my various appearances in the magazine, clothed and unclothed, have put me into the fantasies of tens of thousands of adolescent boys over the years...well, that's not a bad thing, is it? So if you don't mind, let's sashay back to New Orleans for a little while longer and talk pageants, pictorials, and politics—and how, by sticking to my morals, I gained a lifelong advocate that helped me throughout all my many careers.

The Class and Impact of *Playboy*

It's not an exaggeration to say that *Playboy* made my young career possible—probably even more than pageants did. When I was in New Orleans going to college, I was also doing a lot of modeling. I worked with a professional agency and did commercials and some other things. I was becoming well-known and beloved in the city, which was great. People in New Orleans loved me, and I loved them and the city right back.

Then *Playboy* came through town. In an age when nude bodies and all kinds of pornography are a mouse click or swipe right away, it's probably hard to remember just how important *Playboy* used to be, or what a gigantic cultural force the magazine was back in 1976 and 1977. This was long before the Internet was even a gleam in anybody's eye, long before "lad mags" like *Maxim* and *FHM* would take some of *Playboy's* thunder and YouPorn made everybody think they were an erotic *artiste*. *Playboy* wasn't about sex; it was about allure, seduction, urban chic, and intelligence.

Back around the Bicentennial, *Playboy* models, clubs, and bunnies were the epitome of sexy sophistication. While *Penthouse* was sleazy and *Hustler* was gross, *Playboy* was elegant. If you were a top-tier actor or author, you wanted to be interviewed in the magazine. The likes of John Updike, Kurt Vonnegut, Joyce Carol Oates, Anne Sexton, and Saul Bellow published fiction and poetry in its pages. Men and boys learned how to be suave chick magnets from the "Dear Playboy Advisor" column. Hef was every man's idol; wearing a smoking jacket and puffing on a pipe, he was The Man. Around the time that I was getting close to graduating from Loyola, *Playboy* was iconic.

So you can imagine my reaction when *Playboy* came to New Orleans in 1977 to shoot a pictorial called "Girls of the New South" and my modeling agent said, "Are you interested?" Well, of course I was interested; this was *Playboy*! On the other hand, there was no way I was going to take off my clothes. Not only would my parents have flipped out, but I was still the Southern belle who was slightly fearful of men and sex and fiercely protective of her virtue. I also had my eye on a career as a newscaster. I had a reputation in New Orleans as a good girl, and I didn't want a nude pictorial to pop up and sabotage that in a few years. But I was curious if they would pick me in spite of that.

So I went to meet David Chan, the photographer, who was lovely, sweet, and complimentary. I said to him, "David, I guess I'm wasting your time, because I'm not taking off my clothes. I just wanted to meet you."

However, he surprised me by saying, "Well, that's fine, because we shoot totally clothed girls on some of these layouts. I'd love to shoot you, but I can't guarantee your picture will be in the magazine. If they use it, you'll get paid $250. If they don't, then we'll have a great day together."

That sounded awesome, so I agreed. We did a shoot together and he took my lead on locations. I choose Oak Alley, a famous former plantation with beautiful old oak trees that line the road up to the mansion. I wore a romantic, white, off-the-shoulder, antebellum dress that I'd had made for one of my pageants, with a big hoop skirt and a parasol that made me look like Scarlett O'Hara, and decorated with fake magnolia blossoms. I was getting ready to wear the dress to reign as Miss Floral Trail (remember that name, because I'll come back to it), and I figured I would get some more mileage out of it.

> **Shear Honesty:** *You never know the pivotal moments of your life when they're happening. How could you? You can only see them for what they are in retrospect. That's why I think it's so important to always bring your best: stick to your morals and ethics, keep your promises, and treat people with kindness and respect. You never know what will change your life. Playboy and Miss Floral Trail coming together in that New Orleans spring of 1977 changed mine forever.* **Be a good, honest person; you never know who's watching.**

David shot me at the plantation, totally clothed, with my arms crossed over my chest in such a way that my thumbs were covering up where my nipples would be. (That's a small detail that will become important later.) I wasn't trying to be sexy; it wasn't a "Here are my boobs, but I'm hiding them" thing. I was actually just posing in character. We finished at Oak Alley and moved on to other locations, shooting all over New Orleans with me wearing various outfits.

A few months later, the issue of *Playboy* with the "Girls of the New South" pictorial came out—and there I was! I was in the center of a page, surrounded by naked girls. In 1977, *Playboy's* poses had gotten a little more...spread-eagled, shall we say. They were showing a lot more, so the feel of the whole pictorial was pretty racy. But I was thrilled. I'd gotten into *Playboy* on my own terms and made $250.

I thought that would be the end of it. I would bask in my brief glory and move on to my career in television journalism. Unfortunately, the Girls of the New South were about to run face-first into the conservatism of the Old South.

The Floral Trail Controversy

That conservatism was embodied in the Greater New Orleans Floral Trail Society—more importantly for our story, in the queen that the Floral Trail Society chose each year. Now, this wasn't one of those blue-blood, debutante titles where you had to be a Protestant, be raised in a certain family, and attend a certain prep school to be eligible (the city had plenty of those, and as a Jewish girl I didn't qualify). However, that didn't mean it was any less prudish, proper, old-fashioned, snobby, or protective of its supposedly pure pedigree.

The Greater New Orleans Floral Trail had been founded in 1934 during the depths of the Great Depression. Supposedly, the president of the city's Parkway Commission purchased trees, flowers, and other plants to help beautify New Orleans and stem the feeling of decay that came along with economic hardship. Well, the Big Easy is all about audience participation, so it wasn't long before citizens pitched in to beautify their homes and front yards, creating a "floral trail" that wound through the city.

In 1934, the Floral Trail Society was founded and a Queen and Court were chosen to reign over the "Festival of Flowers," a celebration of the Floral Trail and a parade through the French Quarter. It had nothing to do with Mardi Gras but was its own thing, an annual spring festival that was (and still is) a *very* big deal for New Orleanians—who will, God love 'em, take just about any opportunity to crown a queen, stage a festival, hold a parade of beautiful debutantes, and dance and drink in the streets until sunrise.

Just a second ago I said that the Queen of the Floral Trail was chosen. That's a *little* white lie. In reality, the Queen was purchased with cold, hard cash—in my case, $1,500 that my parents put up, a fair amount of money back in 1977. My father's truck parts and equipment business was doing very well by then, so we were sort of *nouveau riche*. I was more than qualified to represent the Floral Trail Society: I was a beauty pageant winner, known and loved around the city, and a girl of sterling reputation. But the fact remains that I didn't win this crown. It was a social honor that gave my parents bragging rights, so after the Floral Trial Committee selected me, they gladly paid their $1,500.

Then, in April of 1977, the issue of *Playboy* with my pictorial in it came out. The Festival of Flowers, where I would be crowned Queen of the Floral Trail at an elaborate coronation ceremony in Jackson Square, was to take place in May. Now, believe me when I tell you that New Orleans takes its queens and its coronations *seriously*...like no other city can. In addition to the Queen, the Floral Trail Court includes a selection of Maids, Misses, Demoiselles,

Princesses, and Flower Girls, the details of whose outfits and escorts are breathlessly reported on each year by the *Times-Picayune*. It may seem overwrought to someone not from NOLA, but down South, it's serious tradition and really very sweet. For some gals, being in the Floral Trail Court is the high point of their lives.

So when the dear ladies of the Floral Trail Society saw my photo (fully clothed, mind you) in David Chan's layout, surrounded by all those other girls in their birthday suits, they had what is called in polite society a "hissy fit." Without informing us or returning my parents' $1,500, they decided that I was not fit to reign and dethroned me. They made one of my Maids the new Queen.

Well, I do declare! That was completely unfair! I had been totally clothed in the magazine, so I saw the whole affair as overblown hand-wringing by a bunch of old-lady, white-haired society prudes. Hell hath no fury like a beauty queen scorned, not to mention my parents, who had paid good money and were ready to see me crowned Miss Floral Trail Society. So I did what any good Southern girl would do: I filed an injunction in district court to be reinstated as Queen of the Floral Trail. I had done nothing wrong, the dress was made, the press had been notified, and by God, I was going to reign!

FOURTH WALL BREAK!

Court? Over a beauty title? Was it really worth it? In my mind, yes. First of all, I hadn't done anything wrong. Second, you have no idea how important titles like this are to New Orleans society. That was the first real sting of adult reality. They didn't care if they broke the heart of a young woman, and I knew I had to fight back and stand up for myself. The whole thing was embarrassing to me and my parents, and as far I was concerned, I was either going to be reinstated as Queen or the world was going to see a bunch of hen-pecked husbands dethroning me because of their prude wives. After my day in court, the public knew I was right and that silly organization got more press than they could ever imagine. When it was all over, I felt vindicated and knew I would have to fight for what I felt was right.

That's how I came to spend six tedious, surreal hours sitting in court. Wars have been won in less time than it took to decide whether I would be crowned Queen of the damned Floral Trail or if it title would be given to some other girl. As I've said, I was well-known in New Orleans by this time, so it was quite a scene—a moveable media feast. Jimmy Fitzmorris, the lieutenant governor, spoke on my behalf, saying that I was "a lovely young lady." Blaine Kern, a New Orleans legend as *the* float builder for Mardi Gras (and still going strong at ninety) testified to my sterling character. After they did their thing, the Floral Trail attorney, Gasper Schiro (remember that name), had his turn at bat.

Remember that I told you that in David Chan's photos, I'd held my arms crossed over my chest? Gasper told the court that my thumbnails—which in the image were maybe the size of a pencil point—were actually my nipples. Horrors! Scandal! I think I'm having an attack of the vapors!

This was my introduction to the blatant double standard that exists in so much of our society, even today, when it comes to men's and women's bodies. It was obvious that Gasper and the Floral Trail ladies were playing on the commonly held belief that a young woman who showed or even *hinted* at anything remotely sexual or come-hither was a woman of low character—today, we'd call her a slut. But if a young Loyola fraternity brother had posed bare-chested for a magazine, rippling six-pack abs all but inviting women to drop their panties, there might have been some vigorous fanning of faces but nobody would have said a word.

It still burns me a little, even today. Women are expected to be both seductress and saint: society values us for our thigh gaps and our cheekbones and begs us to show more skin, but as soon as we try to capitalize on that sexual obsession, we're labeled as whores. That's why with Rhonda Shear Intimates, I've always been conscious of designing things that help women *feel* sexy and seductive while *appearing* classy and put together. It's a tough balancing act, but a necessary one, as hard experience has taught me.

Anyway, the "nonexistent nipple" gambit was nonsense, but it worked. Since the pinprick in the photo *could* have been a nipple and the court's first interest was to protect the (ahem) purity and heritage of the Floral Trail (and to give in to social pressure), Civil District Court Judge Melvin Duran ruled against me. I was out. He did say that I could sue the Floral Trail Society for monetary damages, which, since my career was just getting going, wasn't worth my time. So my brief reign as Queen of the Floral Trail was ground under the well-turned heel of old-line New Orleans politics.

Newsworthy

There was an undercurrent of shame and punishment in the Floral Trail Society's actions—what we would today call "slut shaming." I was to be punished and shamed publicly for having the nerve to be...what? A pretty girl who wanted to pose for a top professional photographer in a way that wasn't at all sleazy? Anyway, the idea was that I would slink away, keep my mouth shut, and be a good, compliant little Southern lady.

Yeah, I know. Makes me laugh, too. But you can't blame them for trying.

That didn't happen. See, the silver lining to all this little Southern Gothic drama was that there was a lot of media interest in my case. If Facebook, Twitter, and Instagram had been around back then, the whole thing would have gone viral. The press covered the affair like it was the greatest thing since the Watergate hearings. *Associated Press, United Press International,* and the *Times-Picauyne* ran coverage of the hearing and the decision...and so did *Playboy.*

Their editors loved it! Not only had I appeared in the magazine, but the whole controversy was happening *because* I had appeared in a pictorial, so readers felt like they had a stake in the outcome. The editor of the news pages in the back of the magazine, Gretchen Edgrin, wrote a whole sarcastic, disbelieving story about me being dethroned. She also started following my career, running little news items on me from time to time. That was the real beginning of my relationship with *Playboy.*

Over the years, while I kept appearing in sitcoms and episodic TV, *Playboy* kept writing about me. I had become a reader favorite, and they felt protective of me, their former model who'd gotten in such hot water for appearing in the magazine. From time to time, articles or short news items would appear talking about what I was up to, what TV shows or movies I was in, and later, what comedy clubs I was headlining. It gave me something I would come to value later in my career: consistent coverage that kept me in the public consciousness.

Shear Honesty: *My relationship with Playboy was part of a pattern I've kept up my entire adult life, one that has benefitted me in more ways than I can count: maintaining personal connections over the long term. I don't burn bridges. I don't throw away business* cards. *I reach out on Facebook, send birthday wishes, and stay on good terms with people. I've done it with photographers, agents, politicians, you name it, and it's helped my career in every sense.* **Stay on good terms with as many people as you can. You never know who will become your angel down the line.**

Pretty Girls Aren't Funny

In 1979, I decided to break free of my beauty queen image and try my hand at comedy. I took an improv class and moved on to doing two or three minutes at whatever LA venues I could find. I was a natural and loved it; comedy became my secret passion, and it wasn't long before I could see myself becoming a full-time standup comic. But after a few months on the minor league club circuit, I noticed that there was a real bias against attractive women in comedy.

Standup comedy was a male-dominated business to begin with; look how hard Joan Rivers had to work to break through the gender barrier back in the 1960s and get time on stages dominated by male comics like Henny Youngman, Marty Allen, and Jackie Mason. Multiply that headwind by ten if you were good looking or didn't "dress down" and look frumpy or masculine on stage. There was as unspoken rule among club owners and comedians: beautiful, sexy women couldn't be funny.

I was sexy *and* self-deprecating *and* funny, too. But in trying to work my way to better and better comedy gigs, I hit a brick wall. In about 1986, after I'd spent years working my way ever-so-slowly through the standup comedy ranks while still acting, modeling, and studying, comedy impresario Sammy Shore, co-founder of The Comedy Store, had the nerve to tell me that I should give up comedy and go back to law school, because attractive women just weren't funny.

That pissed me off. What, if you had boobs you couldn't have timing, too? Hearing that I can't do something has always motivated me, and when I get motivated, look out. I decided to capitalize on my ongoing relationship with *Playboy* to show the know-it-alls what happens when you try to deprive a beauty queen of her rightful place on the stage.

FOURTH WALL BREAK!

Can you believe the way Sammy dismissed me like that? At that moment, it felt like he had slapped me in the face. I could feel my face getting red and hot with anger. How dare this person tell me what I should do with my dreams? It was another moment where an old man was telling me right and wrong. Bad idea. I was going to work harder just to show Sammy Shore he was wrong. One day, I swore I would make him eat those words—and one day he did, quite nicely, when we were booked on the same show! The episode taught me that when someone else decides what you can and can't do, you have two choices: accept it or say, "I'll show YOU." It was like arrogant little Sammy had waved a red flag in front of a bull. Sometimes, feeling slighted can be your best friend...if you know what to do with the feeling.

I went to the editors with an idea for a "Women of Comedy" pictorial. They responded, "Are there pretty comics out there?" *Sheesh.* The "pretty women aren't funny" stereotype had even gotten into Pretty Women Central.

I enlightened my *Playboy* friends. I informed them that beauty and a funny bone were not mutually exclusive and that I would find them some beautiful and funny female comics posthaste. I brought them a couple that ended up in the layout, and they also did their own national search, and in June of 1991 "*Playboy's Women of Comedy*" came out. It featured nude and semi-nude layouts of yours truly along with Rosanne Katon, Ria Coyne, Kitt Scott, and Diana Jordan. I was photographed in Las Vegas, scantily clad and posing in front of one of the billboards that advertised me opening for Smokey Robinson. It was groundbreaking for both *Playboy* and in the comedy world. The layout got a lot of attention, and definitely got me more club bookings.

At the same time, The Playboy Channel was going strong on cable TV, and I was also talking to *Playboy* about doing a "sexy women of comedy" show. They loved that idea, too, but it sort of fizzled out. I was either way ahead of my time or I'd missed out on the glamour days of Hollywood.

Shear Honesty: *This is a lesson I've found to be true over and over—when you're ahead of your time, you make people uncomfortable, and the harder you push, the harder they push back. People don't like change. I attacked the "pretty women aren't funny" stereotype head-on with Playboy and it was great. But when I tried to do it again with a TV show, I got nowhere. Remember, no one ever believes something can be done until it's done, and that's especially true when you're blazing trails and breaking boundaries. If you succeed once, be ready to push ten times harder to make the next opportunity happen.* **Trust your vision; ignore the naysayers.**

Rhonda Is Up All Night

I moved on, landing headlining positions on the comedy circuit and doing endless comedy TV shows like *Evening at the Improv, Girls Night Out,* and *Into the Night.* Then in 1991, I was hired to host *USA: Up All Night.* More on the show later; right now, let's talk about how it brought *Playboy* back into my life again.

In 1992, the success of *USA: Up All Night* caught *Playboy's* attention. The editors approached me and offered me a celebrity pictorial. Wow! It was incredibly flattering. In a sense, it was confirmation that I'd made it.

Wait a second. Wasn't I Jennie Weaker Shear's daughter, raised to value my sex appeal—to tease but not give in? And wasn't posing nude going against that? *Yes* to the first question; *no* to the second. The second question wasn't even relevant anymore. Part of me was still that demure New Orleans belle who won tiaras in beauty pageants, but a stronger part of me was an experienced television star of thirty-seven who felt fit and gorgeous and fully in command of her sexual power. I *wanted* to redefine myself. I *wanted* to be a little bit racy and shocking. I *wanted* to dare people to judge me based on my...assets. This was my time.

Of course I said yes.

I ended up with a six-page layout titled "Rhonda Is Up All Night" (which appeared in the October 1993 issue of the magazine) and a large paycheck. The issue was quite sought-after, as it featured Jerry Seinfeld on the cover at the height of his *Seinfeld* fame, as well as the "Girls of the Pac Ten" spread and Jenny McCarthy's first layout. Shot by the late Richard Fegley, my pictorial depicted me in settings that were typically open all night. There are shots that show me as an overnight DJ at a radio station, shopping at an all-night grocery store with my dog in tow, at a 24-hour laundromat, swimming in Mardi Gras beads at a pool hall, doing a split at a bowling alley, and playing a judge in night court.

The really funny thing was that a lot of these locations were actually open for business when we shot, including the bowling alley. The crew erected a huge tarp up around the lane we were shooting on, but I could see other bowlers, so couldn't they see me, too? (More on that "if you can see them" conundrum in a bit.) Well, the photo of me doing a split while bowling became iconic. I owe some of that to my fabulous makeup artist, Teri Groves, who suggested that I do that shot with my rear facing the camera. She knew I was flexible, and the *Playboy* contract stipulated "full nudity, front and back." I really didn't want to highlight my backside (a reluctance that went back to my pageant days) but there was something so flattering and funny about the pose that I couldn't resist.

I'm in an unbuttoned orange and black bowling shirt, hair falling halfway down my back, with an "Oh no!" look on my face as my bowling ball rolls down the lane, obviously headed for the gutter. The crew did a terrific job; there's not even a hint that they blocked our lane from view. And my butt actually does look pretty good.

There was a lot of humor involved in every shot in the layout, and *Playboy* and Hef loved it. It was glamorous, funny, sexy, and over the top, and my hair was even bigger than it was on *USA: Up All Night!* That version of Rhonda was campy and overtly sexy but still self-deprecating, but in *Playboy* I was free to sex it up as much as I wanted to. I've really never taken the "sexy" thing too seriously; it makes me giggle to act all smoldering and seductive. But doing it with such a group of great professionals was a blast.

Women ask me all the time what it was like to pose for *Playboy*, especially now that they're not doing nudes anymore. Well, it was a lot of things, but glamorous wasn't one of them. The "Rhonda is Up All Night" pictorial took a week to shoot, working eight to ten hours a day. Every muscle in my body ached from the long hours of posing (if a pose is unbearably uncomfortable, it is usually the best shot).

A celebrity pictorial begins with a storyboard, which lets the editors know the shot they're looking for before they shoot it. Of course, I had my say, as well. Marilyn Grabovski was the tough, demanding photo editor and scared the shit out of everyone. If you and a photo passed her approval, you were really something. There were only a few *Playboy* photographers back in the day, and they were artists long before there was Photoshop and digital imaging. I had the honor of working with four of them: David Chan, Steve Wanda, Arny Frietag, and Richard Fegley. There were also tons of lighting guys and women on the set who magically disappeared when the shooting began.

Next, the photographers took test Polaroids (I don't know if anyone knows what those are anymore; good thing I snuck a few of them in my robe pocket for posterity) to check lighting and poses, and then they went to work with big Hasselblad lenses. They didn't have to do much airbrushing because the lighting was so amazing. But the weirdest and most uncomfortable thing about that shoot wasn't the shoot itself, but the fact that the makeup artist asked me to go into the ladies' room with some bleach and see if I could... make the carpet match the drapes, if you know what I mean.

FOURTH WALL BREAK!

OMG! What a WTF moment! I was completely embarrassed, being in that bathroom. I was thinking, "What am I doing here feeling like a pervert at a peep show, standing in front of a small mirror in a small bathroom combing my pubes with bleach? I don't think this is normal." I just wanted to grab my clothes and make a run for it. "Maybe they won't notice if I leave and make them waste thousands and thousands of dollars? Could I flush myself down the toilet?" Worst of all, after fifteen minutes of staring down at my "foofie," the hairs were not becoming blonde, but a nice strawberry color. I had always called my mom for everything, but there was no phone in the bathroom and no cell phones back then. So I took my strawberry-blonde vajayjay out of the bathroom, swallowed my embarrassment and gave that shoot my all. I'm glad I did. It was a beautiful layout and the lighting went perfectly with my new lower curtains.

That was the one time I questioned what the hell I was doing there. In retrospect, I'm very happy that I stayed and did the shoot. I have loved every part of my life's eclectic journey, and although I was a bit prudish in some ways, I also used my looks to get ahead, and *Playboy* was a big part of that. I am happy that I have these beautiful pictures to remember my days in the sun and the spotlight. You can't get those years back, but sometimes I like to pull out the magazine and remind my hubby how lucky he is.

What Sexy Is

Posing nude in *Playboy* didn't get me cast in major films, but it did open some doors. My rates went up for live shows. I got more headlining comedy gigs, and requests for personal appearances rolled in. I also got a season of hosting a comedy showcase TV show out of WWOR in Secaucus, New Jersey, called *Spotlight Café*. At age thirty-seven, I was having the career I wanted and proving that sexy could be funny and funny could be sexy.

I was past the age when women are supposed to be desirable in showbiz, and my pictorial was a validation that I wasn't too old to be sexy. Hollywood is obsessed with gorgeous young things with no body fat and a closet full of size zero clothes, but that sort of beauty is, frankly, a dime a dozen. As you age as a woman, you learn that there's a big difference between *beautiful* and *sexy*. Katy Perry is beautiful; Beyoncé is sexy. I don't think women become *sexy* until we're in our thirties, at least. That's because real sexiness is part attitude, part intelligence, part eyebrow-raising wit and sass, part knowing what looks good on you, and part knowing how to strut what God gave you. Posing for *Playboy* was validation that I had finally graduated to sexy.

The thing is, sex appeal is still part of any actress's portfolio, so young women in particular have to choose early in their careers: go serious and be committed to the craft, or go for quick fame by getting in reality TV or using your sex appeal. When I went out to Hollywood, there were still remnants of the old studio days when you could still be put under contract by a network to be used as they developed you. I was all about creating attention and getting in front of as many decision makers as I could: casting directors, writers, producers—whoever could hire me! But sexy was a young woman's game; once you hit forty, you were cast as the mom or the sidekick, not the sexy leading lady.

Back in those days, you would still be able to get what were called "general meetings" with casting directors in which they would meet with you, but not for a specific role. Those were moments every actor coveted, and I got a few, like the one with Joyce Selznick and one with Bill Sheppard of Disney. My goal was to get their attention and then show them my talent. It backfired some and worked some. Overall, I think you have to decide on the end result you want and stay focused on that path. I did it years ago without any help. But then, flying by the seat of my pants is pretty much the story of my life. I wouldn't recommend that path to every woman, but being spontaneous—and being able to not look back or second guess your decisions—is important.

Today, with women like Jennifer Aniston, Angelina Jolie, and even Pamela Anderson, who graced the pages of *Playboy* sans clothes at the age of forty-eight, we're finally seeing an appreciation of the true sexiness and hotness of older women and seeing women opening blockbusters, producing their own films, and becoming players in entertainment. It's about damned time.

A Midsummer Night's Dream

When I turned forty, I talked with *Playboy* about another layout based on some of the famous entertainers I used to play on USA: *Up All Night*, like Lucille Ball, Barbara Eden, and Cher. It never happened, but *Playboy* remained a positive presence in my life. Once you're a part of the family, you're always part of the family.

The editors kept writing about what I was up to and would ask me to do their radio shows now and then. And even though I had never been a Playmate, I was always on their party list. That led to being invited to the Playboy Mansion, and this chapter would not be complete without my Playboy Mansion story.

I think just about every straight man on the planet has "Go to the Playboy Mansion" on his bucket list. That's all well and good, but getting on the *Playboy* party list is almost impossible. You have to be a gorgeous young gal or an old friend of Hef's, period. If a girl wants to bring a date or a husband, he has to be approved by Hef based on a picture and résumé. That's the way it has always been, and it's Hef's mansion, so he can do what he wants. The upside was that his parties were always filled with gorgeous, sexy guys and girls.

Part of the glamour of *Playboy* parties was the beauty of the invitations. Hef approved each one, and I still have many of them. Gracing each one was an illustration by Alberto Vargas or Olivia De Berardinis, Vargas's protégé. I was blessed in the late '90s to become a subject of Olivia's, but I told her that I could not take the sexy, pin-up girl thing seriously. I asked her to paint me with toilet paper stuck to my shoe.

That's who I am. I giggled about sex for years and tittered my way out of some pretty uncomfortable sexual situations. Humor was my defense mechanism. More than once, I really did walk out of a bathroom dressed to the nines with six feet of toilet paper attached to my shoe—then laughed my ass off about it when someone pointed it out. One thing I have never done is take myself seriously. Life is a lot more fun when you can laugh at yourself for being the ridiculous person you are!

Olivia wouldn't paint me trailing a toilet paper streamer, but she did capture my sense of humor by painting me wearing a space outfit with aliens encircling me. In another painting, she had me wrapped in a stole made of Pomeranian puppies, wearing a dog collar and bones. But Olivia's most famous painting of me was a bust shot named *Why Men Leave Home*. It sold for more than $20,000 and a collector friend owns it to this day. I received a signed giclée of that painting as a thank you for posing; I cherish it, and it adorns my bedroom wall.

Anyway, the first time I went to the mansion was in 1979 for the August Midsummer Night's Dream Party. I don't think I got my mouth fully closed until October. Floating around the grounds were ethereal goddesses dressed (barely) in long, flowing negligees. It was incredible to see such beauty under one roof. The guests would roam from the dining room and the famous movie room to tents that had been erected over the entire back gardens—and of course, to the famed grotto. It was truly an adult wonderland.

However, Hef did not tolerate disrespect towards women. If a guy went a bit too far or got too pushy with any female guest, he was promptly escorted out of the grounds. If you were lucky enough to be one of the men to receive an invitation, you didn't want that to happen, because that invite would never be extended again.

FOURTH WALL BREAK!

"Hold up," you're saying. How could I call myself a feminist and not look at all those young playmates, objectified for their tight bodies and dressed like courtesans, with horror and anger? It's simple: there are a lot of ways to be a woman and be happy with who you are, so it's silly to judge.

I always appreciated beauty growing up. My mom lived it and preached it. The truth is, attractive people tend to get hired faster. I was never jealous of someone more attractive than me, because for the most part, I was happy in my own skin. But I was flabbergasted at the sight of all those women at the mansion. I felt like a babe in the woods at twenty-three. They all looked so sophisticated to me. I was familiar with the world of pageants, but grown-up women floating across the Playboy Mansion lawn in negligees was a sight to behold. They were like living works of art. They were not showing as much as you would think and wore billowing chiffon gowns and robes that floated in the light breeze of Bel-Air. It felt like an old Hollywood moment. It was surreal and fun!

For me, the bottom line is this: if you're confident enough to rock what you've got and it's helping you get what you want in this world without hurting you or anyone else, who am I to judge you?

I dated plenty of men who were dying to get inside the mansion, especially after I turned forty. One of my favorites was Sam Simon: director, writer, producer, boxing manager, philanthropist, animal rights activist, and one of the original creators of *The Simpsons*. Sadly, Sam lost a battle with colon cancer in 2015, but not before doing more good for animal rights, zoos, and PETA than any person on the planet. Sam was beyond sexy and I enjoyed his company. So I made him my arm candy for another Midsummer Night's Dream Party and he quickly became a regular.

The party was an eye opener for him. This was the 1990s, when the mansion was in its glory and the grotto was in full swing. Nights there were always nights to remember. On this night, the usual suspects were there: Scott Baio, Bill Maher, Pauly Shore, Jack Nicholson, and Cory Feldman of *Goonies* and *The Lost Boys*. Back then, Hef was with his first set of blondes, years before the Heathers and Hollys. Anna Nicole Smith was taking a fully clothed dip in the pool.

I gave Sam and my niece, Brigitte, a tour of the mansion, grounds, zoo, and grotto. The grotto was like a steam room and people were having sex everywhere, including in the water.

Somehow Sam, Brigitte, Cory Feldman, and I wound up watching this gorgeous couple fuck in slow motion while we ate shrimp cocktail. It was surreal, like watching a live porn film. It was quite an initiation into mansion life, even for Sam, who hadn't exactly been born yesterday.

There really was no place like the mansion.

If You Can See Them...

The most important man in my life discovered the inhibition-lowering power of the mansion in 2001. A few months into my marriage to Van, we got a coveted invitation for the year's Midsummer Night's Dream bash. I was excited to show my new hubby and childhood sweetheart the mansion, but a little self-conscious at the same time. I was no longer a nubile twenty-something. I was forty-five, and although I was in great shape, I was still twice as old as many of Hef's beauties.

Then we arrived and it didn't matter. The place worked its magic. We enjoyed a couple of cocktails, and Van was careful to ogle the shrimp cocktails more than the Playmates. After we'd sampled the food and beverages, I showed him the grounds, the zoo, the monkeys, the freely roaming peacocks, and of course, the grotto.

We got a little ambitious and went skinny-dipping in the dim lighting, something I had never come close to doing on past visits. But we were still in the honeymoon stage of our marriage, and I decided to get a little naughtier. I showed Van the secret trail that led up to the top of the grotto, a secluded spot where the famous orgies of the 1970s took place. I thought it would be cool to make out with my hubby up there.

We started messing around, and things quickly got hotter and heavier than I had intended. I hesitated. Van looked around and said, "I can see all the other guests down by the pool and bar."

I said, "Don't worry, they can't see us." Well, you know how they say, *If you can see them, they can see you...?*

It didn't matter. I was in the throes of passion with my new hubby, feeling empowered and sexy and fabulous. I was showing him a part of my life that had been going for years but sharing it with him in a way that I never had with anyone else. It was hot as hell.

We did our thing, and as we got up to straighten ourselves out... we got a rousing round of applause and cheers from the crowd below—the people I was sure couldn't see us! I think I blushed down to the roots of my hair. We dressed and scurried back down to the grotto to the approving smiles of the other guests, grateful that smart phones with high-definition cameras hadn't been invented yet.

Playboy was always surprising, always alluring, always doing something wonderful for me. You don't find many allies like that in life.

~ ON THE WAY TO TODAY ~

What did I take away from all this pube-whitening, tradition-smashing, steamy grotto craziness? Let's see...

- [ ] Never underestimate the ability of repressed people to overreact to sex.

- [ ] Having a good agent is like having a big brother or sister watching out for you.

- [ ] There really is no such thing as bad publicity. If people don't know who you are, opportunities can't come your way.

- [ ] Karma is a bitch (you'll see in the next chapter).

- [ ] Forget about news and politics. Facebook is the world's best tool for maintaining relationships with people you haven't seen face to face in years.

- [ ] Sometimes you have to create your own opportunities.

- [ ] Sometimes you have to create your own opportunities. (That one's so important I wrote it twice.)

- [ ] Hot and funny are not mutually exclusive.

- [ ] Sexy is about your wink, walk, and smile, not the size of your ass.

- [ ] If something makes you nervous (or scares you), it's probably worth doing.

- [ ] Pitch your idea. Don't presume the answer is no.

- [ ] Remember, it's the embarrassments, uncomfortable surprises, and shit shows that make the best stories. Go for it.

LESSON THREE
Speak Up

—— *In which our heroine deals out some karma, shakes up the political gentry, does some same-sex campaigning, discovers that she has a voice that people will take seriously, and, against all odds, nearly wins.* ——

*P*layboy was like a guardian angel hovering around me for nearly thirty years (and more; my relationship with them remains close to this day), watching over me, and helping good things happen in my life. If that's true, then my brief, totally unplanned foray into New Orleans politics was the result of a devil sitting on my shoulder, sticking me with a pitchfork and goading me: "Do it, Rhonda! Do it! You know you want to."

Angel or devil, both had something in common: they led me to try things I had never imagined myself doing, and excelling at them. This time in my life marked the beginning of a pattern that you might have already spotted, in which someone told me what I couldn't do and gave me no better reason than, "It's simply not done" (or worse, told me that I couldn't do it because I was a girl), and my natural response was to become more determined than ever to do it and make the doubters eat their words. I'm proud to say that I've made a lot of people choke on "Rhonda, you can't" over the years.

I think that's one of my keys to success. In fact, these days when I see doubt, scorn, or fear in the eyes of people when I tell them I'm going to do something, I treat it as good news. It means I'm on the scent of something big and important, because it's big, important goals and radical changes that make others around us nervous. I want to say to them, "I'm sorry that you're afraid I'm going to make you look bad by doing what you couldn't do, but your fear isn't my problem."

We've experienced some radical change in our country in the realm of politics, to be sure. I'm proud to say that I played a small part in it—came full circle, you might say. But my interest in politics—and my awareness that I really would take any risk to prove someone wrong about my abilities—began in New Orleans in 1978.

Register of Conveyances

April of 1978, to be exact. The hubbub around my *Playboy* pictorial and the Floral Trail Society had just started to die down, and my mind was set on going to Hollywood to try my luck at a career in entertainment. Right around this time, things started revving up in New Orleans for local elections. Politics in New Orleans, as it is throughout the South, is a tradition-bound, syrupy, good-old-boy institution where somethings are Just Not Done and family ties mean everything. As the 1978 election season slowly got underway, I noticed that one Gasper Schiro was running for the arcane office known as Register of Conveyances.

You remember Gasper, right? The attorney for the Floral Trail

Society who cost me my crown when he convinced a judge that my fingernails were actually exposed nipples? Well, Gasper's uncle had been mayor of the Crescent City in the past, and the Schiro name was well known in local political circles. Family ties, remember? Everyone figured that Gasper was a shoo-in to win election to an arcane, barely known office that was mostly responsible for keeping track of official documents like leases, deeds, sales contracts, and plans for subdivisions.

I certainly had no interest in the Register of Conveyances or any plans to run.

But I failed to count on two things: my own desire to get a touch of revenge against the Floral Trail Society in the person of Gasper, and the mischievous, devilish nature of my older sister, Nona. Nona was and still is a naughty person who loves to provoke people and stir up trouble. I've become more that way as I've gotten older, but back then I was too much of a "good girl" to think of such things. Nona was my surrogate troublemaker and a great big sister.

When she read the news of Gasper's candidacy, she said, "You need to run against Gasper." I said I wasn't interested, but she pressed me and insisted that it would be fun to watch him squirm in shock. The more she talked about it, the more I relished the idea of bringing a dose of karma to that pompous lawyer and his political cronies. Imagining his shock and consternation at seeing my name on the ballot next to his gave me a warm, tingly feeling inside.

Remember at the end of the last chapter when I wrote that karma is a bitch? Off I went to City Hall, and I registered as a candidate. With the stroke of a pen, I not only became the youngest person ever to run for office in New Orleans, but the first woman to run for office in the entire state of Louisiana.

A Reality Show Election

For all my youth, this wasn't my first experience as a candidate for elected office. In high school, I ran for secretary of the student council. My campaign slogan was, "Jump on your Honda and go vote for Rhonda!" Clever, right? Well, I lost by three votes. I did work hard, though. Talk about a wake-up call. I kept thinking that I could have begged three more students to vote for me, or campaigned a bit harder. But sometimes you don't get the result you want.

Running for office teaches you a lot about fear: that it's exactly as much of an obstacle as you let it be. Sometimes you don't want to make a phone call or ask for something. But you have to push yourself to make it happen, because nobody's going to do it for you. You have to get out there. That's why I encourage young people to take an improv or public speaking class. Get out of your comfort zone. At some point you will have to speak in public, even if it's just in front of a neighborhood group, your kids' teachers' association, or at work. At some point, you'll have the opportunity to get up in front of an audience and try to convince them to do something important. Be prepared. You have no idea how far you can get just on audacity and guts.

With my hat thrown into the ring, so began the strangest election anyone in New Orleans could remember. The candidate slate looked like something out of a reality show. We had me, a twenty-two-year-old beauty queen and disgraced *Playboy* model; Ernest Hessler, the eighty-four-year-old incumbent whom no one had seen in years; Gasper, who had a limp and a harelip; and Melvin Bush, who had no interest in winning the election at all, but ran for another reason.

This was Louisiana, home of Huey Long. The state was no

stranger to political corruption; bribes and payoffs were as commonplace as the humidity. In New Orleans, people would enter races they had no chance of winning just so viable candidates would pay them to quit so they wouldn't split the vote. That's why Melvin Bush ran, and I presume he got his money, because he quickly withdrew from the election. Then things started getting really interesting. Gasper was well known in the city, but I had years of experience on stage and in front of a microphone and was a former Miss Louisiana. As awkward as he was on the stump, I was charismatic and well-spoken.

I figured that I had no chance in the race, so I ran a daring, rule-breaking campaign. I handed out glamorous head shots to voters. I started making speeches in front of the New Orleans Young Democrats, and I was shocked when the local media showed up to cover them. I shouldn't have been; this was a great story! You had a member of an old-line New Orleans political family running against a photogenic young underdog whom he'd trounced in court in a widely covered scandal. It was journalism gold, a real David and Goliath tale.

I tried to look as old and mature as I could on my campaign flyers and lawn sign. In fact, my campaign brochure read, "A serious young woman who will serve the people of New Orleans with integrity, intelligence, and hard work." They were collector's items! Remember, I had already won many pageants (including Miss Louisiana), appeared in *Playboy*, had a rift with the Floral Trail Society, been the Shape Spa gal, and had danced on the *John Pela Show*, so I was well-known. When the lawn signs came out, people were taking them as souvenirs. And I could never have paid for all the publicity that my past notoriety was giving me for free. Every time there was an article in the *Times-Picayune* about the election and the first black mayoral candidate, the little office I was after would get as much ink—or more. In today's terms, I had "gone viral." Even the back editorial page of *Playboy* was having fun rehashing the whole Floral Trail episode.

But I still had to prove myself as a serious candidate. I don't know if it was my competitive nature, my desire to get back at Gasper for the Floral Trail fiasco, or the power that came with winning a political office that made me want to win so badly, but I wanted to prove I was more than a beauty queen. I spoke in front of church congregations, every little back alley political group, and the Young Democrats (who endorsed me, which was huge). The *Times-Picayune* endorsed me, too. I became more and more confident with every speech.

A Candidate for Change

At that time, I was friendly with Dutch Morial, who the year before had been elected the first black mayor of New Orleans, and he endorsed me. Once that happened, I got some other major endorsements and my campaign began to pick up some steam. I thought, "Oh shit; I'd better learn something about this office I'm running for." To my relief, it was basically a record keeping position with thirty-two jobs under it, and at the time its office was located in the basement of City Hall. Even so, a position with thirty-two people reporting to you was considered a "political plum" in the Big Easy.

FOURTH WALL BREAK!

Dutch Morial was an amazing, brilliant, handsome man. I became friends with his brother Frank and his son, Marc, who also served as mayor of New Orleans and is now president of the National Urban League. Dutch had greatness in store but also a thing for the ladies. He respected me, endorsed me, and encouraged me to continue with my campaign. He promised me a job with the city and put me on a committee to check out all the potholes in the city. That lasted a month before I moved to Hollywood, and was the only real job I ever had except for my brief stint as a Playboy bunny. Dutch was about change...and so was I.

But I was a pretty sharp cookie, if I do say so myself. I immediately saw an issue I could own for the election. If you haven't seen it yet, think for a second about what I just told you about the office of the Register of Conveyances. Millions of paper records. Stored in a basement. In New Orleans, a city where the water table is so high that we don't bury our dead but lay them to rest in above-ground mausoleums. It was a recipe for disaster in case of a major flood, which in my city was always a risk, even though Katrina was still twenty-seven years in the future.

My platform became that if elected, I would move the Register of Conveyances office out of its damp basement and put all the documents on microfilm. It was a smart idea and people really liked it, and as I kept speaking, the endorsements kept flooding (pardon the expression) in. Before long the race for this odd little office that no one knew about was getting more press coverage than the mayoral race—including coverage from the national press. *Playboy* got hold of the story and of course they wrote the whole thing up in detail in the back of the magazine, which marked the third time I'd appeared in *Playboy*.

I think what everybody loved, apart from the contrast between

Gasper and me, was the vitality and new ideas I brought to my campaign. New Orleans politics at the time was like the Floral Trail: *fossilized*. Things had always been done a certain way and that was just how it was. Family dynasties passed offices down to the next generation, endorsements were bought and paid for, and nothing much changed. First Dutch Morial changed things with his election, and then I came along saying that the emperor had no clothes. I didn't have anything to lose, so why not be creative and have fun? That made me a dangerous candidate!

The last night before the election, to get a few more votes, I really went out on a limb and dialed up the shock value by campaigning at all the gay and lesbian bars in the French Quarter. I was shocked by what I saw. I had thought I knew my seamy, seductive city really well, but I really was a very innocent young lady. Well, I got an education and became an adult right then and there! Everything was going on at these clubs: guys on guys, girls on girls, you name it. I was propositioned by more than one lesbian, but it was worth it because I think I gained a few votes in the process.

FOURTH WALL BREAK!

On that last night, trolling for votes on the city's adult side, I ended up in what looked like a house down in the Bywater neighborhood at 634 Louisa Street, but was actually a clothing-optional private club called The Country Club. It was a big New Orleans mansion with a central hallway and rooms to the right and left. Well, the things I saw! Left and right, there were guys and girls mingling, then I went further and there were orgies, boys and girls, three people at time, you name it. I walked down another hall and saw men doing stuff. In the back were cabanas, and everything you can think of (and probably some things you'd rather not think of) was going on back there. I was twenty-two, and my mouth flew open and stayed that way. That was how I picked up votes. Who knows? A few more shady sex clubs and I might've won!

The whole election was fun and exciting, and when election night came I actually got more than 35,000 votes! But sadly, it wasn't enough. Gasper beat me by only 135 votes. Incidentally, he stayed in that office for the next thirty years, only being ousted in 2008 when the city finally eliminated the office of Register of Conveyances altogether. As for me, I wasn't disappointed. In fact, I was thrilled. I'd become a candidate on a whim, run a no-holds-barred campaign, nearly won, and probably given the eventual winner a heart attack in the process.

But something else had happened, too. When I'd spoken in front of audiences during the campaign, they hadn't laughed at me. They treated me like I was a serious adult, not a ditzy twenty-two-year-old girl. The experience showed me that my age didn't matter unless I *made* it matter. I'd gone into my campaign with real ideas and something to say, insisting that people take me seriously, and they had.

Politics is a tough business, and I learned more in six months of campaigning then I did in four years of school—at least when it came to growing up fast. When you throw yourself in that arena, no one cares if you're single, young, old, black, white, or female. You are on the firing line. I learned to associate names with something about the people I met on the campaign trail. I learned to ask for votes. I did something few twenty-two-year-olds ever have the opportunity to do.

There were even some people who wanted me to stay in

New Orleans politics and run again. Dutch Morial, Blaine Kern, and Lieutenant Governor Jimmy Fitzmorris all wanted me to stay around and stay in politics. Maybe I should have; I would have won practically any office I'd run for because I was known and liked. But I was ready to move on and have the entertainment career that I'd been dreaming about.

> **Shear Honesty:** *My experience speaking as a candidate showed me a side of New Orleans—and people in general—that I hadn't appreciated before. The city could be a rather sexist place, as were the South and the entire country at that time. But if you defied that sexism and came to the table with confidence, eloquence, and real ideas, the people were generous, welcoming, and respectful about what you had to offer. New Orleans may have a reputation for style, but I saw its substance. I've found the same to be true everywhere. If you take yourself seriously and go into a situation thinking—KNOWING—that you are someone to be reckoned with, you will be.* **No one can trivialize you without your cooperation.**

Blaine Kern Jr.

I can't end this election tale without a brief coda about my campaign manager, Blaine Kern Jr., son of the Mardi Gras legend, Blaine Kern Sr. The elder Blaine had worked himself up from a poor artist and become *the* epic float builder of our time, the New Orleans version of Walt Disney.

When I became involved in Mardi Gras, first as a Maid, then as Queen of Endymion, I got to know Blaine Sr. better. Although he was twenty-six years older than I was, he was handsome, charming, romantic, and had an energy like no other man I had ever known. I really enjoyed dating him (though we never consummated the relationship; remember, I was a very sexually conservative young lady), and could have seen myself marrying him. But he claimed I was too young, which is interesting because his beautiful wife, Holly Kern, is about fifty years his junior. But I must say they are a perfect match; Blaine Sr. is younger mentally than ever. We both talk about having an inward drive that keeps people young and that you just can't extinguish, and Blaine Sr. has it.

In any case, Blaine Sr. and I are still friends to this day, and I am proud to say that he and Holly were at my big sixtieth birthday party, and he was dancing late into the night at the tender age of eighty-eight.

Around the time I ran for office, I began dating Blaine Jr., who was a couple of years younger than me and quite handsome and charming, like his father. When my candidacy took off, Blaine Jr. volunteered to jump in and be my campaign manager, even though I had no money. He was great for me and for my campaign, and we learned a lot about campaigning and each other. A crush was growing in both directions, but it bothered me that he was younger than I was.

After the election, I was itching to get to Hollywood, and the relationship sort of fizzled. I don't think Blaine Jr. ever really forgave me for choosing Hollywood over him. I've thought about that relationship over the years. You know how they say that sometimes, you let the good ones get away? Well, Blaine Jr. was a good one. He eventually made it big on his own with his own company, Mardi Gras Productions, decorating for huge international events.

Funny thing: Blaine Jr.'s son is now doing well himself in Hollywood as an actor and has gotten some big starring roles. The beat goes on. So things really do eventually come full circle, jealousy and rivalry notwithstanding.

⮜ ON THE WAY TO TODAY ⮞

What did your obedient authoress learn from her nearly successful toe-dip into the world of politics, gay strippers, and stump speeches? Well...

☐ Sometimes, it's fine to let yourself be talked into something you wouldn't do on your own.

☐ You never know what you can do until you try.

☐ Some people will write you off, but not everyone will. Find allies and hold them close.

☐ Politics is full of hidden motives.

☐ Being an eloquent, convincing speaker is one of the most valuable skills you could ever learn.

☐ Give it your all, even if you think it's hopeless. You might surprise yourself and win!

☐ Sometimes, tradition just needs to be defied and the "way things are done" just needs to be blown up.

☐ Fortune favors the provocative and fearless.

PART Two
HOLLYWOOD YEARS

LESSON FOUR

A Wink and a Smile
Go a Long Way

—— *In which our heroine narrowly escapes the notorious LA Parking Garage Slasher, starts her own one-woman society, ducks the amorous advances of several sports legends, rides the roses, rubs elbows with Golden Globe winners, and loses a shot at Miss America over $1.98.* ——

*I*n 1977 I graduated from Loyola University at age twenty-two with a bachelor's degree in communications. While I thought about going to law school, I couldn't resist the pull of Hollywood any longer. Finally, in the summer of 1978, I talked my parents into letting me move out to Los Angeles. However, they set conditions they felt would keep their baby safe halfway across the country. First, I had to be in some sort of school situation, so I enrolled in the American Academy of Dramatic Arts in Pasadena. It's the oldest acting school in the English-speaking world, where everybody who's anybody trained, from Lauren Bacall to Robert Redford.

The other condition was that I had to take girlfriends with me. I found two college girlfriends, Susan Sherlock and Cindy Reed, who were willing to come out with me for the summer, and when my parents heard that, they said yes. They flew out to California with us and got us settled into our first apartment. They made sure it was a nice apartment in a safe neighborhood in West Hollywood, which made them feel good. Later, they put me in another apartment on the ninth floor of a high-rise on Wilshire Boulevard, near UCLA in Westwood. So I never had to work as a waitress on the night shift to afford the rent on an overpriced fleabag apartment in Hollywood. I was thankful for that.

But even though my first LA apartment was in a very safe neighborhood, my mother had made me so paranoid about sexual assault that I spent half the time looking over my shoulder for the inevitable ski-masked rapist. It was ridiculous, and it led to a true sitcom moment. Susan and Cindy had done laundry earlier in the day in the laundry room of our apartment complex on Cynthia Street. Like many apartment buildings, ours had the laundry room off the parking garage, which could be creepy at night. Late that night, we realized that we had not removed our clothes from the dryer, and I was terrified to go into the dark, empty, echoing garage to get them.

Who could have been waiting for us in our gated garage? I don't know—the bogeyman? Bill Cosby? The point is, I made the other two gals so nervous that we ended up calling a cab to drive us—this is true—from the front of the building around the corner and into the garage so we could rescue our laundry! I can't even imagine what the cabbie thought when three young actresses entered his cab and asked to be driven fifty feet into a subterranean garage to get some ratty underwear. I'm guessing he thought we were out of our minds. Talk about an easy fare!

Shear Honesty: *Let's talk about fear. I'll be the first one to admit that for all my brassy, bold talk, I'm as vulnerable to fear* as anyone. For instance, I'm a hypochondriac. But it's one thing to feel fear and another to let it stop you from doing what you want to do. When I was young in LA, I feared men lurking in the shadows. But that didn't stop me from auditioning everywhere, because I believed in my ability to handle whatever came along. In whatever ventures you pursue, you're going to feel fear. It's normal. Feel it, own it, and decide whether or not it's rational. If it is, adjust. If it's not, push past it and do what you need to do anyway. **Fear is only important if it stops you.**

The Bachelor Women Society of America

Ridiculous antics aside, I gradually settled into a new life that could not have been less like my life in New Orleans. In the evenings, I went to acting and comedy improv classes. By day I worked my butt off to do everything I could to get noticed by people who could cast me in something—*anything*. I worked the phones, did dinner meetings with would-be agents, dropped off résumés and head shots—anything to get noticed and stand out from the tens of thousands of other girls doing the same thing. The original Schwab's drugstore on Sunset Boulevard—where Lana Turner was supposedly discovered while sitting on a stool and sipping a milkshake—was still around, and I would even drop in there. I figured it couldn't hurt; maybe a little magic would rub off. It never hurts to have a little luck.

But **creativity, determination, and moxie matter more than luck**, and I knew that I had all three. So I used them. I had bakeries send beautiful cakes to producers with icing that read, "What do I have to do to get a meeting with you?" I never heard from any of them, and until now I never realized how that must have come across. I was always a goody-two-shoes, in my twenties still naïve about double entendre. Fortunately, that changed in my later life, and risqué humor is now my favorite form of humor.

It was hard to stand out from the crowd. Remember, those were the days before the Internet; there was no YouTube or Facebook to help with self-promotion. You did what you could, and when you did a show or commercial, you got a videotape and built your résumé. My goal was to catch people's attention with my looks, then, once I had them looking, wow them with my brains and my talent. I still feel this way. In any business, you get your message across by first capturing your audience's attention. Packaging matters in any business, from acting to selling clothing, the business I'm in now. There's a psychological principle called the *halo effect*, and it says that a good first impression makes someone more likely to see you in a positive light later on.

That's why it's so important to dress immaculately and carry yourself with charm and professionalism at any interview or audition. First, you get people's attention so they look up from their smart phones (Flattering dress? Check. Great hair? Check. Dazzling white smile? Double check.) and when they see you, you make it so they can't imagine giving the job or the part to anyone but you.

Shear Honesty: *Oh my God, do first impressions matter! They matter in an audition more than just about anything, because you might only get a minute or two in front of that director, producer, or casting director. But what in life isn't an audition? A first date, a job interview, pitching a product, or trying to get an investor to fund your company—they're all auditions, and you need to put your best foot forward. Show up on time, even early. Be dressed and groomed perfectly. Know about the person or company you're* *meeting with. Be calm, articulate, positive, and succinct in what you say. Have your opening planned: how you'll sit, where you'll put your hands, what you'll say. Have some smart questions prepared. None of this will guarantee you getting the job, the part, or the second date, but they will improve your odds!*

Of course, getting producers and other players to notice me in a city of two million was easier said than done. One classic Rhonda trick came about not long after I'd gotten to Hollywood. My parents took me to see Gene Shefrin, one of the great, big-time, old-school publicists. I had minored in public relations and marketing, and my dad really believed that it would make a difference in my career, so I signed with Gene on the spot. (Mom and Dad footing the bill, because Gene was way out of my price range.)

Right away, he started coming up with some very old-school ideas, the most outrageous of which was the "Bachelor Women Society of America." It had one member: *Rhonda Shear.* But once a year for the next three years, Gene put out a press release announcing that the Bachelor Women Society of America had selected the top bachelor in the world. One year it was Woody Allen; another it was Prince Charles. One year it was George Burns, and we actually did a photo shoot with George in his office that was picked up by *UPI* and the *Associated Press.*

But as hard as I worked and as many wild ideas as I tried, nothing made me a star. Nobody was going to walk up to me and hand me my own TV show. Things didn't work that way. There were hundreds of thousands of young, hot, talented men and women in Los Angeles who were all dying to do the same thing I was dying to do, and only so many jobs to go around. Becoming successful was a matter of some talent, a lot of determination, even more hard work, and no small amount of luck.

ABOVE: *My beautiful mom and dad, Jennie and Wilbur Shear, before a Mardi Gras Ball in 1983.*

RIGHT: Me before losing
my two front teeth.

Rhonda Shear

ACROBATICS
MECHANICAL MIME
S.A.G./A.F.T.R.A.

ABOVE: *Glossy 8x10 publicity shot submitted by my agents to casting directors for gigs.*
These two shots show off my acrobatic and mime abilities.

Noel Blakely
NEW ORLEANS, LA

RIGHT: *A program photo from my days at the Ann Maucele School of Dance in 1972. I had just become a graduate dance instructor.*

LEFT: *My mom and me before the taping of a Maury Povich Valentine's Day special. The episode featured female comics and their moms, and my mom tried fixing me up on national TV.*

LEFT: *Back when high school sororities and fraternities were huge, Van and I attended a formal for Van's fraternity together. Taken at my parents' home, you can see the love light in our eyes.*

RIGHT: *Van and me walking up the aisle after our wedding ceremony. We had already eloped but did it all over again for our families in New Orleans at the Royal Orleans Hotel.*

ABOVE: *After winning my first of three Miss Louisiana titles, The Times-Picayune photographer took me to the top of a building close to the Louisiana Superdome, now the Mercedes-Benz Superdome. It was under construction at the time, but one of the pictures appeared in the newspaper in 1973.*

LEFT: *Van and me on Lake Pontchartrain in New Orleans. We had stayed up all night with my parents to watch Joanne Woodward and Paul Newman shoot a scene from a film. We sat where they sat, and I had stars in my eyes.*

ABOVE: *Posing right after winning Miss Hollywood-USA. This led to the Miss California-USA pageant and on to Miss World-USA and Miss Universe.*

ABOVE: Publicity shot taken of the newly chosen "elevens" for The Starmakers, which was a take off on Bo Derek's 10. Career starter for me!

BELOW: With my parents in full Queen of Endymion attire.

BELOW: Walking the runway in the Miss World-USA pageant. Bob Hope was the owner of the pageant, and Dick Clark was the emcee. He also became my manager years later.

LEFT: Presenting a gift to the notorious Governor Edwards as the newly selected Miss Louisiana-World.

RIGHT: Taken by famed Hollywood photographer Harry Langdon for my own use. I was showing a little more brunette, circa 1996. As I always like to say, "Behind every great woman is a great behind!"

LEFT: *Taken at the famous plantation Oak Alley, the same location and in the same dress as the infamous Playboy photoshoot. The dress was my state costume for the Miss World-USA pageant and Miss Louisiana-World pageant. It was also to be used for my reign as Floral Trail Queen.*

LEFT: *Taken by Harry Langdon for a magazine shoot. Harry photographed many stars and the covers of albums. His dad was the famous silent film star of the same name.*

LEFT: *In full queen attire in Washington, D.C., just minutes before being presented to the court and guests at the Washington Mardi Gras Ball in 1976.*

RIGHT: *My "Go for the Gold" poster taken by famed Hollywood photographer Dick Zimmerman. It became a billboard on Sunset Boulevard during the 1984 Olympics, causing some fender benders.*

Thank *you* for your service!

To all the brave men & women who keep our country safe...

Sizzle Kisses! XOXO

Rhonda Shear

ABOVE: *A photo taken for our military by USA Network in 1991 to be sent overseas.*

ABOVE: *With my loyal friend and beautiful model, Regina Marlow. This was a press picture for our boutique and Rhonda Shear brand. Everyone always says we look like sisters!*

LEFT: *Publicity photo taken right after my marriage to Van in 2001. I'm a natural brunette, but once you go blonde, it's hard to go back.*

LEFT: *Sassy publicity shot taken by Playboy photographer David Mecey when I was thirty-eight. Never too old for sass!*

ABOVE: *Another publicity shot taken by the iconic Harry Langdon. I'm wearing the same teddy that was used in the opening shot of Rhonda in the UAN layout in Playboy in 1993.*

ABOVE: *Publicity shot taken for the fans of UAN.*

ABOVE: *Van and me at the star-studded red carpet opening of our boutique, Maison Rouge, in St. Petersburg in 2007.*

RIGHT: *With my niece and best friend, Brigitte Pailet.*

RIGHT: *Presenting the Lace Crossover Ahh Bra with superstar host Colleen Lopez on HSN as Today's Special in 2017.*

BELOW: *Advertisement for the Rhonda Shear brand with Playmates Jessa Hinton (left) and Alana Campos (right).*

RHONDA SHEAR

Find your *Ahh* Moment!

Shapewear
Sleepwear
Loungewear
Bras & Panties
XS-3X

www.RhondaShear.com

ABOVE: *Live on air with HSN pitching my line of "Ahh Dreams" cozy-licious loungewear.*

LEFT: *Some of Shear Enterprises' team and my best friend, Chuck Anderson, right after winning Ernst & Young Entrepreneur of the Year 2012 for Florida.*

LEFT: *Presenting the Ahh Bra as Today's Special on HSN in 2017. We've sold 35 million of these award-winning bras worldwide!*

LEFT: *Taken for the Rhonda Shear catalogue. From left to right: Kayla Collins, me, Jessa Hinton, and Alana Campos. All are gorgeous Playmates and successful women. My beloved Yorkie, Tiki, makes a guest appearance, too!*

The Los Angeles Press Club

I decided that I needed an edge over all those other young, would-be starlets, a way to get seen and known. So I started entering beauty pageants in California. It hadn't been long since I had held multiple Miss Louisiana titles, so my pageant chops were still sharp. Heck, I could take down these big-city amateurs!

My mother had never given up her dream that I would win Miss America, and she kept pushing me to enter the Miss California pageant. If I won, I would have qualified for Miss America. But I was more interested in meeting people who could further my career, and that meant entering more pageants that would get me known in and around the City of Angels. (Think of it as networking with shoulder pads and a push-up bra.) And that is how I became Miss LA Press Club after being in the city for only a couple of months.

The Los Angeles Press Club has been around since 1913 and its members and mission statement speak passionately about upholding the standards of great journalism and recognizing the finest members of the Southern California press corps. To be fair, it does those things, including honoring bright new voices in the local media. But back in the late 1970s, the Press Club had the same core mission as most of the professional boys' clubs of that era: to be a place lecherous old reporters could go to get loaded and swap war stories with their buddies. They were a bunch of colorful characters and were incredibly kind to me. That's what the LAPC was like when I won my crown.

Trivia time: who was chosen as the first Miss Los Angeles Press Club in 1953? If you said Norma Jeanne Baker—otherwise known as Marilyn Monroe—bravo! She graduated from being chosen as the Press Club's "Miss Eight-Ball" in 1948 and set a standard that nobody else could live up to, really. She and I were bookends, because I was the very last Miss Los Angeles Press Club. Times were changing, and the women's movement was making private club beauty cuties seem like relics of a time when men were men and women were barefoot and pregnant. But I had a ball wearing that crown while it lasted, and it really helped my career.

FOURTH WALL BREAK!

Miss Press Club was a pageant like the others I had entered in New Orleans. You had to go to the club, leave a picture and résumé, and they called to let you know if you had made the cut. I did, and I did an interview with members of the Press Club—in a bikini—and ended up in their Behind the Eight-Ball *magazine. The final contest was on stage at the Press Club and was typical: evening gown, swimsuit, answer some questions. It was old hat to me and I won. That's when my love affair with the LA Press Club started. They took me under their wing; I was their unofficial hostess, and they were wonderful. Despite what you might think, they were respectful and never lewd with me.*

Unlike most of my past pageant titles, this one came with a job: to represent the press corps and the *Los Angeles Times*, which sponsored the LAPC. I spent a lot of time walking celebrities up to the dais at events like the Annual Journalism Awards dinners at the Biltmore Hotel. I also got to hobnob with legends like George Burns while fending off the advances of legendary sportscaster Howard Cosell.

If you're over, say forty years old, then you remember Howard Cosell. If you're younger than that...how do you describe Howard? Picture a homely, balding little man wearing a toupee and a perpetual squint, who even when he was twenty-one probably looked like he was fifty-five. Now add a slo-mo delivery that sounded like he'd just taken a handful of Valium and washed them down with Crown Royal. Now make him the absolute biggest name in sportscasting in the 1970s and 1980s. There you have Howard Cosell, the voice of *Monday Night Football* and championship boxing (if you've ever heard someone use the phrase, "Down goes Frazier!" you've heard Howard's work).

Back in 1979, I was invited to a roast for Los Angeles Police Chief Daryl Gates. There I was, sitting on the dais with this star-studded group that included Muhammad Ali, Sammy Davis Jr., Gene Autry, Slim Pickens, and Cosell. Howard was as much a horny old goat as any man there, and he spent a good part of the night trying to slip me his room key. This was the beginning of my using flirtation and sarcasm to deflect men's advances. For anyone who's assumed for all these years that I used my boobs and my feminine charms to sleep my way to the top (or wherever it was I got in entertainment), here's a news flash: I *didn't*. I may have cultivated a sexpot image, but I remained very much Jennie Weaker Shear's "Let them look, but not touch" daughter. I knew I was funny, and I used humor to discourage potential paramours without bruising their egos or making them feel rejected. When you're getting excited and I'm making you laugh, it's not much of a turn-on.

Plenty of young women were (and still are) willing to sleep their way into roles or representation, and the power brokers in Hollywood knew it. So they would try, try again. If I offended them it would hurt my career. But if I made them feel good even while I was rejecting their advances, who knows? Remember, my rule is no burned bridges. So while Cosell kept pushing his big, ornate hotel key toward me, I'd push it back towards him, giggle, and make some tittering joke about how huge and hard it was, and he'd get a kick out of it and not notice that I'd just cock-blocked him. It was pretty skillful, I have to admit.

Tournament of Roses

I adored reigning as Miss Los Angeles Press Club. One of the best things about it was riding the Press Club float in the world-famous Tournament of Roses Parade. You know how I feel about parades and floats, but parades in Los Angeles are nothing like they were when I was growing up in New Orleans, and the floats are completely different. The floats of New Orleans are huge, ornate, garishly lit, animated "super floats," like glitter-bombed wedding cakes. The riders, always masked, throw beads and trinkets to the crowds below, often in return for girls of all ages flashing their, um, assets.

Well, I was shocked to see how civilized and proper the Tournament of Roses Parade was. You've probably seen it on television: gorgeous floats made of hundreds of varieties of flowers, foliage, and seeds. They remain on display for a week or two after the parade. They are often animated but spectacular in their floral beauty. But the biggest difference is the people. They're dignified. No one throws anything to the crowd. The crowd sits and waves, and you just wave back. How dull. For a New Orleans girl it was unheard of to have nothing to throw, but it was fabulous nonetheless. I rode in the Tournament of Roses Parade for the Los Angeles Press Club three years in a row. Other than having to be on the float at five in the morning (ugh), it was an amazing day. Pasadena is old California, and the parade is a marvelous tradition.

FOURTH WALL BREAK!

I rode in three Rose Parades, and they were some of the most exciting times I ever had. In the first one, I wore a white leather cowgirl outfit. It was freezing out (yes, even in California, January is cold), but it was so beautiful and it was such an honor to be part of the event. It was a completely different vibe than Mardi Gras: people sitting, waving, and behaving themselves, completely civilized and sophisticated, very respectful.

Still, give me the parade crowds in New Orleans: drunk, screaming, offering to show boobs for the beads and trinkets that the revelers throw. That's how I roll and that's how I reigned as Queen of Endymion. The super parades of New Orleans, Bacchus, and Endymion have always had celebrities as King, from Bob Hope, years ago, to Tom Jones, Dolly Parton, The Beach Boys, Britney Spears, Taylor Swift, Kevin Costner, and all the way up to Aerosmith's Steven Tyler in 2016. The parades culminate inside the Superdome, where guests in black tie wait with outstretched hands for the last of the beads and trinkets. Most of the old-line *krewes* (organizations that participate in Mardi Gras) hold their balls (no, that's not what I meant, shame on you) before the parade, but the newer organizations have their galas inside the Superdome after the parade. The floats serve as the backdrop for the evening. Their twinkling lights and animation are awe-inspiring.

(When Van and I got married on January 11, 2001, we went to Endymion the next month as newlyweds. There we were, in full formal attire, a couple of drinks in, while the float riders unloaded hundreds of pounds of beads onto the crowd inside the dome. I was smiling and waving—until a long, heavy faux pearl necklace collided with my face and turned my front tooth to powder! Three weeks into my marriage and I looked like a character from *The Beverly Hillbillies* until I got back to my dentist in Los Angeles. It was like being six years old again and waiting for a new tooth to come in.)

Golden Globes and Beyond

Being Miss LA Press Club was wonderful, but Old Hollywood was dying fast. The boys' network was becoming obsolete. After my reign ended in 1980, the LA Press Club did away with the pageant for good. But wearing that crown had some benefits for my career. I met members of the Hollywood Foreign Press Association through the Press Club, and in 1983 they chose me to be Miss Golden Globe. That's a major honor, one usually bestowed on a star's offspring. Only a handful of people who weren't stars' children—including Donna Douglas and Linda Evans—have had the same chance. More often, presenters were Hollywood kids like Melanie Griffith, Joely Fisher, John Clark Gable, Freddie Prinze Jr., Dakota Johnson, and Rumer Willis.

Being a Miss Golden Globe meant I got to hand the winners their statuettes and escort them off the stage. It was great fun, and I got to meet idols like Joan Collins and Sir Laurence Olivier. This was back when the Golden Globes didn't get a lot of respect; they were the poor stepsisters to the Oscars. The year before, Pia Zadora had won Best Newcomer for the film *Butterfly*, and it was rumored that her billionaire husband, Meshulam Riklis, had bought the award for her. Who knows, but from 1983 on, the Golden Globes got a lot more serious.

(Interesting factoid: I dated Meshulam Riklis on and off for a year or so after he and Pia divorced in 1993. I had begun my standup comedy career and he owned the Riviera in Las Vegas.

He kept holding out the proverbial carrot: if I would sleep with him, he would make me the regular comic in one of the casino's production shows. I didn't give in, so I didn't get that gig or win a Golden Globe, either. The price of virtue.)

My venture back into pageant life really paid off. For a city of millions, Los Angeles is a surprisingly small town, and my pageants and award show gigs put me in contact with agents, casting directors, and people who became lifelong friends. Like any business, entertainment is all about connections and contacts, and I was already building a great Rolodex (that's where we used to keep business cards before we all had iPhones). But I wasn't through with the pageant world just yet—and it wasn't done with me.

Shear Honesty: *From time to time over the years, it has occurred to me that if I had slept with more of the many, many powerful men who wanted to get me into bed, I probably would have had a bigger career. I might have starred in my own sitcom, which was my dream. But I don't regret saying no to Meshulam Riklis or any of the other producers, directors, and celebrities who came on to me, some of whom were, apart from their position and influence, extremely attractive and charming. Why? Because that would have been a violation of who I was, and you don't get that sense of self back. There are women who might say, "Come on, Rhonda, it's just sex!" but that's not true. I would have been compromising my values. More importantly, if I'd jumped into the sack with every mogul who hit on me, I would have been admitting that I didn't have what it took to make a career on my own merits. I would have devalued myself, and no woman should ever do that.* **Be true to your values.** *It might cost you in the short term, but compromise will cost you more in the long term.*

Chuckie Baby

After my reign as Miss Los Angeles Press Club ended, I figured I was through with beauty pageants. After all, I was in Hollywood to become an actress and comedian. On a whim, I entered the Miss Hollywood pageant—and I won. That opened up the possibility of the Miss California-USA title and fanned the embers of Mom's big Miss America dream back into a flame. At this point I was ready to devote all my energies to getting seen and cast, but this meant everything to my mother, who had done so much for me. It was my last chance at Miss America, so I decided to give it a try.

To be eligible for Miss California, I had to win a local, Los Angeles–area pageant. I chose the Miss Torrance contest (Torrance is a suburb about thirty minutes south of LA). I still had my dance chops, so I pulled a mime/acrobatic/jazz routine out of mothballs and started practicing again. The Miss America people loved routines that mixed different talents, and mine had it all, including a puppet I named Gasper Schiro, who beat me for Register of Conveyances. I figured I had a good chance of knocking 'em dead in the talent competition and using my charm and pageant savvy to walk away with the Miss Torrance crown. From there, it would be a straight shot to the Miss California pageant, where anything could happen.

Talk about great moments in bad timing. As I was getting ready for the pageant, along came Chuck Barris. You're not familiar with Chuck Barris? Well, he was a true original who, sadly, passed away in 2017 at the age of eighty-seven. Chuck was a television producer and host, a pioneer and a genius who changed the face of television—especially the game show. Like most pioneers and geniuses, he was also a little bit...eccentric. All you really need to know about Chuck can be summed up in three titles: *The Dating*

Game, *The Newlywed Game*, and *The Gong Show*. He created them all.

Wait, you've never heard of *The Gong Show?* No, no, that won't do at all. Google it right now and watch a few clips. Seriously. I'll wait.

(hums the tune you hum while waiting for an elevator)

Okay, wasn't that insane? As you probably figured out, *The Gong Show* was a cut-rate talent show that became a cult smash starting in 1976 by featuring a really strange collection of "talent" and semi-celebrity judges like Arte Johnson and Jaye P. Morgan, who looked like they didn't have anything better to do. When they hated an act, they'd bring everything to a halt by ringing this giant, cheesy gong. It was crazy, weird, fun, and totally Chuck. He hosted the show, sported all sorts of bizarre outfits and props, and became as big a hit with fans as the show. Everybody called him "Chuckie Baby."

I adored Chuckie Baby. I'd done a couple of shows for him, including *The Gong Show* in 1979 (I did an acrobatic dance number in a sexy softball uniform and nearly gave NFL great Jack Youngblood a heart attack) and *The Dating Game*. But mostly, Chuck hit on me and wrote me funny letters trying to date me. Once, he'd broken his arm in an accident and was in a cast, and he called to ask if he could come over for breakfast. When I said no, he wrote me a note: "How tricky can a cup of coffee be? Imagine what you might have said if I'd wanted an egg?????" There wasn't anybody like Chuck.

Shear Honesty: *Chuck Barris was a little nuts. But we're still talking about him today while a lot of conventional producers are gone and forgotten. Why? He was an original. Hollywood and every other industry have a bad habit of recycling old ideas—not because they're good but because they're too lazy or scared to* *think of something original! But only the truly creative and daring can be great. Don't think like everybody else. Don't be part of the herd.* **If your idea scares the shit out of you and everyone else tells you that you're nuts, that's a great sign.**

$1.98 Beauty Show

Chuck was an odd duck, but he was also a visionary and he knew that my poise, sass, and comedic timing were perfects fits for his shows. So he kept casting me. That was fine with me, because it got me in front of the camera. A more serious actress might have turned down jobs on cheesy game shows, but I just wanted to be on TV. Chuck had another show, *The $1.98 Beauty Show,* a beauty pageant version of *The Gong Show* where the winner won a whopping $1.98 and a bouquet of vegetables. While I was getting ready to compete in the Miss Torrance pageant, Chuck was begging me to be on *The $1.98 Beauty Show.* I resisted.

I said, "Chuck, if I lose this, it's going to look really bad." But he kept asking me, because it was a new show and Chuck knew that his audiences loved me. Finally, I gave in. Any opportunity to be on camera, right?

On my episode, Willie McCovey (the home run-hitting San Francisco Giants first baseman) and Alan Shepard (the first American in space) were the judges. Naturally, they both hit on me. Willie and I went on some dinner dates, and he tried to get to second base with me (see what I did there?). As for Alan, you've heard the rumor that astronauts are relentless poon hounds, right? It was completely true in Alan's case. He definitely had a thing for this heavenly body; he hit on me for years with no success. I did get an autographed picture of him, though, one of many that I cherish.

Anyway, I taped *The $1.98 Beauty Show*. It was funny as hell, and I won, of course. The trouble was, my episode aired the same week that I was competing for the title of Miss Torrance. Whoops. The judges saw the show, and the sponsors thought that *The $1.98 Beauty Show* and I were making fun of Miss America. Long story short, I was first runner-up for Miss Torrance, and I have no doubt that my *The $1.98 Beauty Show* episode cost me a fair chance at the title. But win or lose, that was the end of my pageant career and any shot at Miss America.

FOURTH WALL BREAK!

Willie McCovey and Alan Shepard were judges on that $1.98 Beauty Show episode, but otherwise it was like Chuck's other shows: goofy, with women of different age groups doing crazy acts, but very professional. Remember, I was running for Miss Torrance and I didn't want to do the show, but Chuck talked me into it. I respected Chuck and knew the show was crazy and silly, but I loved the comedy side of it and that Chuck was so far ahead of his time. I didn't think the show was disrespectful of women at all. I had been in so many pageants that I was probably more at home doing the $1.98 Beauty Show than in the Miss USA Pageant.

My parents—especially my mom—were heartbroken, but I wasn't. It was time to move on and hang up my tiara. I'd gotten everything I could out of being in pageants: poise, confidence, unearthly skill at ducking men making passes at me, a stack of showbiz contacts, and a foot in the door of Hollywood. Now it was time to focus all my energies on building a career.

✎ ON THE WAY TO TODAY ✎

What did the last Miss LA Press Club learn from my turn on the Rose Parade catwalk? Judge for yourself...

☐ If people with money want to help you and expect nothing in return, let them.

☐ If you're scared, bring friends along, but go.

☐ Being audacious and daring might get you noticed, but there's a big difference between being noticed and being called.

☐ Class, poise, eloquence, and ability stand out more than stunts and party tricks.

☐ Even the biggest, most important people love a good laugh and somebody with pluck and courage. Always reach out. "No" is the worst that can happen.

☐ There are ways to discourage someone without making them feel insulted or judged. We could use more of that on Facebook.

☐ What's customary in one place might be terribly inappropriate in another. Wherever you are, learn the rules of conduct.

☐ If it ain't fun, why do it?

☐ Sometimes, chasing one opportunity will cost you another. Make sure the cost is worth it.

☐ Don't waste too much time chasing someone else's dream.

LESSON FIVE
Quit Being Your Own Worst Enemy, Start Being Your Own Best Friend

—— *In which our heroine stays at the* Pretty Woman *hotel, learns to stop worrying and love auditions, becomes a mannequin, nearly fractures Bob Hope's skull, embraces her inner bimbo, has the world's first R-rated nose job, and accidentally goes to war with one of television's biggest stars.* ——

I may have moved out to Los Angeles in 1977, but it wasn't my first experience with Hollywood and showbiz. That came in 1975 when I was only nineteen, and it was like a dream: effortless, filled with fantastical events, and totally misleading.

I had won Miss Louisiana-USA, and that title was associated with a popular jewelry line, Sarah Coventry. To my delight, the company selected me out of all fifty Miss USA state title holders to fly out to California and shoot a Sarah Coventry catalog. It was a paid job, but more than that I was terribly excited to be in LA. This was the beginning of my dream!

Well, things only got better. The Sarah Coventry people picked me up in a limousine and put me up at the Beverly Regent Hotel, which would later become famous as the hotel from *Pretty Woman*. So it's my first time in LA, I'm there by myself, and I'm shooting in a professional studio with a top pro photographer. After I did my own tour of Rodeo Drive and Universal Studios, I was thinking, "I could get used to this."

Well, it turned out that the publicist for Sarah Coventry was also the husband of the casting director of *Happy Days*, and he said, "You should meet my wife, Pat Harris. You are the perfect age, and you would be so good for *Happy Days*." Keep in mind, this was 1975. *Happy Days* was in its second season and had become a huge hit. Henry Winkler, Ron Howard, and everybody on that show were my idols. My head was spinning. I went to Pat Harris's office on the backlot at Paramount Studios, and we talked for a few minutes. Then she said, "You know what? There's a part coming up this week that's perfect for you. Do you want to read for it?"

Are you kidding me? I come to LA and get offered a part on the number-one show in the country, just like that? Doesn't this happen to everybody?

Of course, it wasn't that easy. Normally, when you read for a part, you read with the casting director, which is still nerve-wracking but tolerable. But because all my planets were aligning, I ended up reading with Henry Winkler and Ron Howard! So there I was, nineteen years old and terribly star-struck, with only one or two bit parts on my résumé, my SAG card earned mostly through work in New Orleans, and a terrible case of nerves, reading opposite Richie Cunningham. My reading showed my nerves more than my talent.

Afterward, I sat outside and could hear everybody talking; the casting director said, "She's adorable, but still a little green." I didn't get the part.

It turned out that they were casting for a big Christmas episode, and I was mortified. But when I took a moment to look at the big picture, I was excited. I was still in college, had little experience, and I'd come to Los Angeles and been driven around in limos and auditioned with television stars. It had been an amazing experience that got my feet wet in the best way imaginable. Most of all, I was hooked. This was the life I wanted.

From the time I got back to New Orleans, all I could think about was getting back to Los Angeles and starting what I was sure would be a superstar career as an actress. I mean, how hard could it be?

The Hollywood Hustle

A few years later, I was all-in for Hollywood: taking acting classes, going on endless auditions, making contacts, and putting together the portfolio of image-building tools that every actor had to have in the days when *Backstage West* and *Variety*, not Instagram and Twitter, were king: head shots, a sample reel on VHS tape, and business cards.

FOURTH WALL BREAK!

This was before the Internet, so we got a lot of work from ads in Backstage West and Drama-logue. There were also open calls at networks and commercial auditions. A regular day for me was scouring Drama-logue for auditions, sending out pictures, going to acting classes, and doing everything I could to get in front of casting directors. Classes were great: I had cold reading, scene study, typical stuff. I took classes with Bobby Hoffman, the casting director of Happy Days; back in those days, casting directors would hold seminars and actors would attend so we could get in front of their faces. I also spent a lot of time building up my store of clips on tape; I was really good at collecting footage. I would haunt people until I got footage from them. That's what we had to do before YouTube.

I was also learning that, as easy as my Sarah Coventry experience had made "the business" seem, the odds of anyone making it—if you define making it as being able to earn a decent living as a professional entertainer (actor, comedian, dancer, musician), not "being a star"—were longer than long. Even today, with Netflix, Amazon, Hulu, YouTube, and a million cable networks, there are maybe 200,000 recurring jobs for actors and other performers in the entire country. Back when I started, back when there were only three television networks (ABC, NBC, and CBS) and no such thing as streaming movies, forget about it. Ninety or 95 percent of aspiring entertainers like me were unemployed in their chosen field, so they had to hustle and take other jobs—usually waiting tables, which offered the flexibility they needed to go on auditions during the day.

When you add the fact that Hollywood was the dream factory, the fantasy of riches and fame that so many young girls and strapping boys aspired to, the result was a cutthroat, brutally competitive business that ate a lot of people alive, especially young women. Then again, I've never been opposed to tough competition; in fact, I love it and encourage it. Competition is Darwinian: it separates the people who can step up when the pressure's on from the ones who wilt in the spotlight. For the people who can handle it, competition brings out their best. From my pageant days to today, I've always welcomed competition because I'm confident in my abilities. **Confidence is a self-fulfilling prophecy**. Is that self-esteem? I don't know. I just know that whatever it is, I've always had it. You need it to survive in Hollywood.

Wait a second. Just what is "Hollywood," anyway? A lot of people think it's a city in Southern California, but it's not. It began as a self-contained town in the 1870s, named Hollywood by a developer named H. J. Whitley, who thought *holly* would reflect his English heritage and *wood* would honor his Scottish blood. Today, Hollywood is just a neighborhood in central Los Angeles. But in the early twentieth century, when major film companies like RKO and Paramount built huge studios in the community, the broader definition of Hollywood was born: the symbol of the American film industry, fame, fortune, bright lights, the red carpet, and glamour. That's the Hollywood I was after.

But for someone new and undiscovered, that Hollywood wasn't about glamour. It was about one word: *auditions*. When you're trying to make it, you basically do three things with your time: work, go to classes, and go on auditions. A young actress auditions for all sorts of jobs, and to get those auditions, you sign with a talent agency that takes a commission from any pay you might get. To increase my odds, I signed with a talent agency, a modeling agency, and a commercial agency, each of which looked for jobs that pertained to their expertise. I would get a call from an agency saying that there was an audition or interview for such-and-such a job at such-and-such a place. I would get the details, grab what I needed, and go. You had to hustle or you didn't have a prayer.

Shear Honesty: *Does hard work come before confidence or the other way around? I think it's a "fake it 'til you make it" proposition. If you don't have a natural supply of self-confidence, you can't just announce, "I'm going to be confident today!" and have that be that. Go out and do the work, again and again. The* more you put yourself out there and do your best, the more you'll start to believe in your capabilities. Eventually, that will turn into self-confidence.

Audition Blues

In fact, I and others like me hustled so fast and so hard that we often forgot all about how brutal auditioning could be for your self-esteem and confidence. That was a good thing, because if I'd thought too hard about what I was subjecting myself to, I might not have put up with it. I was one of the more daring girls among my peers, though you wouldn't have known it to meet me. Dad had always referred to me as a powder puff, and I was certainly soft and feminine, but I had some spine, too. I didn't wear suits or try to dress to be a tough broad; instead, I used my smile and sex appeal to sell decision makers on who I was, not who I thought they wanted me to be. Even so, the scrutiny of the audition process could shake the poise of even the most self-assured young woman.

FOURTH WALL BREAK!

You needed an agent to get a reading for a network sitcom. Your agent would submit your picture and résumé and you might get a call from the casting director's office saying, "I would like to see this person." The first call might narrow the field down to thirty, forty, or fifty people, which gives you an idea of the odds we all faced. If it was a recurring role, there would be even more people. You would read, and if they liked you, you might get a callback, maybe two. Commercial callbacks were the killer because of the money. Everybody wanted commercials, so you'd be out in the hall, which would be full of people reading to themselves but also trying to intimidate you.

It was the same routine for me, again and again. After being scrutinized from head to toe by a dozen or more casting people, producers, and directors, I would inevitably leave the room ass-first, backing out because I didn't like people staring at my butt, just like in the pageant days when I used the "Rhonda Walk" to get judges to look at my eyes, not my derriere. Then I would sit in my car in the parking lot and go over every word of dialogue I had just said, breaking it down and finding fault with every choice I'd made. "I should've done this, I should've said that" became my mantra.

It took more than fifty auditions before I finally stopped doing that. I just interviewed. I had meetings. I put my very best foot forward. I never looked back on what I should have said or done. I moved forward with enthusiasm. And you know what I figured out? The people holding the audition *wanted* to hire me. They wanted to be wowed and to stop looking. They were hungry and tired of hearing the same thing from a hundred look-alike, sound-alike actresses. So I gave them something unique. I sparkled. You don't do that with teeth whitening strips, but with deep confidence. Compete only with yourself. Love every little job you get. Ask questions. Don't shrink from the challenge. Stand out. You are an individual. You have what it takes. You can win the job, the gig, whatever you want.

It's hard to see all of this while you're going through it. Every tiny obstacle looks a hundred miles high. That's why I'm sharing my journey. If I had a buck for every tear I shed over a career setback, I would own my own island by now. Every loss is a teacher. Every time someone tells you "No," figure out why and address it. Now that's one more weakness you don't have. You can stop looking left or right at what others are doing and look only at your goal.

By the way, the auditions where I thought I had screwed up

the worst and completely humiliated myself? Those were the ones where I usually got the gig.

> **Shear Honesty:** *Failure isn't the end of the world. Overreacting to it can be. Everybody fails, but if you go off the deep end with the drama and self-blaming and run away with your tail between your legs, you're your own worst enemy. The truth is, most people are very forgiving of failures, and failure is your classroom. Why didn't it work out? What could you have done better? What did you do right that no one appreciated? What's the missing "x-factor" that you can bring to your next venture that could get you over the top?* **Treat failure as what it is—opportunity in disguise.**

When I Went Bust

Some of those gigs were great, some were terrible, and few led to anything more than a one-time paycheck. But the goal was to land a commercial. Every actor coveted commercials because they paid well. If they ran for a few cycles, you could get residuals, which meant a nice payday, a luxury for any actor.

Meanwhile, even though at five-foot-four I was too short to get some of the elite modeling gigs, I relied on modeling to build my portfolio of photos and pay the bills. One of my most interesting modeling jobs was as a sculpture model for a high-end mannequin company, Greneker Mannequins, which is still around today. They made mannequins for couture displays at exclusive department stores like Neiman-Marcus.

It was a surreal experience. I thought they would throw some plaster on my face and make a cast, but no. I posed, stock still, for hours while an artist sculpted my face. I had just turned twenty-five, and the artist told me he thought that a woman's beauty was at its peak between twenty-five and thirty-five. This was before my nose job, and I thought it was quite flattering, as well as pretty cool! How many young women can say they've been a mannequin? The most macabre part of posing was going into the factory and walking past all the dismembered mannequin body parts: heads, arms, and legs. I would not want to get locked in that place by myself at night!

The neatest part of the whole thing came the first time I saw my mannequin in a store window. It was a unique experience and a nice payday, and I also got a life-size mannequin and a bust of myself, which I still have. The mannequin lived on for years as part of my bedroom set on *USA: Up All Night*. The ironic thing was, I had pretended to be a mannequin in a mime act for years. Now I truly was one.

A Sexist World

If you're a youngster or don't remember what a weird, sexist, over-the-top place Hollywood was back in the late 1970s and early 1980s, let me refresh your memory. It wasn't just the age of cocaine and excess. It was also the age of the blockbuster, when movies like *Jaws* and *Star Wars* turned films into genuine cultural milestones. It was the heyday of geniuses like Woody Allen, Sidney Lumet, Francis Coppola, Roman Polanski, and Robert Towne (together, the last two men made *Chinatown*, maybe the ultimate movie about Los Angeles). Cable TV wasn't yet widespread, so it was the last time when the three networks dominated the airwaves and the sitcom was king. It was when standup comedians like Richard Pryor, George Carlin, Steve Martin, and Robin Williams not only became superstars but showed that comedy could be a force not only for commenting on culture, but for changing it as well.

More than anything else, when I arrived to seek my fortune, Hollywood was totally a man's world. The industry was unabashedly sexist, and women were mostly sex objects—eye candy for some director's show or some mogul's arm. From *Baywatch* to *Charlie's Angels*, your prospects were less about acting and more about tits and ass. There were plenty of frauds with "Producer" emblazoned on their business cards whose only goal was to get poor, unsuspecting would-be starlets into the sack.

Hollywood is still a sexist world where women still have to fight for the meaty roles (and, based on Amy Adams' account from her work on *American Hustle*, equal pay) but it's gotten better. Stars like Jennifer Lawrence have changed the pay scale and the rules. Hell, someone like Amy Schumer wouldn't have had a prayer of making a movie like *Trainwreck* back in the day, and now she's one of the biggest names in comedy. Good for her!

When I started my career, sex wasn't anywhere near as rampant on television as it is today (and on the public airwaves, nudity was nonexistent), but neither was feminism. Do you believe a show like *Charlie's Angels*, where three gorgeous women were tarted up as bikini-clad secret agents to work for some hidden male boss, could have been made in any era but the '70s? I was an extra on *Charlie's Angels* once, wearing a gold lamé bikini, and I got sent home for pulling attention away from the stars. Was that a compliment or an insult?

At least *Baywatch*, which launched a few years later, had a beach setting as a reason for showing Pamela Anderson's boobs in every other shot! But in my era, pretty girls were commodities both on screen and off screen, which meant that to advance my career, I had to be willing to be sexy and embrace my inner bimbo. It also meant that I got into more than a few creepy and/or scary situations with men who saw me as one more potential conquest.

At first, when I landed in Hollywood, I went after one kind of part most aggressively: the girl next door (because it suited my good girl self-image). Oops! That was a mistake; no one would cast me in those roles. After one failed audition after another, I realized that my strong features, big hair, and ultra-curvy body weren't conducive to being cast in the background or as the ingénue. I finally got tired of trying to play against type and just went for it. Now I got the parts, mainly sexy bimbos and airheads, and mainly in comedy. But that was fine with me—I started working!

FOURTH WALL BREAK!

It didn't bother me to audition for the sexy femme fatale roles. I was used to strutting in swimsuits in pageants, and that's what Hollywood was about then for women, like it or not. If that's all you know, that's all you know. I was too young to think, "I'm being used." I did what I had to do with an eye on getting bigger roles down the line. I could rock a swimsuit, so I embraced it. Plus, every time I went for the girl next door parts, I never got them. I embraced what I had. A door was opening and I was ready to break it down. My timing may have been off—I was too late to be Marilyn and too early to be Sarah Silverman. I wasn't going to change Hollywood, so I did the ditzy neighbor or the ditzy girlfriend. But I opened some doors for women to be funny, and I'm glad I did.

I played the next-door neighbor on *Married with Children* who wanted Al to help her move her couch. When Al asked what I did,

I replied, "I dance on tables for men near airports." I played Bambi on the remake of *Love, American Style.* On *Happy Days,* I played a nude model who Chachi (the photographer's assistant) drooled over. I didn't care that I was being typecast; I was working regularly. I was becoming an actress who casting directors knew could deliver lines with good comedic timing and look good doing it. I really wanted my own sitcom, but if I couldn't beat them at their game yet, I would join them. I went deeper into comedy.

Through all this, I was well aware of what Hollywood was like and how it chewed up and spit out beautiful young women who went in with an "I'll do anything to be a movie star" attitude. Too often, those girls found themselves on a bus or plane back home in a few months, broke and bitter. That wasn't going to be me. This was the first time I intentionally decided to play the system even as it was trying to play me. I knew producers and casting directors wanted me to be little more than a hot number delivering a breathy line while flashing my cleavage in a little dress, and I wasn't going to be able to change that as Rhonda Shear, powerless bit part actress. But if I had to play the game for the time being, I would use my work to get what I wanted. I would use my work to get what I wanted: experience, relationships, influence, access to important people. I would use my sex appeal and pretend to be the *bimbo du jour,* but I would also work hard, wow them with my brains and comedic talent, and think like a businesswoman. It was a great training ground for my many future lives.

Shear Honesty: *You won't always be in a position to make the rules or even to influence them. That doesn't mean you have to submit meekly to them. Work on making yourself indispensable to people in power. Learn everything you can from them and go above and beyond to earn their trust and respect. There are very* *few people in this world, male or female, who can be counted on to keep their promises and deliver excellence again and again. Be one of those people. Before long, you'll find that you are influencing the rules and shaping the world around you. When you get to that point, use your powers for good!*

Taking Advantage of Naïve Girls

If you were thinking that this was going to be a story about Rhonda sleeping her way to the top with a list of Hollywood movers and shakers, I'm sorry to disappoint you. I would never compromise my virtue for a part, even for my "big break." Still, I had to be careful.

There have been people on the lookout for young, naïve starlets just arriving in Hollywood as long as there's been Hollywood, and it wasn't always sex they were after, either. For example, head shots and résumés were the tools of the trade in getting seen by agents and casting directors. After you had those, you had to build your video montage of acting roles. You'd copy those onto videotape and send them out in the hopes that a casting director would watch them and think you were right for a specific role.

Your photos had to portray you with different looks for potentially different parts: athletic girl, businesswoman, young mom, girl next door, seductress, and so on. As I've said, girl next door parts always got the most work, so I had plenty of pictures depicting me with that look. *Nothing.* Not a sniff of a "girl next door" in twenty-six years. But I still needed that photo on my résumé and business card, and that meant I needed a photographer.

My first photo shoot was with a photographer who an agent recommended. He was nice and a decent photographer who didn't charge an arm and a leg and didn't make a pass at me. He did ask me out to dinner and to a disco (it was that era, remember), and I liked him, so I went. Now, I had been wearing a heart-shaped diamond that my mom had given me. She had painstakingly saved up for it without telling my father, and it was a beautiful stone: pinkish, two carats, heart-shaped. I treasured it and wore it all the time. Apparently, I didn't get the memo to look like a starving artist.

I'm sure my photographer noticed the stone. We were at the disco, dancing close and fast. At the end of the evening, he dropped me off at home with a peck on the cheek. But when I got inside, I realized with horror that the necklace was gone! I never could prove it, but I'm sure that the snake lifted my diamond necklace from around my neck while we were dancing. Later, I asked him if he had found or saw my necklace, and he radiated guilt. But I never saw my necklace again. Mom had insurance on it and was able to recover some of the value, but I never recovered from the sentimental damage. I learned not to wear pricey jewelry on shoots or anywhere else.

Assaulting Bob Hope

After some more hard lessons, dozens of auditions, and more failures than successes, I got my first big break in 1978, after I'd been in LA less than two years. At the time, Bob Hope was still one of the biggest names in showbiz; he had been doing TV specials since the 1950s and had done at least eighty of them in the previous two decades. So when I found about an open casting call for a new special—appropriately called *The Starmakers*—that would star Bernadette Peters and Robert Urich, I jumped at the chance. This was right around the time that Bo Derek did *10*, so their shtick was that Bob Hope was looking for six "elevens" to be in his special. Yes, it was typically sexist, but I didn't care.

My modeling agency had called to tell me about the audition, and I figured that it would be me and maybe five or six other girls vying for the part. Uh…no. Little did I know that this was an "open call," which meant that every newcomer and wannabe in town showed up. I was about to come face to face with some of the same women I would audition against for years to come. I showed up at NBC Studios in Burbank, and there must have been *a thousand* girls in swimsuits in a line all the way around the corner of the building and down the block! It was fantastic PR for the special, but it was hell standing there all day in the Southern California heat.

However, the old workhorse pageant girl in me came out. If these girls could do this, so could I. I just needed to catch the producers' attention and then show them my talent! So I waited. And waited. Finally, I got inside, and the producers narrowed the girls from a thousand down to fifty, and then to twenty-five, and each time I made the cut. Then we went home. When we came back the next day, we each met Bob Hope. The plan was to cut down from twenty-five girls to the final six. When my turn came, I stood in front of Bob and his daughter, Linda, and I told him I was a New Orleans girl and a dancer. I did the mime act that I did a lot back then, and then I smiled and did a high kick—and to my absolute horror my shoe came flying off and landed on the table inches from Bob's head!

I stopped breathing—but everyone laughed and I got the part. I certainly got their attention! I still have the original photo of Bob holding up my picture and résumé and smiling at me. I still like to call that the day I nearly killed Bob Hope.

FOURTH WALL BREAK!

Wearing a bikini for that audition didn't bother me; I was as comfortable in it as in a jogging suit. I understood that Bob Hope needed the PR because of the competition on TV. Having a thousand girls in line at NBC was great press for him. He was a legend, and the thought of meeting him was too much for me to handle at that age. I was super nervous, partially because I thought this could be my Lana Turner "big break." When my turn came, there sat the man I grew up watching in the den with my parents: the ski jump nose, the voice. I had three minutes to make an impression. I didn't plan on my shoe coming off, but he liked me, I think in part because I didn't look like every other girl in line.

The search for the perfect "11" girls got a lot of press coverage, and that opened doors for me. After that special, a couple of the other girls and I started getting most of the "sexy girl" roles on shows like *Happy Days* and *Sheriff Lobo*. I also got my first personal agent (as opposed to being part of the stable for a talent agency) from that special, so it was a nice career starter. This is a perfect example of how I played the system even while it *thought* it was playing me. Sure, I let Mr. Hope and the producers use me as a piece of meat for their "11" concept, but I knew exactly what was going on and I played *them* like a fiddle: flashing my Southern charm to get the part, then turning the role into a great springboard for my career.

Another amazing early part was for a show called *Two Top Bananas*. It was a TV special starring Don Rickles, Don Adams of *Get Smart* fame, Carol Wayne (Johnny Carson's sexy sidekick on *The Tonight Show*), Murray Langston (The Unknown Comic, who wore a paper bag over his head during his act) and me. It was a play on vaudeville—fun physical comedy working with some of the greats—and I loved it. Once again, I thought my comedy acting career was off to a roaring start. Even though vaudeville skits always portrayed females as the dumber sex, I was funny and worked really well with these comedy greats.

But the highlight of this whole period came when I played Scarlett O'Hara to Johnny Carson's Rhett Butler on *The Tonight Show*. It was an infamous "Alternate Ending to *Gone With the Wind*" bit in which Johnny's Rhett announced at the end that he was gay—a shocker for that time. That was *really* cool. For the sketch, I wore none other than the same antebellum dress that I wore for my infamous *Playboy* "Women of the New South" pictorial. I also wore it in the Miss Louisiana-World and Miss World-USA pageants. That dress got around—not as much as Monica Lewinsky's—but it got around!

Anyway, Johnny was totally professional and never even flirted with me, unlike so many men in the business who seemed to think that young actresses were their personal harem. But that didn't stop Johnny's director, Bobby Quinn, from asking me out.

Shear Honesty: *I got hit on A LOT in Hollywood, and women ask me from time to time if I got sick of it. No, as long as the guy was respectful and could take no for an answer, which most could. Being asked out is a compliment, and I took it that way. I didn't find it objectifying, but flattering. A lot in life is like that: it's all about how you choose to see something. Are you insulted or amused? Hurt or motivated? Scared or challenged? If your reactions are holding you back, maybe it's time to rethink them.*

Joan Rivers and My Nose

As my career began to pick up speed, I became uncomfortably aware of my appearance. I was born with curly, frizzy hair that boys and girls made fun of all the way from kindergarten through sixth grade. My mother worked tirelessly to straighten it, but she couldn't do anything about my prominent nose. There wasn't anything terrible about it, but it wasn't as perky as Christy Brinkley's, and I was insecure about it.

Shear Honesty: *As a feminist, I am not promoting plastic surgery or suggesting that women should be ashamed of any part of their bodies. We're all beautiful, and you should never feel like you have to live up to artificial beauty standards set down by men. Plus, the models and actresses who make us all feel inferior when they splash their impossibly toned, gorgeous bodies on magazine covers invest a lot of time and money in fitness trainers and personal chefs in order to look that great. After all, being beautiful is their job. With that, two caveats.*

*First, if you want to get something nipped or tucked or lifted and it's **for you** (not because your significant other is begging for the double-D upgrade), then go for it. Second, if something about your appearance is holding you back professionally, you don't need to justify a damned thing. In either case, just make sure you work with the best surgical team, and remember, less is more. Also, try eating well, exercising, and getting more sleep before you resort to surgery. That won't shrink your nose, but it will give you a fitter body and better skin, get rid of those eye bags, and improve your health. After all, pretty wrapping doesn't matter if what's in the package is falling apart.*

My nose had become an issue during a general casting meeting in Hollywood with the great and powerful Joyce Selznick. I call her that because she was like the Wizard of Oz: hard to see and really intimidating. Joyce was pure old Hollywood. She had discovered Tony Curtis, helped launch stars like George C. Scott, Faye Dunaway, and Candice Bergen, and cast some major films, including *The Buddy Holly Story*. To get a meeting with her was a major coup, and she was brutally honest when she told me, "You are a beautiful gal, but initially you will be cast as the young femme fatale. They won't light for you, but they will light the scene for the star. Your profile may not look good and could lose parts for you."

That was all I needed to hear. I ran, not walked, to the Beverly Hills office of Dr. Frank Kamer, known as *the* surgeon for noses in Hollywood. There, to my astonishment, I ran into one of my idols, the great Joan Rivers! It wasn't surprising to see her in a plastic surgeon's office; after all, she would become infamous for having the most surgically altered countenance in entertainment. But seeing her in the flesh—what a treat!

It got better when she asked me, "What are you doing here? You are a beautiful young lady."

I quietly said, "My nose."

"Turn to the side," she insisted. I did, and without hesitation she said, "Yeah, you can take a little off the top." My idol gave me her blessing with her beloved dog Spike in her lap. So I had the surgery, and it was something of a comedy. At the time, I was dating a very conservative sitcom writer named Fred Fox Jr. who looked like the watermelon-smashing comedian, Gallagher, with long hair on the sides and no hair on top. I was also appearing in a play where I had to use some very blue language—fuck, cunt, the whole dictionary. Fred came with me when Dr. Kamer did my nose and waited for me during surgery, and after I was in recovery, they brought him in to see me. Well, I don't know what kind of happy gas they gave me, but I slipped right into my play's foul-mouthed character. I have it on good authority that I called Dr. Kamer a cunt and asked Fred why he was wearing a bald shower cap. It's probably good that I don't remember any of it.

Temporary bad behavior aside, surgery was a success. The nose job freed me from my insecurities about my profile, allowing me to be a more animated performer and comedian. You have to do what makes you comfortable. You have to overcome your own demons. If that means taking a class to overcome your fear of speaking in front of a group, do it. Confidence is a life changer.

Ponch and the Fonz

Compared to the stories some women told, my experiences working my way around Hollywood were pretty positive. I did have a few unpleasant experiences, though, especially when I came into conflict with the ego of a star. One incident I'll never forget involved Henry Winkler and *Happy Days*. It was 1980 and I had already been on the show twice, and one day I got a call from Bobby Hoffman, the casting director, about playing Fonzie's girlfriend. Because they knew me, I didn't even have to audition. So I went to the set and for the next two days we read the script and blocked the scenes. Piece of cake.

At the same time, I was going out on a lot of commercial auditions. Commercials may not win Oscars, as I said before, but actors love them because you can make a lot of money doing national spots. I'd gotten a few good commercials before, including Coke and Mitsubishi, and the same week that I got the call from

Happy Days, I auditioned for a national Church's Fried Chicken commercial and got it. Hooray! The spot was shooting on Thursday, which was perfect because my *Happy Days* scenes wouldn't shoot until Friday. I spoke to Bobby Hoffman and the director, Garry Marshall, and asked if I could possibly miss the Thursday rehearsal. They said it wouldn't be a problem because my scene was already blocked and Henry knew I was a pro.

I filmed the Church's commercial, but when I showed up on the *Happy Days* set Friday morning, my name was no longer on my dressing room door. Nobody was talking to me, and I was walking around like a fool. Finally, someone said, "Henry wants to talk to you." I was twenty-three and terribly intimidated, but I walked right up to the biggest star in TV and asked what was going on. Henry said, "I want to tell you that you did something wrong, taking the commercial. I hired your stand-in on the spot when I found out you weren't here for blocking." I was horrified. I thought I had gone through the right channels, but that didn't matter.

FOURTH WALL BREAK!

Working on Happy Days was a complete dream because I'd auditioned when I was nineteen. It was the hottest show on the air and embodied everything good about the sitcom at the time. If I couldn't have my own sitcom, then I wanted to work on a sitcom like that. I got to work with the great Jerry Paris and Garry Marshall. Everyone was completely professional.

Weeks would start with a table read, where we would just take the script and everyone would read it. The second day, we would start blocking scenes. For me, it was easy to memorize my lines because my part was always small. But what I loved about the sitcom format was that it was shot before a live audience, so it was like a mini-play. You got feedback from the audience. It was a dream come true...until Henry fired me. Henry had always been nice to me on the couple of episodes I'd worked on in the past: friendly and encouraging. But by this time I think he was on a head trip. It was his last year on the show, he had been a star for many years, and he was going to show me what happened if I dared take another job. But what he showed me was how easy it was to be blackballed. And you know what? They never ever ran my Church's Fried Chicken commercial, either.

Henry said, "If you're going to take acting seriously, you should take *acting* seriously, not commercials." That was bullshit and he knew it; he knew exactly how financially important commercials were to actors. But that didn't matter. I cried like a baby right in front of him, and he still fired me. It was a cruel, egotistical thing to do. Because of it, I was blackballed not only from *Happy Days* but from the other hot shows that Garry Marshall produced, *Mork & Mindy* and *Laverne & Shirley*. I'll never know how much damage that incident caused, but I do know that *Happy Days* ended in 1984 and Garry never called me in for another role. I have no doubt that I lost out on some great opportunities because Henry Winkler felt that he had to teach a lesson to a struggling young actor.

It was one of those moments in your life that you don't forget. I was light-years from disrespectful or arrogant. I would never have done the commercial if I had known I was going to make Henry or anyone else upset. But I was too young and naïve to understand the superstar ego. No one told Henry what I was up to, and he didn't find out until the day of the taping, but by this time he and *Happy Days* were synonymous, and nobody was going to go up against the show's superstar—not if they wanted to keep their job.

(I told that story in an interview not too long ago, and the interviewer tried to get in touch with Henry's publicist to get Henry's side of the story, but the publicist just said that Henry wouldn't have done that kind of thing. He has the reputation for being one of the nice guys of Hollywood, but I've seen another side of him.)

Another unpleasant and downright strange incident came when I appeared on the last season of CHiPs in 1983. We were filming on a barge out in the Pacific Ocean off the coast of California. Now, Erik Estrada, who played "Ponch," was normally a nice guy, but he was also the star of the show and had a massive ego. On that day I guess his ego got the best of him because he suddenly grabbed a megaphone and shouted to the entire cast and crew, "I want you to know that the reason you're all here is me! Watch your Ps and Qs or I'll have you all fired!"

It was bizarre. *Happy Days* had already happened and I was terrified of losing another job. I'd already had some kissing scenes with Erik, he was flirting with me, and I was afraid I would get fired because I wasn't going to sleep with him. Worse, we were offshore on a barge, so it wasn't like I could sneak off the set and hide in the ladies' room! But I worked with Eric later on and he was a gentleman, so I'm going to chalk that one up to too much sun.

Shear Honesty: *Ego is a dangerous, dangerous drug, and there's a lot of it in showbiz. One of the reasons I treasure my self-deprecating sense of humor is that it keeps me humble; I know better than anybody how ridiculous I can act! I've had a lot of successes in my life, but I've had them because I've stayed humble. Humility prevents you from feeling entitled, so you work your ass off for everything because you presume that's the only way you'll get it. As soon as you feel like the world owes* *you something, you're done for. I try to remember that all my opportunities and all the people who bless me with their love and support are gifts that I'm always working to deserve.*

My Dad

The worst moment in my TV career, however, came away from a set, though it did profoundly affect my career. In 1984, my father died suddenly of a heart attack at age sixty-nine. After his death, I was consumed with guilt because I hadn't been with him when he died. I had rushed out the door to some appointment, and my last words to him were, "Oh, Dad, you talk too much." Then he was gone. I was so close to my parents, and even though my mother was a huge influence, my father was my greatest cheerleader. My grief was overwhelming.

At that time, I had landed a meaty guest-starring role on the marvelous sitcom *Cheers*, playing a flight attendant with brains. But I guess I didn't realize how hard my dad's death had hit me. I've always been a bit of a hypochondriac, and when I showed up on the set of *Cheers* a couple of months after Dad's death, I started having psychosomatic illnesses. For a while, I felt I couldn't take a step. It was weird, even for me. I don't know what a nervous breakdown is, but I was having something like that. Finally, it was too much: I went up to the producer, quit that episode, and left the set. I thought I was done, maybe for good. But Ted Danson and everyone else involved with the show were incredibly sweet and professional. A few months later, they even brought me back for a smaller part. Talk about compassion and class. They're a lot more common in entertainment than big egos.

I went back to New Orleans and saw a doctor who put me on

some antidepressant medication, and slowly, I felt better. But I still spent a year back home getting my head together before heading back to Hollywood to resume my career. I loved my father very much, and he is still in my heart every day.

ON THE WAY TO TODAY

What tips did I pick up from Bob Hope, Johnny Carson, Joan Rivers, and the other legends I encountered in my early Hollywood years?

- ☐ *It's never as easy as it seems at first. Usually, it's a LOT harder.*
- ☐ *You're going to fail more often than not. Get over it and move on.*
- ☐ *You can't change the game until you win the game, and to win you have to play. So play well.*
- ☐ *Watch your valuables.*
- ☐ *Most people are good and kind, but there are always a few who will prey on the well-intentioned.*
- ☐ *If you see an opportunity, odds are that other people will, too. Be prepared to compete.*
- ☐ *Make 'em laugh and they'll remember you. Bland never wins out.*
- ☐ *Sometimes, doing what's fair and right still gets you kicked in the teeth. It's a tough world.*
- ☐ *When in doubt, tell them you love them, always.*

LESSON SIX
Don't Wait for Opportunities, Create Them!

—— *In which our heroine bares all (briefly), meets the partner every actress dreams about, becomes a mannequin (again), rocks a gold bikini, crashes a black-tie power party, gets advice from God, and proves that you don't need to sing to deliver one hell of a singing telegram.* ——

By the early 1980s, you would have had a hard time cruising through the weeknight network lineup without seeing my face. I did *Dukes of Hazzard, Happy Days, Married with Children, Three's Company, Full House, Dallas, CHiPs, Hart to Hart, The A-Team, Cheers, The Young and the Restless, The Fall Guy, Misadventures, Sheriff Lobo*... you name it, I was in it. I was on fire back then.

In 1984 I made my first moderately successful feature film, *Basic Training*. It was directed by Andrew Sugerman (who would go on to garner an Oscar nomination as a producer) and produced by Emmy winner Gilbert Adler and starred people like Anne Dusenberry, Angela Aames, Walter Gotell, Morty Brill, and Will Nye. That film launched many careers. We even had a red carpet premiere. The only hard part for me was the nudity. There was a sex scene, and the only way for me to get the role was to show my boobs. Remember, I was still very much the Southern good girl who lived according to my mother's moral code.

But I was also realizing that I had been blessed with a bad girl's body that could open doors in my career. So I agreed to the nude scene, but my agent put very specific language into my contract: the director could only shoot my boobs in profile and for only one shot. So there's a three-second shot of me in the throes of lovemaking where you can see one breast.

Those three seconds became an *eternity* when the movie came out in 1984, and my father got to see it before he passed away. We had a premiere in New Orleans, and it was really cool that my father got to attend, even though I was horrified at the idea of him seeing his little girl's hooters up on the screen. He died later that year, so he didn't get to see a lot of the other things that I accomplished, but I was really delighted that he got to see that movie and things like *Happy Days* and all the other TV appearances that I was starting to get one after another.

FOURTH WALL BREAK!

I was so nervous about what my parents would think, but it was a starring role and I had their best wishes. Even though I was comfy in tiny bikinis, there's a big difference in removing that top. It felt dirty, and I was modest. In the scene, my female costar walked in on me and this wonderful actor, Mark Withers, making love. Mark and I practiced the scene and blocked it with the director with our clothes on. The next day, I kidded with the director and producers that they had to be in their underwear to shoot. Then it was time to film and they cleared the set of grips, technicians, and extra people. Mark came to the set and gave his wife and me each a rose, which was such a classy gesture.

Then it was time to film, but the scene only took a couple of takes. It was hot but choreographed. We were in bed and I had underwear or a bikini bottom on, and I had the sheets up high so there was no butt showing. You could only see the side of my breast. But what was a very fast shot on camera seemed like forever when I watched it. I actually did another topless scene on a USA Network show, but because it was cable they couldn't actually show anything, so they put moleskin on my nipples! But it's actually hotter because it was after my boob job.

The Marvelous Kenny Ellis

Unquestionably, one of the reasons my career was going so well, apart from my own stubborn work ethic and pageant-bred chutzpah, was the endless, amazing, unconditional love and support of the brilliant Kenny Ellis. Kenny was (and still is) a warm, funny, absolutely golden-voiced comic and actor who's now a cantor, and he's been one of my greatest friends and supporters for nearly (good Lord!) forty years. I can honestly say I would not be where I am today without Kenny.

Life is a cutthroat business, and I don't just mean Hollywood. I mean any part of life. It's tough, and people and circumstances will conspire to take you down. I think everyone needs a sidekick, someone who'll be with you through thick and thin, no questions asked. Someone with no hidden agendas, whose crazy complements your crazy, and who's loyal to the end. We all need someone like that, someone we can count on, who brings out the best in us...who *gets* us. For me, that was Kenny. I hope you're lucky enough to find somebody like that on your journey.

If Miss LA Press Club and the Bob Hope special were two early turning points for my career, meeting Kenny was the third. I met Kenny in 1978 in Harvey Lembeck's Comedy Improv Class. Everyone studied with Harvey. He had coached people like Robin Williams, John Ritter, and even Bryan Cranston of *Breaking Bad* fame. You may remember him as Rocco Barbella from the *Phil Silvers Show* or as Eric Von Zipper in the beach party movies. I loved his class, and I knew right away that I wanted to work with Kenny because he was so obviously talented (I've always been turned on by talent). Kenny was a Jerry Lewis type of comedian: very physical, rubber-faced, and wonderfully improvisational with a gorgeous singing voice. He performed at my sixtieth birthday gala and had me crying like a baby in under a minute.

"Rhonda was auditing this class and sitting in the back, being very quiet and un-attention-getting," Kenny said in an interview. "She was wearing a hat to hide her hair, jeans, and a t-shirt, and nobody was going to look twice at her. She didn't want to be the center of attention. Rhonda's always known what to do and when. Anyway, she came up to me during one of the breaks and said, 'I think you're the funniest person in the class.' We talked and she told me that she'd won an audition at NBC from being Miss Los Angeles Press Club and needed a scene partner, and she thought I would be the perfect person to do it with.

"People come up to you in Hollywood all the time and tell you things," Kenny continues. "So I said, 'Sure, whatever.' But then she handed me a business card that said 'Rhonda Shear' with her phone number, which was very businesslike, and asked me to call her and we would set up a time to rehearse. I'd never gotten a business card from a girl before, so this was interesting. We got together and she'd asked me to bring any comedy scenes that I had. Well, I had tons of comedy scenes that I'd purchased at theatrical bookstores, but as we started reading through them, we realized that they weren't very funny. Right on the spot we started improvising and writing our own scenes, and that was how we started doing an act."

Shear Honesty: *Packaging matters in any line of work. Today, they call it your "personal brand." Back then, I don't think we had a name for it. But I knew from watching my father run his business that for people to take you seriously, you have to present yourself as a professional. I knew there were a hundred thousand would-be actresses out there, all trying to be taken seriously. Business cards and a no-nonsense attitude were a way to stand out—to let someone like Kenny know that I was about working hard and making a living. Today, you'd do the same with a great website. The tools don't matter, but the intent does: be polished, smart, and professional. A great first impression can be what convinces someone to give you a chance.*

For the NBC audition, Kenny and I did a scene from a Neil Simon play. It didn't lead to anything, but now I had footage that I'd actually performed on the original *Tonight Show* set. More importantly, Kenny and I quickly became bosom buddies and partners in crime, both of us trying everything to get seen, get noticed, and get that big break that we were *sure* was waiting out there. We were absolutely inseparable, a match made in comedy. Like Lucy Ricardo and Ethel Mertz from *I Love Lucy*, we would do *anything* to get in front of anyone with the power to "put us in the show," and in the process we met some of the biggest names in Hollywood. Kenny would even make calls for me, posing as my manager, if we couldn't get in the door ourselves.

The late 1970s and early 1980s may have been a sexist era, but it was also a magical time in Hollywood. You could still see glimpses of Old Hollywood and the studio system, though both were fading fast. It was an era when you could still beat the pavement, dropping off pictures and résumés to producer's and casting director's offices. We should have gotten an award for pure moxie and wacko creativity.

In the endless fight to get seen, known, cast, and paid, Kenny was the best friend a young actress could have hoped for: phenomenally talented, inventive, and always pushing me to try things I might never have tried on my own. For the next seven years, we did the craziest things you can imagine, things nobody else would even try, to get the attention of the bigwigs. We spent hundreds of hours writing comedy sketches and bits, because we were natural foils. Most of the time, I was the straight man, like Gracie Allen to his George Burns. Kenny has brilliant comedy timing, so I would play it straight (which is sometimes harder to do) and Kenny would be Kenny. It worked perfectly, because nobody expected the pretty girl to also be funny. We wrote hundreds and hundreds of comedy routines and performed them for years, all over Hollywood, Las Vegas—anywhere we could work.

That's hustle. That's making your own work, folks. That, right there, is the difference between success and failure, not luck or destiny or other such nonsense. I knew actors who sat around waiting for their agents to call, bemoaning the fact that there "wasn't any work." Bullshit. There was work; they just weren't willing to hustle and either find it or make it. Most of those actors (some very talented) never did make it; they left LA and went on to something else. That's one reason I don't believe in doing things halfway. Don't dip your toe; jump in. You're only going to be motivated to stick your neck out if it's a matter of survival.

This was survival for me, and with Kenny's encouragement I was able to do things I never thought I could do. That "leap, then look" mentality is with me even today.

> **Shear Honesty:** *This whole era with Kenny taught me that there is so much to be gained from being bold, audacious, and outrageous. So many women lose out on wonderful things because they're afraid of looking silly or offending someone; they don't chase their dreams, or they're too shy. Who cares? Your dignity will recover—go for it! Nobody's going to hand you anything— you have to go out and grab what you want! You make your own opportunities by speaking up, tricking your way in the door, and breaking the rules and a few eggs along the way.*

A Real Live Girl

Kenny and I were a fantastic team not only because we pushed and helped each other but because we had a nose for opportunity. "At the time, there was a TV show called *The Shields and Yarnell Show*, and they had done this robot kind of mime," Kenny says. "Rhonda told me, 'I can do that,' and I thought 'Wow, this could turn into something.' We wrote a sketch based on Barbie and Ken, called 'Rhondie and Ken,' and that was the first time we ever did the mechanical doll thing."

The mechanical doll act is what Kenny and I are still best known for. Kenny played the nutty professor who had invented this life-size doll—me. I would dress up in a leotard and a nice top and put a big bow in my hair, and we would do our vaudevillian shtick. I might have Tic Tacs in my mouth and while Kenny did my hair onstage, the Tic Tacs would fall out...one...at...a...time. Kenny would sing songs to me like "If You Were a Real Live Girl," a parody of "I Enjoy Being a Girl" from the musical *Flower Drum Song*. I had a knack for that sort of slapstick, physical comedy.

Then we had an epiphany: why not put me in a nude body stocking so I'd look like a mannequin? After all, I'd already been sculpted as a real mannequin, so this was the logical next step. Kenny had studied with the great Marcel Marceau and was a wonderful mime, so he helped me perfect my robot movements. That act became our greatest hit.

In a typical performance, Kenny would carry a real mannequin onto a department store set, and then he'd carry me on stage, usually wearing a nude skullcap that made me look like I had no hair. He'd position my arms and torso just so and then turn away to style the wig he was going to put on my head. While he wasn't looking, I would change positions, and when he looked back he'd do a classic comedy double take. From there, I might elbow him in the stomach while he brushed my wig, fall into the splits and make the poor guy lift me back up, and generally mess with him. It was classic vaudeville clowning, and audiences loved it.

In fact, the act was so popular that we had a harebrained, Lucy-and-Ethel idea. "We came up with this idea as a publicity stunt and a way to get into offices," Kenny says. "I would deliver Rhonda as a mannequin. I would pick her up, knock on the door, and walk in with her slung over my shoulder. The reactions were so amazing that I wish we'd had a cameraman with us to capture them. I delivered her first to Dick Clark, because I had some connections at Dick Clark Productions. They said, 'Let's do it, bring her over. We'll deliver her for Dick's birthday.'

"So we went over, went in, and did our shtick," Kenny continues.

"Dick was on the phone at the time and his jaw practically fell off. He didn't know what to say. Then at the end, he said, 'Thank you very much,' and I carried her out. Rhonda got a Dick Clark special as a result of that. That's also how we met Larry Klein, which led to her getting USA: Up All Night."

FOURTH WALL BREAK!

Getting into Dick Clark's office was nerve-wracking, but because I had Kenny there, I wasn't completely terrified. I guess when I donned that leotard and ball cap I became like Supergirl and just did it. The act got us an entrée into many places, and I'm glad we did it. The worst that would've happened was extreme embarrassment, and I'd already had that. I think that's why I can go on live TV and sell stuff, because once you've gone in front of someone in a ball cap and a nude body stocking, you really can't be embarrassed.

Kenny and I pulled that stunt all over Hollywood as a way of getting into the offices of shows we wanted to be on or important figures we hoped would hire us. We crashed our way into the offices of Johnny Carson, John Davidson, and the Smothers Brothers, who were the only ones to kick us out. Everybody else was wonderful. One especially lovely instance stands out: during a writer's strike, NBC had asked the great Steve Allen to produce a variety show. Kenny knew Steve a little and knew where the show was rehearsing, so he picked me up, put me on his shoulder, and carried me right into the rehearsal that Steve was doing with Louis Nye and Don Knotts!

They could have kicked us out for interrupting them (and most big stars would have), but this is how wonderful Steve Allen was. As I started into my live doll routine, Steve started making ratchet sounds with his mouth as I was moving. He laughed the entire time, and then said, "They would be great on show number seven." Well, it turned out that NBC only produced six episodes of that variety show, so we missed out. That was a bummer, but the memory remains precious.

Starving actors that we were, Kenny and I would work anywhere that would pay us. The live doll thing was just one part of our larger act. We won first prize at a talent show at the Palomino Club in North Hollywood, and even though it was a country and western club, they would put us on anytime we wanted to go back. "We did a lot of stuff with the Press Club and the Masquers Club, an old Hollywood actor's club," Kenny says. "We did a show there and got to meet people like Janet Blair and Ginger Rogers. They would bring us back as part of their variety show. We performed in New Orleans, in the French Quarter, at a place called Clyde's Comedy Corner. It was me, Rhonda, and some girl named Ellen DeGeneres."

It was a great time in my career. People started comparing Kenny and me to Lucy and Ricky or to George Stiller and Anne Meara. We kept hustling and being creative. We really had no choice; it was either do that or get a night job!

The Emmy Awards and Honey Bunny

Just like Lucy and Ethel, Kenny and I would do anything to meet influential people or generate press coverage, always hoping to be cast in something big. And when I say anything, I mean *anything*. We used to bluff our way onto studio lots from Paramount to Universal to Warner Brothers. You can't do that today because of tight security, but back then security was pretty lax. We couldn't drive onto the lot, but I could usually talk my way on by saying that I had an appointment with so-and-so. We'd get a walking pass, Kenny would be in a suit and carrying a briefcase full of our pictures and résumés, and we would go from office to office, dropping them off. Then we would go to the studio commissary and have lunch with the stars.

We also used to crash big parties. The craziest one was in 1988 when we crashed an Emmy Awards dinner at the Century Plaza Hotel in Century City. "We knew all the ins and outs of those places. So we walk in the door, Rhonda goes to the ladies' room, I go to the men's room, and we meet up at the escalator," Kenny recalls. "We went up the escalator and nobody stopped us. Rhonda was wearing a gown and I was wearing a tuxedo. We were mingling with all these stars and it was very nice, and then she looks at me and says, 'What are we going to do when we have to sit down?' I said, 'I'll think of something.' We see a table that has two chairs with nobody sitting, so we sit down and start talking to the people next to us. Then two people came and said they were supposed to be at this table, and I said, 'Oh, I'm sorry, we must have the wrong table.'"

Kenny continues: "Then we see another deuce that's empty up near the dais, so we go up and I say, 'Is anybody sitting here?' A guy said no and we sat down. Again, small talk with the people next to us and so on. Then the guy next to me says, 'I'm Daryl Hickman. I'm the president of CBS.' I said, 'Nice to meet you, Mr. Hickman,' and almost choked right there.

"Everything is going smoothly—until the waiters come around to ask us for our dinner ticket. And I say, 'My gosh, I think I left my ticket at the other table.' We had to think fast. So I get up and run to the other table and ask if anyone has found my dinner ticket.

I don't like lying and I don't like doing things that are shifty, but this was fun. Finally, I go to back to the other table and Hickman leans over to me and says, 'I know what you're doing. I'm not going to have you thrown out, but don't try this again.' I almost passed out. He shook my hand, and the second dinner was over, we left because the jig was up."

FOURTH WALL BREAK!

Thank goodness for youth; you can get away with so much! I'm sure everyone at the awards knew immediately that we were crashing, but you could see right away that we were good kids from good families, not grifters or fame whores. I'm also sure that some of those bigwigs had pulled similar stunts at one time. Yes, I was embarrassed, but not as embarrassed as I would have been today. That's what youth is about: getting away with things you wouldn't even try when you're older.

With Kenny and me, it was one screwball idea after another. Another time, we started our own singing telegram company, Hot Lines. This was the height of the singing telegram era, and it seemed like another great promotional stunt. Trouble was, while Kenny is blessed with a gorgeous voice, I couldn't carry a tune if it came with handles attached. No matter. I went out as the Honey Bunny. We wrote a song called, "I'm a Honey Bunny," and I would go into offices, hop around, smile, and charm everybody so they wouldn't notice how bad my singing was.

Shear Honesty: *You won't always be the perfect fit for the opportunity. When that happens, instead of trying to bullshit people into thinking you have a skill you don't have, rock what* *you DO have. I can't sing. So of course, a singing telegram job made perfect sense! Actually, it did, because I could smile, dance, move, make just about anybody laugh, and charm the socks off a room (thank you, pageant experience!). Bring your best to the table no matter what you're doing. You still won't always be the right fit, but you might impress people enough that you get a chance you didn't know was there.*

It worked so well that a couple of years later, when I wanted to do a portfolio photo shoot with the famous photographer Harry Langdon, I went back into singing telegrams to raise Harry's $5,000 fee. That time, I worked for a company called Live Wires. They had all these young actors with amazing voices, but they loved my look, so the Honey Bunny was hopping again! One time, I got a call from Live Wires that said, "We're sending you to Paramount." I was thrilled. Paramount Studios! Then they gave me the address, and it turned out that I was delivering a singing telegram to a guy alone in his house in the city of Paramount, a blue-collar suburb of LA.

It was my very own Lucille Ball moment, and looking back, you have to laugh. Young actors have those kinds of moments, and I certainly had my share of them. But during that one summer, I was able to make my $5,000 and book my Harry Langdon photo shoot. Live Wires loved me and wanted me to stay on, but I had bigger things in mind. Honey Bunny went into permanent retirement.

Another highlight of that wonderful period was when we got advice from the great George Burns. Kenny and I had met him at a Press Club event, and he invited us to the studio where he had his office. We met with him, and he lectured us on what we should do as a male and female team. He was very sweet and he said, "You know, I was in a male-female comedy team, too," referring of course to himself and his beloved wife, Gracie Allen. If you're too young to remember George and Gracie, look them up on YouTube. That's how to be smart, funny, and sweet at the same time. They're still hilarious.

George said, "If I were you, I would recommend that you never do dirty," as he chewed on his famous cigar. "Put it in the minds of the audience. Let them think it, but don't you say it." I based my act around innuendo, using his advice. Maybe it was old school, but it suited me. When the time came for us to go, we walked toward the door we'd come in. But he pointed us toward a different door. We opened the door and behind it was a brick wall. We turned around and George said with a twinkle, "Gets 'em every time." He was one of a kind.

Stopping Traffic

The year 1984 rolled around and Kenny started managing me, turning his focus toward building my career. He really cared about helping me, even more than he cared about his own career. As a result, my career continued to grow, although we never really made it as a comedy duo. Our material was very old-school; comedy was becoming edgier, more topical, more political, and more profane. We were doing sketch work better suited for something like *Saturday Night Live*. Speaking of that, Kenny reminded me that we actually got an audition for *SNL*, but I backed out at the last minute because I didn't want to live in New York. I still kick myself for that one.

Anyway, Kenny was relentless in making calls, and that resulted in some interesting opportunities. The Olympics had come to LA, and this was also the time when posters were huge in American culture. Remember when half the boys in America had Farrah

Fawcett in her red swimsuit hanging in their bedrooms? Well, the always-resourceful Kenny decided that I needed a poster for the Olympics. He contacted the StarMaker Poster Company in New York and put together a poster deal for me, just like that.

> **Shear Honesty:** *If you're ever in a position where you can hire someone to represent you as an agent or manager, do it. It's worth every cent of the commission. There's a reason that actors and writers are always dying to find representation: it opens doors. An agent has access that you don't have, can work tirelessly to find opportunities for you, and can be the bad guy in negotiations so you don't have to. I put in years and years of hard work, but without great representation I would not have had the career I enjoyed.*

In my poster, I wore a gold leather bikini with water dripping down my body; the type read, "Go for the gold! Love, Rhonda Shear!" The poster was shot by famed Hollywood photographer Dick Zimmerman, whom I would later coax out of retirement to shoot the first catalog for my clothing brand. To our delight, my poster started selling well. But Kenny took it a step further.

"Rhonda is into publicity, and she really likes to make a splash," he remembers. "So as a publicity stunt we had a billboard made from the poster and we actually hoisted Rhonda up on one of those cherry pickers to promote its unveiling. We put out a press release, and it was in the newspapers." The billboard stood at a sharp bend in Sunset Boulevard and Roxbury on the world-famous Sunset Strip, right by the old Carlos & Charlie's restaurant; it cost us $900 a month, which was a small fortune back then. But it stayed up for six months, turned a lot of heads, and probably caused a few accidents.

This was another time that I used Hollywood's obsession with the hot female body to my advantage. Call my billboard "cheesecake feminism" if you want, but it was empowering because, even though I was posing in a swimsuit, I decided how I would look and where my image would go. This was me flexing the power not only of my sexuality but my marketing savvy. The billboard was me not only playing the game but *winning* it. If Hollywood was going to use me for my body, then I was going to benefit.

After the billboard became a thing, I got a lot of modeling gigs wearing swimsuits or modeling for the covers of fitness magazines. Bodybuilding legend Joe Weider actually approached me about becoming the next Rachel McLish, the first famous lady bodybuilder in the 1970s. Joe said that I had a better natural body for bodybuilding than Rachel and that he would personally make it happen, but I said no thank you. I liked my curvy, feminine body and I didn't want big muscles. Also, I didn't want to work that hard. Of course, if I'd known how hard I'd have to work now just to keep from collecting extra cup sizes, maybe I'd have taken him up on it all those years ago.

Unfortunately, though everybody knew me because of the poster and billboards, nobody knew that I was an actress. Was I on a show? Where could they find me? I didn't have a body of work that someone could really create a strong PR campaign around, so while my name was getting out, nothing was really happening. I had always thought that if you got out there, people would call you and cast you. But that was magical thinking, and it just wasn't true in a city where beautiful girls were a dime a dozen.

Also, I was becoming confused with a local legend named Angelyne. Oh my God, where to start with her? Before Paris Hilton and Kim Kardashian made "famous for being famous" into a million-dollar enterprise, there was Angelyne. She was a bit part actress who, in 1984, started putting billboards up all over Los Angeles and became a local icon for her pouty lips, enormous platinum coif, gigantic boobs, and bubblehead persona. Sighting her driving her pink Corvette down Sunset was considered a good luck charm, but being confused with her was irritating and even sort of insulting. I was an experienced actress and comedian with hundreds of credits; she was somebody who'd appeared in a few movies and performed with a punk band and was desperate to be famous.

Despite this, all the attention did help me get some modeling gigs, but I'm only five-foot-four, which is short for a model. I got some fashion modeling work, and a lot of gigs in swimsuits or shorts, and I continued landing small parts in sitcoms and episodic shows, but I was making more money from my mechanical mime act than anything else. Still, I didn't mind paying my dues. With every gig, I got more exposure, made more contacts, and got closer to my big break. I knew that I was a lot luckier than most people.

Shear Honesty: *Not every opportunity will be a good one. I could have jumped at the chance to become a bodybuilding star, but would that have served my larger goal? No. It would have typecast me. Don't be so anxious for the right opportunity that you jump at ANY opportunity. There's a fine line between ambitious and desperate. Early in your career, you may have to say yes to just about everything because you need experience and contacts. But as you progress and figure out who you want to become, start curating your time and only say yes to what moves you in the right direction. Remember, being able to turn away work is a sign of success.*

End of an Era

From 1978 to 1984, Kenny Ellis and I tried just about every oddball, harebrained, *I Love Lucy* scheme we could think of to get seen and get cast. But by 1985, we had put the live doll gig on the shelf and our run of wonderful, zany stunts mostly came to an end. I was working pretty much all the time as a talk show guest and getting small parts in movies, so the time came when I no longer needed the mime act. Meanwhile, I think Kenny, who always wanted our relationship to be more than a friendship but was too sweet and too much of a gentleman to press (God, he was wonderful), was ready to move on as well.

It wasn't just our relationship that was changing. For better or worse, 1984–1985 marked the beginning of the end of an era in Hollywood. The studio system was dead. Cable television was starting to become serious competition for the networks. Women were getting bigger roles, bigger jobs, and bigger salaries. I was there to see it happen. When I came back from New Orleans in 1985 after recovering from the death of my father, I would be ready for a new phase in my career.

ON THE WAY TO TODAY

What advice did I distill on the journey from starving actress to billboard icon, comedic foil, and Honey Bunny that I still rely on? Let's see...

- ☐ *Find an ally who's got your back and pushes you to be better.*

- ☐ *Get an agent. Seriously. A great agent is your best friend.*

- ☐ *A little embarrassment isn't going to kill you. Just don't compromise on your values.*

- ☐ *Even the biggest names are still people, and everyone respects somebody with the guts and desire to get their foot in the door.*

- ☐ *You have to create your own opportunities. You can't sit around waiting for the phone to ring.*

- ☐ *Always present yourself as a polished professional, especially when you're not.*

- ☐ *Crash. The worst that'll happen is you'll be escorted out, and you'll have some awesome stories to tell.*

- ☐ *Doing silly, crazy things to get ahead is fun and an adrenaline rush. What's the point in doing anything if it's not fun?*

- ☐ *When you're hanging your ass out over the edge, you're making progress. Not comfortable progress, but progress.*

LESSON SEVEN
Barriers Are for Breaking

—— In which our heroine becomes a comedy junkie, hits the road, dodges airborne shoes, becomes a headliner, covers Bill Clinton's nomination from her décolletage, and learns that despite what everyone told her for years, pretty, sexy women can indeed be funny as hell. ——

Though I didn't know it, that new phase began in 1986 when Chuck Barris (remember Chuckie Baby?) cast me as the sexy bailiff in the pilot for his show *Comedy Courtroom*. Each show would play out a real small-claims court case, but with comedians playing the judge, attorneys, plaintiffs, and defendants. Playing the prosecuting attorney for the pilot was a wonderful standup comedian named Bobby Kelton, and I fell a little in love with him.

Bobby was a topical comedian with a wonderful command of the English language and a stage presence that was smooth as silk. He had appeared on *The Tonight Show* twenty-one times and opened in Las Vegas for the likes of Paul Anka, Tom Jones, and Gladys Knight. He was awkward offstage, with limited social skills, but when we worked together on *Comedy Courtroom*, I thought he was really cute. When the show wrapped, I handed him a business card. He called, but I kept breaking our dates, nervous that somewhere in him was the hidden rapist my mother had always warned me about. In my heart of hearts, though, I knew Bobby was a good guy—cool on stage, pleasantly nerdy offstage.

Finally, ten months after we met, I invited him to a big Hollywood party and we started seeing each other regularly. He was the first guy who took me to a diner, instead of a nice restaurant, for a dinner date. I thought it was novel and charming, but it struck me as odd that he ordered fries and blotted the oil from each one individually. By the time we were done eating, he had a pile of oil-laden napkins on the table next to him.

Our second date was even stranger. He took me to a friend's wedding. The reception was going to be at the Santa Monica Pier, and it was going to be lavish. I hadn't eaten all day, had too much cheap champagne at the wedding, and got sick. Bobby took me home and tucked me in, but instead of babysitting his new girlfriend, he left to go back to the reception so he could get the free jumbo shrimp. We never stopped fighting about that. Bobby was dry and antisocial while I was bubbly and outgoing, and he never saw a penny he wouldn't try to pinch. People always wondered why we stayed together for thirteen years, but I knew.

Shear Honesty: *Life is too short to stay with the wrong man for the wrong reasons. Bobby liked taking care of me, but the real reason I was with him for so long was that I could hide behind him. I still carried that mom-induced apprehension about men, and so many men hit on me that if I wasn't feeling brave, I could tell them I had a boyfriend. Bobby and Kenny Ellis were my shields, which is not a healthy thing.*

It was his standup comedy. I watched him on stage all the time doing his act and he was great. In the process I caught a serious case of the comedy flu. Before long, I was continually begging him like Lucy begging Ricky: "Put me in the show, put me in the show! I could open for you! Please?" I'd learned to speak to an audience and tell a joke during my pageant days and polished my patter when I was running for office. Most of all, I *loved* comedy. I was dying to get in front of the mic. After years of pageants, classes, improv, and working with Kenny, I was ready to give it a shot.

The trouble was, no decent club wanted to give me any stage time. The prevailing wisdom was that women weren't funny, and pretty women were the least funny of all. Stupid, right? Well, by now you know my pattern. Tell me that I can't do something and you wave the red flag before my inner bull. My father's name was Wil, and his saying was, "Where there's a Wil, there's always a way!" I had the will to create more stage time for me and my new female comic friends, so I did.

I was still working with Kenny, and he and I decided that if female comics were not getting enough stage time at the clubs, we would create our own female showcases that would welcome gals just starting out in standup. We talked a Westwood deli into letting us use its upstairs space on a weeknight and launched "Babes of Comedy." The show was a hit, and before long we were featured in the "Things to Do" section of the local newspapers and had brought "Babes of Comedy" to the legendary Laugh Factory. Slowly, we were earning respect while showing audiences that women could be good-looking and funny at the same time.

Shear Honesty: *I know I've said it before, but it bears repeating. If no one will open a door for you, get out a chainsaw and cut your own. That's what being a feminist means: refusing to accept limitations imposed by other people, especially because you're* *a woman. If you're not finding the job of your dreams, if no one will publish your book, if you can't get someone to take you seriously—take the decision out of their hands. Make your own path and don't worry about whose feathers you ruffle. Remember,* **it's much easier to apologize than to ask permission.**

An Uncompliant Woman

It was never easy, though. I've always been a little ahead of my time. I was the first woman to run for office in Louisiana. I started my own, one-woman bachelor society. When no one would give pretty girls a chance in comedy, I started my own show. I loved trailblazing. It took some guts and a knack for selling, both of which I had. Trouble was (and this is still true today), the system was run by men, and some of them didn't take kindly to a woman pushing her own cause as persistently as I did, even when she did it with a Southern drawl and a winning smile.

It wasn't just comedy club owners, either. More than once, I became frustrated with agents and managers who I didn't feel were selling me with enough gumption. I wasn't a big star, so maybe it wasn't realistic to expect agents to spend all their time working on my behalf, but I did expect them to be creative, put forth effort, and believe in me. As I saw it, agents and managers should have been grateful to represent someone who was constantly kicking down walls and trying to make things happen instead of sitting home on the couch waiting for roles to be dropped in their laps. So if an agent didn't hustle at least as hard for me as I hustled for myself, I dropped them.

Because of this, after a while I was labeled as "unmanageable" and uncompliant. That was unfair, but I wasn't about to become meek, mild Rhonda just to make a bunch of agents happy. I had half-jokingly promised my dad that I would buy him a Rolls-Royce when I made it, and I wanted to have some real success for him. For the record, the best I could do was get him a 14-carat gold charm, which he kept until the day he died.

Meanwhile, while all this was going on and I was working in TV, I was searching for a way to hone my comedy chops. The show Kenny and I had created was great, but it was friendly territory. You can't become a standup performing for your mom; you've got to be out on stage with nothing but a mic and your mouth, naked and alone in front of an audience that doesn't give a damn if you bomb. If you're good, maybe you get a few laughs. If not, you get deadly silence. It's brutal, which is what Bobby said after his twenty-first *Tonight Show* appearance when I told him that I wanted to start doing solo comedy.

"Oh no," he said with a groan. "If you start doing this, working the tiny clubs and all that, I will have to go through it all over again." He was talking about the jokes that bomb, the awful hecklers, the club owners that don't pay, and all the rest that he'd already lived on his way up through the comedy ranks. He said, "It's hard, Rhonda. Your ego gets bashed day in and day out, and it's a thankless job, especially when you're starting out."

I heard him, but I didn't care. I was going for it, with or without Bobby's approval. But I also knew that despite my experience as an actress, beauty queen, and model, I was starting from scratch. But I was committed. I loved every sound that came from an audience, even the sneezes. No one was going to stop me.

Shear Honesty: *Men who stand up for themselves and refuse to take no for an answer are go-getters; women who do the same thing are often labeled as "bitches" who "want to be like men."*

Well, guess what? Men made the rules in this world, so if you want to get anywhere, you'd better be prepared to play by those rules and develop a thick skin when men can't handle it. Don't get me wrong; there are plenty of men who admire and love working with strong women. I've been lucky enough to work with a lot of them. But you'll always find a few unevolved types who'll condemn you for being assertive and going after what you want. Ignore them and keep doing it your way. You're not the problem; they are.

Paying Dues

The thing is, Bobby was one hundred percent right about standup as a business. There are no shortcuts. You elbow your way on stage past a hundred other wannabes trying to do the same thing, deliver your best five minutes of material, and then do it again and again and again until you get good. So that's what I did. I started going to small-club showcases all over Los Angeles just so I could get stage time.

You'd write your name on a board along with musicians and other kinds of acts, then sit outside waiting to be called. If you got called, great. If not, you'd go home and try your luck again the following week. The first showcase where I got to perform was at a Holiday Inn bar and was organized by a famous talk show host and actor, Skip E. Lowe.

Skip, who died in 2014 at age eighty-five, was beloved by everybody, in part because he loved to put young people on stage so they could get some professional experience. I went on right after four little black kids who did a knockout Michael Jackson impression, did my two minutes, and walked off to scattered applause. I have no memory of what I said, but somebody sneezed and I assumed it was a laugh. Just like that, I was hooked.

From that point on, in between TV and modeling gigs and commercials, I wrote concepts, setups, payoffs, and one-liners. I tried being a character that wasn't really me, which was a disaster. I even tried mime (don't try this). But slowly, I became the real Rhonda on stage. Slowly, I got funnier and funnier.

FOURTH WALL BREAK!

The first time I walked out on that stage, my heart was pounding, but I forced myself to do it. That's what you do when you want something so badly. I loved the comedy club scene; I was a night owl from New Orleans, after all. I loved the late hours and dimly lit rooms. It was wonderful: the smell of liquor, the laughter, comics running through routines and one-liners.

One time, when I was in New York, Larry David was in the back of the room with one of those school composition notebooks, walking back and forth with Bobby and me and saying, "I don't know how this crowd is. I don't know about this." It's hard to believe he was the same guy who became a zillionaire after Seinfeld. But comics are insecure, even the successful ones.

What I was doing was exciting and fun, but audiences looked at me like I had two heads. I wasn't a housewife or doing the frumpy thing. If a joke bombed, I giggled through it. Of course, it still wasn't easy. In those early clubs, there were times I had an audience of two or three people, but I went on. It didn't matter. I loved the whole journey of standup.

In the beginning, I was also looking for myself on stage. I went on in skirts and petticoats, with a higher voice like a little girl, but that wasn't me. Then finally, I settled into myself. Today, the few times I've gone on stage and just riffed, it's been so easy. Writing today would be so easy; it would just be reality. But I don't want to be a sixty-something rising star.

After a year of local showcases, I got my first paying gig in 1987, opening for Wayland Flowers and his puppet, Madame, in Atlanta. Not long after that, I unofficially opened for Robin Williams at the City Zoo in San Francisco, which was a thrill. As we moved into the late 1980s, I started to work regularly all over Los Angeles. But it was still a challenge to get stage time at the major comedy clubs: The Improv, The Laff Stop, The Ice House, The Comedy Store, and the Laugh Factory. Those were the prestige clubs and getting on stage was tough, mostly because of that same frustrating prejudice: *pretty women weren't funny.*

My hunger for stage time led to an incident that Bobby still hasn't forgiven me for. He tells the story: "It was 1988, and we were at Dodger Stadium for Game One of the World Series, the famous game where Kirk Gibson hit his game-winning home run off Dennis Eckersley. It was the bottom of the ninth and Gibson came to bat, and then Rhonda said to me, 'There's a club in West Hollywood that gave me a spot tonight. We have to be there in 45 minutes.' My God, we're at the World Series in the bottom of the ninth! But it was a big deal to her, because it was one of her first solo spots. I couldn't fight her off and so we had to leave.

"We were still leaving the parking lot and I had the radio on in the car," Bobby continues, "and then the announcer shouts, 'It's gone! I can't believe what I just saw!' I just stopped the car and stared at her. This was for a club that probably wasn't open for more than three weeks, a little hole in the wall on Santa Monica Boulevard in West Hollywood. There were maybe one or two people in the audience, but Rhonda did her act. And for that, I missed one of the greatest moments in baseball history."

Shear Honesty: *I felt really bad about making Bobby miss that baseball moment, but he got a little solace years later. We met Kirk Gibson at an event and he sat with us privately and told us every behind-the-scenes detail of that magical at-bat. It wasn't the same as being there for the home run, but it was still pretty cool.*

Comedy School

In fact, it was so hard to get stage time as a new comic in LA that over the next couple of years, I spent most of my time on the road, which turned out to the best comedy school I could have ever attended. At the out-of-town clubs I was usually the opening act and emcee, which is the lowliest and hardest job in comedy. You have to be funny, give out information (who is playing at the club next, the old "Remember to tip your server" thing), and introduce the next comic without upstaging him or her. The featured act (the middle comic on the bill) or headliner rarely even acknowledged you, but I was cute, and that helped.

I paid my own way on those trips because I refused to stay at the "comedy condos" that the clubs would spring for because they were always disgusting. So I would foot the bill for my own motel room. Since the airfare usually cost about whatever the club was paying me, the trips were usually a financial wash. But I wanted experience as a road comic, and this was the way to get it.

My mother would have freaked out if she'd seen some of the dives I worked. I went to smoke-filled bars (before non-smoking laws passed) that turned into comedy rooms on the weekends, in towns as far away as Anchorage, Alaska. They loved me in Alaska. It's a state with five men to every woman, so even if they hadn't heard a word I said, I would have killed.

In Alaska I overheard people talking about their first bear hunt, stood on a glacier, and ate the most outrageously fresh and delicious salmon I ever tasted. I loved traveling to perform standup. I met wonderful people, saw this great country, and got the on-stage confidence that led me to a starring role on TV and enabled me to do what I do today.

My road experiences changed me. I may have started out as the genteel, naïve New Orleans girl who my father thought was too soft to make it in Hollywood, but I grew balls doing standup. Once you've stood in front of a room of strangers, many of them a few drinks in, all of them basically daring you to make them laugh, you can handle anything. I worked a college once and a shoe came flying at me. It wasn't because I was bad; it was because they were drunken college kids. Another time, I was playing a dive bar with a dance floor and a fight broke out during my act, so I just walked off the stage. Every comic has those stories, but the point is that after I'd dealt with that kind of abuse, what could anyone to do me at an audition?

FOURTH WALL BREAK!

I didn't get heckled a lot. I had a few classic heckle lines, but usually I would deal with them by talking to them. I was an oddity, so it didn't happen much. I was heckled even less after USA: Up All Night because people knew me. But it still happened on occasion. Once, in Dallas, some guy in the front row kept saying, "You really think you're hot, don't you?" I put him down, and he shut it down. The most common heckle isn't really a heckle. It's when people are loud, drunk, and talking through your act, ruining your timing.

The comedy condos were revolting. There would be blood on the wall sometimes, and my friend Carole Montgomery told me that I should never, ever use the mayonnaise in a comedy condo kitchen, because the guys always put their dicks in it. But the worst was waiting for club owners to pay you. It was degrading. I'm in the middle of Podunk or Boise and waiting for some guy to count the cash and pay me, and he tries to gyp me out of $100 because he didn't make his numbers. Meanwhile, some dude in a car with bald tires and filled with McDonald's wrappers is waiting to take me to the airport. I had to get a little tough with some owners. It's never easy to ask for money, and I got as tough as I could.

Only once did hecklers really get to me. I was at a really tough Boston club full of drunk men, and a table of guys at a bachelor party wasn't just heckling me. They were being ugly and filthy. I guess the club was making more money from the bachelor party than from my act. Finally, I got fed up and walked off. But when you consider how many shows I did, in hundreds of little bars and clubs, I didn't have many bad heckling experiences. When I did have them, I learned to deal with them. Being a road comic toughens you up and teaches you to be poised under fire.

That really helped me years later when I started selling my lingerie on HSN, formerly known as the Home Shopping Network. When you're selling on HSN, you can't sit around, because dead air doesn't sell anything. You have to improvise, tell stories, be funny, and have energy. Fortunately, I'm really good at all of that, because it's just like standup. Nothing that can happen on air will throw me, because I've already had shoes and drinks thrown at me. If a mannequin's arm comes off during a segment, I just roll with it and make a joke.

That's why Joan Rivers sold so much jewelry on shopping TV; she was brilliant, funny, and inspirational. Standup prepares you to shine in situations where there isn't a script. Once you master it, you'll never be afraid in a public situation, ever again.

> **Shear Honesty:** *You're going to have to pay your dues. Get used to it. The popular stereotype going around these days is that Millennials want cupcake jobs that don't ask them to get their hands dirty and treat them like special snowflakes. But I don't believe that. I think Millennials work as hard as anyone, but the truth is that NOBODY has ever enjoyed paying dues in lousy jobs. It sucks! But hard jobs and tedious work are part of advancing in any career. That's how you learn the ropes, develop a good work ethic, meet mentors, and earn the respect of people who will give you more opportunities. Don't ever shy away from dues-paying work, especially if you're new to a field. It's the best training ground you could ever hope for.*

Breaking Through in a Man's World

But there was an obstacle I couldn't get past: standup was still mostly a man's world. If you think about the pioneers of standup, going all the way back to the Borscht Belt comedians in the 1950s, you think about people like Alan King, Shecky Greene, Henny Youngman, Milton Berle, and Shelley Berman. All men.

When Bobby Kelton started in the mid-'70s, there were maybe a couple of women out of the few hundred comedians working at the time. By the late '80s, the scene had started opening up to a few more ladies, but just a few. A few women were becoming household names: Elaine Boosler, Paula Poundstone, Rita Rudner, and Roseanne Barr. But none of them played it sexy. If a woman was attractive, the audience wouldn't buy that she could also be funny.

Part of it is role-playing. The father is the jokester of the family. Mom is maternal and takes care of the kids. Even as late as 1990, it didn't feel right for women to be talking openly about sex and orgasms and the like. That sounds strange when you think about world-class stars of today like Margaret Cho and Sarah Silverman, who are so wonderfully candid and dirty in their acts, but there you are. In those days, you had to look funny or be a housewife to have any credibility. Roseanne and Joan Rivers made it by making fun of their looks, sex lives, and marriages. But even today, women comedians are judged as much on their looks as on their material.

FOURTH WALL BREAK!

The sexism was more about being a female—being a female was still new. Because I was a sexy female, comedy didn't know what to do with me. Agents and managers hit on me, but I was used to that. Worse, a couple of big-time managers led me on because they wanted to get in the sack with me. But I never tried to dial down my looks; I went for it more in standup. I was the girl who could get the guy, not the girl who said guys were shitty.

I headlined, did all the comedy shows, and while I didn't ever get my own special, I went pretty far and opened a lot of doors for women. I even did a comedy album: Your Bedtime Buddy, *made from tapes of my sets at the Ice House in Pasadena. But I've never been paid residuals for it. The producer was a slimeball: if you open the CD, he had lifted the few topless shots I did other than for Playboy and used them without my permission, to sell extra copies.*

Pretty women have it tough in standup for a simple reason: the heart of standup is making fun of yourself. Thousands of comedians, male and female, have made millions of people laugh by talking about their goofy noses, weight problems, and bad relationships. But from the audience's perspective, I was young, beautiful, and charming. How could I make fun of myself believably? Ironically, I never had a lot of confidence in my looks. I hated my nose, my hair, and my curvy butt. The Kardashians hadn't come along yet to make a big booty desirable.

So comedy was early training for what would become the Rhonda Shear brand: sexy, self-deprecating, smart, and funny. In my standup shows I made fun of my beauty queen past, guys trying to get to third base on dates, and men in general without putting men down. It worked. People in the comedy world would tell me, "You can't do this. You look like a soap actress." I'd always reply, "What is a comedian supposed to look like?" Crickets in response. I loved the challenge of proving them wrong.

I used another strategy in the clubs: getting the women to laugh first. When I came onstage, young and attractive in a short skirt, the women in the audience felt threatened. They would clutch their dates a little tighter and dare them to laugh. So I immediately made fun of myself or my dating disasters and got the women on my side, laughing. Once that happened, they would loosen their hold and let the guys laugh. Then the room was all mine.

Of course, I couldn't have done any of it without standing on the shoulders of trailblazers like Phyllis Diller, who worked twice as hard to get half as many bookings as her male counterparts and relied on making fun of her appearance. One of the joys of my life was getting to know Phyllis. She hid her fabulous body and great looks behind her wit and incredible laugh, but she paved the way for all women comics. She was an amazing artist and lady—a true broad, and I mean that with respect and love. In my bedroom I have a signed self-portrait that she painted, and it's one of my most prized possessions.

I was lucky enough to hang out with Phyllis several times at the Polo Lounge. Phyllis was fearless. She loved her martinis, wigs, and a diamond the size of a skating rink that Fang got her. Once, at one of those outings, the most incredible thing happened. Phyllis turned to me and said, "Rhonda, I would love you to play me in my life story." I was speechless. I have no idea if she really meant it, though it seemed sincere at the time, but that was enough fuel to keep this comic going for years. Phyllis, I'd be honored to play you one day.

Shear Honesty: *Never pass up the chance to spend time with people who have already mastered what you're trying to do. I took every chance I could get to pick the brains of people like Phyllis Diller, George Burns, and other legends of TV and comedy. If you have the opportunity to have a drink or engage in conversation with a great from your field, never pass it up. It might not come again, and you'll have missed out on what might be wisdom that could change the course of your life.*

The Comedy Store

I was making some progress, but even for experienced male comics, the LA scene was hypercompetitive. In 1979, there was even a comedians' strike focused on The Comedy Store, which refused to pay its comics. The comics even tried to organize their own labor union, though it didn't last very long. I remember the strike well: comedians picketing in front of The Comedy Store location on Sunset Boulevard, and the horrible news that a comic named Steve Lubetkin had committed suicide by jumping off the roof of the Continental Hyatt House next door. His suicide note read, "My name is Steve Lubetkin. I used to work at The Comedy Store." This was life-and-death stuff, not funny at all.

Jamie Masada, an Israeli immigrant who was only twenty-five, decided to take advantage of the ill will aimed at The Comedy Store by opening his own Hollywood comedy club that same year in a building that Groucho Marx had owned. Eventually, the Laugh Factory would become a force in comedy and open locations in Vegas, Chicago, and other cities. But in the late '80s, it was a dump that nobody would play. Still, people showed up for my all-girl showcases, including Los Angeles Lakers owner Jerry Buss, a notorious skirt chaser who came in with his harem of too-young girlfriends.

Still, female comics dwelt in a kind of ghetto. For example, in 1978, Mitzi Shore, who had won The Comedy Store from her husband Sammy in their divorce, turned the upstairs section of the club into a fifty-seat venue only for female comedians called The Belly Room. That was absolutely unheard of in those days, and we were happy to have a chance to work there under the same roof where people would come to see Richard Pryor and Sam Kinison. However, being in The Belly Room was still like being a baseball player in the minor leagues: until you got to the main stage, you weren't really in the game.

The game was winning Mitzi's approval. She was a petite woman with a shrill Bronx accent who wore all black and sat in the back of the club making the ultimate decisions about who would go on. She was terrifying because she had the power to make or break a career. She made Roseanne Barr a star, and bookers from *The Tonight Show* would go to her shows to watch the sets of up-and-comers. We all wanted to be her next favorite female.

The third of the Three Musketeers of LA standup was The Improvisation on Melrose, run by monocle-wearing Budd Friedman. Budd was good to me: he knew I was from New Orleans, and he was visiting New Orleans to scout real estate for a club there. I hooked him up with the best restaurants, got him invited to the best Mardi Gras balls, and fixed him up with my sister, Nona. Yes, I'm willing to pimp out family members for my career. Unfortunately, she didn't sleep with him, so I had to work for my stage time anyway. C'est la vie.

Eventually, I worked my way from The Comedy Store's Belly Room to the main stage, and that was my life for a while. The comics would all hang out and when our chance came, we did our best material and tried to ruin each other. Stars like Seinfeld and Leno were all doing sets right along with us. Through 1991 I worked all over, taking opening, middle, and headliner jobs at clubs big and small. I was meeting booking agents, but I got most of my work on my own. I did it without knowing anything about the business, learning as I went.

One of the things I loved most was the sorority of women comics. We were all in the same boat, so we helped each other. We wrote together. We would get together late after shows at a deli or coffee shop and talk about our sets. I was becoming part of a very special world, and it's still special. Comedy is a tight community. Many of my old pals are still working the road, while some are writing and producing and some are in other fields. Now that we're no longer rivals, we follow each other on Facebook and root for one another. You never get comedy out of your blood. Once you do it, you're a part of the family. It's wonderful.

> **Shear Honesty:** *Women have a reputation for being catty and more likely to sabotage each other than to help each other, but I've rarely found that to be the case. All the way back to my pageant days, other girls were always classy, super supportive, and happy for me when I won. The family feeling among women in comedy was the latest version of that kind of warm, loving female camaraderie. Seek that out as you move through your ventures, because it can be a cold, lonely world. You need people around you who know what you're going through because they're going through it, too. Having a "band of sisters" who have your back, who you can laugh with and cry with and plot the downfall of evil men with…that's priceless.*

The Big Time

Then came 1991 and *USA: Up All Night*, and I began getting bookings at hotel/casinos in Las Vegas and Reno: The Dunes, The Sands, Harrah's, Caesars Palace, Bally's Grand, and The Riviera. All of a sudden I was opening for Smokey Robinson, The Temptations, Johnny Rivers, Al Jarreau, Chicago, and Three Dog Night. Vegas and Reno were wonderful, because even if you were an opening act, you got the star treatment. You stayed in a suite, had a limo whenever you needed it, had your own dressing room with five-star service, and you were respected. As any comedian who's worked the dives will tell you, that sort of thing never, ever gets old. It doesn't get much cooler than seeing your name right below the headliners on the marquee of a Las Vegas casino. You've arrived.

(The only "you're there" moment better than Vegas came when I saw my name on the outside of The Comedy Store. The building is painted all black and it's covered with the white signatures of the top comedians who have graced the stage over the years. One night after my set, I headed for the side door—the performer's entrance—and stopped dead. My signature had been added to the wall, and Mitzi Shore had to have approved it. Every time I go to LA, I check to see if it's still there, and it is. That's better than a star on the Hollywood Walk of Fame.)

FOURTH WALL BREAK!

Vegas was fabulous. Back then they had opening acts, which are rare today. You got paid nicely. Your agent would ask what your rider was—sandwiches backstage, red M&Ms, whatever— and you would get it. They would put you up in a fabulous suite and pick you up in a limo. It was fantastic. I was an opening act, so I still had people coming into the club when I was doing my act, and I had to overcome that. But I was treated great, so I can't say anything bad about any of it. But that world is gone now. Now, it's about "four-walling": you pay for your own hotel room and do all the promotion, and then you hope people show up so you make money. That has been the death of what was a great system.

Standup was evolving. I was appearing on the covers of magazines in Vegas and pre-selling tickets, and that's what club owners love. People wanted to see someone they knew from television, and USA: *Up All Night* was making some noise. I was the woman who dared to throw out double entendres on late-night TV, and people were curious. Still, managers didn't really know what to do with me. Jenny McCarthy and Chelsea Handler hadn't come along yet, and I was something they hadn't seen before. But the female comedy voice was changing. It wasn't just the housewife shtick or male-bashing. Women were talking about real stuff, and the view of us as sex objects was slowly changing. Perhaps I was too early for the revolution, but somebody has to be first, right?

USA: *Up All Night* had another big benefit: my pay went up, which drove Bobby Kelton crazy. He'd been working as a standup for years and now I would walk into a club and get $5,000 for one night's work. That's why so many showbiz couples break up; when one half of the couple is having more success than the other, things can get tense. But my TV show was sexy and fun and broadcast into 90 million households every Friday night, and I wasn't about to apologize for that!

> **Shear Honesty:** *If you're successful, no matter how generous, humble, and accessible you are, there will always be people who resent your success and try to tear you down. That's not about you, but them; insecurity is the root of all unfair criticism. Throughout my life, I've encountered people who were angry at me because I enjoyed the kind of success that they envied, including my siblings for a time. That's unfortunate, but it's also very human. Three pieces of advice when you run into that sort of resentment. First, don't change a thing. Don't stop being amazing just to make other people feel important. Second, don't feel guilty. As long as you're not waving your success in other people's faces, you have nothing to be ashamed of. Third, use these situations as*

opportunities to find out who your real friends are. Hint: they're the ones who are happy when you do well.

Peaking

I was at my comedic peak in the early '90s. All the years testing material and all my years on the road, writing and working my way up from opener to headliner, were paying off. I was confident behind that mic. Early on, my stage presence was ahead of my material, but the material had finally caught up. Woody Allen says that you have to do a joke at least one hundred times before it's good enough to be a permanent part of your act, and that's true. Sometimes you do a joke and it kills. The next time you do it, it flops. Standup is an unusual art because you write it, cast it, and star in it yourself.

I loved the challenge. I loved the power of that mic—not only holding the attention of a paying audience, but getting honest-to-goodness belly laughs. I had found a home, and I'd earned it. It took years of hard work, traveling, and building an act and trying out setups and jokes over and over again. It all came from my life, my experiences, my mind, and my timing.

At that point, I also had the pleasure of working with comedy idols like Sinbad and Bobby Slayton. I co-headlined with the late Richard Jeni. I worked with George Burns, Don Rickles, John Candy, and Joe Piscopo. I also worked with my share of comics who became superstars, including Ray Romano, Jon Stewart, and Jeff Foxworthy. I worked with Jon several times, including in 1992 on a show called *Battle of the Sexes*, which also starred George Hamilton, Dr. Ruth Westheimer, and Judy Tenuta, among others. Jon and I also worked together at the MGM Grand in Las Vegas, where I was the opener and Jon was the middle act. The opening comedian introduces the headliner, but after Jon finished his set, I went on stage to introduce Jon Hayman...and there was no Jon Hayman. I had to ad lib because he was still sleeping off the last show in his suite.

There's nothing like comedy, disasters and all.

I was also a guest on every talk show under the sun: *The Vicki Lawrence Show, Larry King Live!, The Joan Rivers Show, Maury Povich, Sally Jessy Raphael, Nightalk with Jane Whitney, Leeza, The Buzz, VH1 Top 21 Countdown, The Cybil Shepherd Show, Talk Soup, Extra!, Hard Copy, Ricki Lake, The O'Reilly Factor, The Rosie O' Donnell Show, Politically Incorrect, The Richard Bey Show, Geraldo, Mike and Maty, Joan Rivers' Gossip! Gossip! Gossip!, The Gordon Elliott Show*. If it had a couch, I was on it.

The standup comedy shows started rolling in, too. I appeared on *Evening at the Improv, The Rick Dees Show, Comedy on the Road* on A&E, *Lip Service* on MTV, and *Women Aloud* on Comedy Central. But one of my funniest bookings was *Circus of the Stars*. Remember that? It was the show that convinced celebrities to do circus acts. I did an aerial act, flying high above the crowd, doing contortionist acrobatics (thank God for all that dance training!). The twist was that I was playing my *USA: Up All Night* over-the-top bimbo character. It was a funny bit: I was talking on my phone and powdering my nose while getting into these wild positions, and the act ended with me tangled up on the ground with ringmaster Leslie Nielsen. The training was grueling, but it was a blast.

I also did lots of morning radio. I love morning radio; it's a natural medium for me (if only it could be later in the day!). The patter, the inside jokes, making people laugh, the surprises...it's wonderful. You can create visuals in people's minds without them ever seeing you. I had worked the radio stations in New Orleans back when I ran for office, so I knew how to make that work for me. Radio people would call me when they wanted a female guest with a fun attitude and great comedic timing.

I was also a part of the beginning of reality TV. Back in the early '90s it was really live, on-camera improvisational comedy, and the producers knew that with my smarter-than-she-looks, sexy bimbo character, I could rock that. I did 48 Hours, and I was a regular on Hard Copy. Hard Copy would send me out as a reporter, which was funny given that my outfit was more conducive to a hooker than a reporter. Audiences loved it!

My Hard Copy claim to fame came in 1996 when I covered the Democratic National Convention in New York City from my cleavage. The producers wired me up with a camera in my bra, giving the audience "the girls"-eye view of the nomination of Bill Clinton and Al Gore. The problem was that back then, cameras weren't tiny things like today's GoPro. They were big and bulky and didn't have their own microphones or miniaturized features. So I had to have a cameraman following me while I carried a TV station in this huge, heavy bag on my shoulder: microphone and recorder and all the rest, with a scarf around my neck to hide the wires. So it looked like the camera that was following me was capturing me and the scene, but the real camera was in my cleavage.

Hard Copy sent me onto the convention floor dressed in a low-cut top, and the joke was that all the men I interviewed—including Sam Donaldson, a young Brian Williams, Ted Koppel, and other major reporters and delegates—would pretend to be talking to me, but would really be sneaking looks at my boobs. Basically, I was reporting on men's reactions to breasts in a political setting, which was—wait for it—the same as in every other setting. It was very funny, and the footage ended up being highly requested by the news agencies. Quite a combination, boobs and politics. And I don't mean breasts, either.

FOURTH WALL BREAK!

I had a lot of laughs doing Hard Copy. *It was kind of like reality TV before reality TV, goofing on people. You can't do that kind of crazy stuff on TV anymore, because it would be considered sexist. It was good old-fashioned fun and very funny. Everything is so politically correct now, but a lot less fun.*

Lifeline and Fountain of Youth

From campaigning for my own talk show and doing British TV to my busy standup schedule, the mid-1990s were a blur. But even as I moved onto other things, the comedy bug stayed in my bloodstream. A few years later, I decided to revisit the comedy stage with a sendup of the type of scenes I'd played on USA: *Up All Night*. By this time, many of the women I started with in comedy had become headliners in their own right, and I thought it would be great fun to host "Rhonda Shear's Up All Night Pajama Party." So I did. We had an all-star female cast who all stayed on stage for the duration of the show, which was unheard of.

We dressed the stage like the ultimate pajama party, with beds, furniture, food, faux martinis, teddy bears, the works, and invited the audience to wear their bedtime attire to the theater! We staged the show as an on-stage slumber party with skits, contests, and interactive bits with audience members. The women would do their sets but remain onstage in some sort of pajamas during the other performances. It was fun, relaxed, and naughty, and audiences loved it. We took the show to Indian casinos and even did a couple of nights in Vegas.

I loved it because it was a great way to work with some of my favorite comedy friends. We revived the show in the late '90s, again in the early 2000s, and again in 2013. I often think of taking it back out on the road. A pajama party in Rhonda Shear pajamas? What a fun way to connect with my customers!

Comedy will always be a part of my life because, despite everything I've done, I'm a comedian first. I've never felt more alive than when I'm standing in front of an audience telling jokes. All my friends my age who did comedy when I was coming up are still performing: Carole Montgomery—who's still performing for service members around the world and mentoring young comedians in New York—and the Three Blonde Moms—Joan Fagan, Kat Simmons, and Donna Cherry, who keep alive the idea of women working together in comedy.

Shear Honesty: *I've replaced standup with inspirational speaking in front of all kinds of groups. I'm usually speaking as an entrepreneur, but I always get in a few jokes. I can't help it. Not many keynote speakers can tell stories about making out with the Fonz or sparring with Bob Hope. I'm constantly invited to speak in front of business groups, women's groups, and charitable organizations, or on college campuses. It's a real high to talk about making it in business. I never would have put that on my résumé years ago, but now being a humorous keynote speaker is a true pleasure. It feels great to give business advice and answer questions about my years in Hollywood. I always open the floor to questions after a speech. That's the fun part.*

My life today may not include the bright lights of Las Vegas, but I'm very proud of changing career paths in life so successfully. We all can do it. Put your blinders on, don't listen to anyone else, and follow your dreams. There is no age limit to following your passion.

I'm no Joan Rivers, I realize. I didn't carve out a place for women in standup through relentless hard work the way she did. Joan's a hero. But I think I made my mark. I was the first headlining woman to show the world that funny can be sexy, and sexy can be funny. I was a bit of a pioneer in a male-dominated business and opened doors for female comics who today don't have to worry about their looks being more important than their talent. I'm proud of what I did. I was good, and as Bobby points out, being good as a comic is not easy.

"I know comedians who've been doing it for forty years who don't have five good minutes of material," he says. "Comedy is really, really difficult. To do an hour at a top level is not something everybody can do. Rhonda did it."

Comedy also helps women feel better about themselves, and that's very important to me. When I'm on HSN, I talk about boobs and body parts and what I call the "wiggle waggle" but I do it in a comedic way. What I'm really telling women is that it's no big deal if our least favorite body parts have some wiggle or jiggle. Arms, breasts, belly—we all have them, and we should be able to feel proud and sexy, inside and out, jiggles and all. Comedy has always helped me say things that I thought were important, and now I get to talk to 90 million girlfriends through HSN, helping them feel confident and comfortable in the skin they're in. Pat yourselves on the back ladies; we've made it this far, and we've looked damn good doing it.

Comedy is a lifeline like nothing else I've ever seen. It binds comics together. Out of all the people from my life, none have stayed together like the comedy community. Comedy is the great equalizer, because whether you're Chris Rock or a young opening act, at the end of the day, we all sit down and say, "How was the show?" We all want the applause and approval.

Comedy is also a fountain of youth. Comedians keep working at an age when most folks are in the retirement home or looking at the grass from the wrong side. George Burns and Bob Hope lived to 100. Mel Brooks, Carl Reiner, Buck Henry, Neil Simon, Norman Lear—they're all still writing and performing in their eighties and nineties. The bottom line is that while actors might retire, comics never do. Most would rather die on stage, and I don't mean dying in terms of not getting laughs. When their ability to make people laugh is done, so are they.

Comedy keeps you alive and young. It keeps you relevant and working because you have to stay on top of the news and know what's going on in the world. Plus, there's no age limit. Even if you're not comfortable working the clubs anymore at eighty, there are theaters and cruises. If you're good and you love it, you can work until they carry you off the stage feet-first.

My cherished friend Carole Montgomery insisted on weighing in on the Rhonda Shear legacy in comedy, so I'll give her the last word. "Women weren't funny, and God forbid you should be funny and sexy at the same time," she says. "Rhonda was funny and smart and gorgeous, and women especially hated that. If a couple went to a comedy club, women would get really pissed because the guys were looking at Rhonda and getting hot and bothered. The truth is, Jenny McCarthy wouldn't have a career if Rhonda hadn't done what she did. Rhonda was the whole package: smart, funny, and a knockout. She was a pioneer."

Comic and designer. That's what I want on my tombstone. *Many years from now.*

ON THE WAY TO TODAY

Here's some wisdom I picked up on my way to becoming a comedy headliner, talk show staple, and future Phyllis Diller. Take my advice—please!

- ☐ If the road is blocked, take a detour.

- ☐ People will oppose you for all sorts of reasons. Most are about them, not you.

- ☐ Women can be as anti-woman as men. Don't trust someone just because she has two X chromosomes.

- ☐ Aspire to pay your dues instead of dodging the chance.

- ☐ Be patient about becoming proficient at anything. Becoming really good means repeating the same thing thousands of times. Practice, practice, practice.

- ☐ Develop a thick skin. You're going to encounter haters and you can't let them stop you.

- ☐ People who've been through the same things as you are your comrades in arms. Hold them close.

- ☐ Use your talents to give back whenever you can.

LESSON EIGHT
There Are Many
Ways to Be a Star

—— *In which our heroine orders the luna fish sandwich, gets her big break, bites Howard Stern, becomes an object of foot lust, gets inside information about the infamous O.J. Simpson trial, has way too much fun making bawdy, breakneck, boundary-pushing late-night comedy television, and becomes a star.* ——

*A*s the calendar flipped to the 1990s, I was that rarest of birds: a working actress but not a star. I'd had my moments, including one memorable line in *Spaceballs*. They were auditioning every comic in town for the film, and the casting director got me in to read for Mel Brooks, who cast even the smallest parts personally. I wanted to read for the part of the waitress at the Galaxy Grill, but Mel said, "No, just talk." So I did. I found out that Mel was looking for a blonde for the waitress; at the time I was—gasp!—my natural brunette. I told him that I could wear a wig, but he said, "No, just show up, go to wardrobe and we'll figure it out. I like you and I want you in the movie." He was incredibly sweet.

I showed up in my own strapless red rubber dress (it had to be cleaned with Armor All) and waited for Mel to tell me what

I was doing. He had me play the part of one of the Grill's customers and threw me my now-famous line as we were shooting: "I'll have the luna fish sandwich." Out of everything I've ever done, people shout that to me more than anything else, which tickles me to death.

At that point in my career, I was what someone described as "the best known unknown person in Hollywood." The paparazzi knew me as a starlet, and I would often end up in the tabloids, usually wearing one of my outlandish outfits. I knew how to get attention. I was an eclectic personality, and I loved working. There was no job too small, which probably hurt me a little, because stars don't take every job that comes along. I probably did a lot of stuff that other actors wouldn't have taken, but that's just who I was. I loved to work.

One big reason was that I wanted to keep my Screen Actors Guild, or SAG, card, so that I had health insurance. As long as I had health insurance, I was a working actor, and I had it from the day my mother and father dropped me off in Los Angeles to the day I left. There are approximately 160,000 members of the Screen Actors Guild and only about one percent are full-time working actors. I'm proud to have been among that number.

Shear Honesty: *If there's a professional association or union involved with your line of work, join it. That's a huge help, especially when you're just starting out. Professional associations can give you camaraderie, represent your interests, provide things like health coverage and legal services, and mark you as a real pro instead of a wannabe.*

Turning Point

Around 1990, I was at a crossroads in my career. I had done everything under the sun but still wasn't a star. I hadn't hit a big payday, and I couldn't command big roles just by walking in the room. I could have gone either way: gotten a big break and become a household name, or faded into the obscurity of regional commercials, game shows, and more talk shows.

Looking back at that time, I realized something: you don't know when you're at a turning point in your life when you're at it, only in retrospect. That's why it's so important to always bring your A-game to everything you do. You may have no idea when your big break is just around the corner, so do everything you can to increase the odds of that break breaking your way. One thing I did was have great representation.

As I've told you, through the years, I had a lot of different agents because I wanted them to work as hard for me as I did, and few met my standards. Even though I self-destructed a little when I walked off the set of *Cheers* after my father died, my agents always insisted that I was a lock to become a sitcom star. Still, by 1990 it hadn't happened, and I was beginning to wonder if it ever would. I was thirty-five years old, and while I was funnier and sexier than ever, Hollywood was and is all about new, exciting faces. I'd been around for a while; perhaps too long. But as it turned out, this was my turning point.

I was with Dick Clark Management, which had just launched. Larry Klein, whom I had met years before when Kenny Ellis and I barged into Dick Clark's office with our live doll act, was my manager, and he also managed Tim Conway Jr., who was producing *USA: Up All Night* (UAN) for the USA Network. They had an East

Coast version of the show, hosted by Gilbert Gottfried, that ran on Saturday nights. The West Coast version, which ran on Fridays, was hosted by Caroline Schlitt.

Caroline was very good on her version of the show. But in 1990 the producers decided they wanted a sexy, campy, over-the-top host. Cassandra Peterson had become a household name as Elvira, Mistress of the Dark, hostess of *Elvira's Movie Macabre*. In that show (which ran from 1981 to 1986), she would host second-rate horror movies, filling time before and after commercial breaks with witty banter, jokes, sketches, and other funny stuff. She was very good at it, and she made sexy work in her low-cut black gown and a smart, sarcastic Valley Girl accent. Elvira was a smash, and USA wanted its own Elvira.

Larry Klein managed Tim Conway Jr., so he couldn't put me up for the job because it would have been a conflict of interest. But he told me about it and put me in touch with the people from USA Network, and I set up an audition. I talked with Hilary Schacter, one of the New York producers, and he told me that he was looking forward to coming to LA to meet with me. He and I became friendly, and he appreciated my sense of humor. He said, "We have to hold an audition and the whole network has to make the decision. But I like the way you sound."

Not long after that, the USA people came out to LA and auditioned more than a hundred women. Now, here's where my ability to stay in touch with people moved the needle. USA's written description of the job (which all the women who were auditioning got) said that this was a host job. Ninety percent of the women came to the audition dressed like news reporters! Because I'd been talking to Hilary, I knew they were looking for comedic and sexy. That was a huge advantage for me.

Shear Honesty: *Do your research. I can't remember what many of my classes were about in college, but I learned how to research and how to find the answers. Life is research. No one taught me how to do what I did; I figured it out for myself by asking questions and doing the legwork.*

I showed up for my UAN audition wearing a dress cut nearly to my belly button in front and down to my butt crack in the back. I brought a blow dryer, turned it on during the audition, and pretended like I was blow-drying my hair. I did the sexy, funny, outrageous character that I felt they wanted. This was a pivotal moment. For years, people had been telling me I was too sexy to be funny. Joyce Selznick had even told me that my mouth was too sexy! This time I said, "Fuck it." I was going to go in character and go over the top. I had nothing to lose, and maybe I could finally show the world that I was funny.

FOURTH WALL BREAK!

I didn't tell anyone how I was planning to show up to that audition. After the meeting with Steve Feder and Hilary Schacter, they had a lot to mull over. I had been watching Carolyn, and I knew I could make the show mine. I had been doing standup in every gin joint in the country, so I knew I could improvise and be funny. Basically, there wasn't anything on camera that I couldn't handle. So I went for it, and after weeks of waiting, I got it. Sure, it wasn't the sitcom I'd been dreaming of, but I had landed a steady gig on national television, and that was more than most actors could ever dream of.

Afterwards, nothing. And more nothing. I died a little every day. I assumed the worst. I figured that, once again, I had made the wrong decision. It was torture. Then about a month and a half later, I got the call: I'd gotten the job. I hosted my first episode of UAN on January 4, 1991.

With that one decision, Hilary Schacter and the USA people changed my life. Hilary and I have become really close since then, and I'm grateful to him because he saw something in me that no one else did—not just the sex appeal but the comedy, sharpness, and smarts. Getting UAN changed everything for me: my pay scale, my industry clout, my appearance schedule, my confidence level... *everything*. I wasn't getting network money, but I had a regular national show and a great regular paycheck. This was my big break.

> **Shear Honesty:** *When you're facing a challenge, gather all the information you can, ask people you trust for advice—and then trust yourself. That's all you can do. I can't count how many times I second-guessed a decision and then regretted it, and we've all done that. The choice I made in my Up All Night audition was the right one, even if that didn't become clear for a while. Sure, you want to make smart choices based on good information, reading the room, and so on. But once you're ready, trust your gut. You know better than anyone else what you need to succeed.*

Uncharted Territory

USA: *Up All Night* was early basic cable. That meant it was the Wild West, uncharted territory where (almost) anything was on the table. Kay Koplovitz, a mega-force in the television business and a true inspiration, grew the network on her own from something called Madison Square Network. It was one of the first cable networks, and when I signed on it was the biggest basic channel, with about 90 million subscribers. It was big and powerful, which meant only good things for me.

Movie showcase shows have been around for decades. There was Elvira. There was *Fright Night* with Larry Vincent (yes, the movie was based on that show). There was Vampira, who created the genre, the brilliant *Mystery Science Theater 3000*, Joe Bob Briggs' *Drive-In Theater*, *Dinner and a Movie*, and me and Gilbert Gottfried. The content was usually a blend of broad, campy sketches and man-on-the-street interviews.

UAN started at 10:00 p.m. on the West Coast and went until 2:00 a.m. We were also a cash cow for the network. Because of this, we flew under the radar a lot of the time. The B-movie genre, horror genre, and scream queen genre all had rabid fan bases, and the fans ate, drank, and bought the things that USA advertised on late-night TV, including adult services delivered by 900 number. Despite what many fans believed, the shows were not live, because it was a bitch to find interesting locations with late-night hours and events that were still going at 1:00 a.m. That's why we did so many shows in the studio. But we still had that live-TV, anything-could-happen vibe. Because we ran late at night, network executives weren't always paying close attention. Because of that—and because we were insanely profitable—we got away with a lot. It was the most fun I've ever had on TV.

I even got involved in the advertising. I helped make Snapple one of our biggest advertisers and did Snapple ads on the show. It was basic, raw television at its finest. We would even make fun of our own network, and not once did anyone come to the producers and say, "We have to reshoot this because you said this or that." We had near-total freedom, and the same was true for the movies we showed—three per night. Name a cheesy, B-grade, low-budget flick and I hosted it. Fun fact: the first film I hosted was *Basic Training*, which I had starred in years before. A few other favorites:

- *Attack of the Killer Tomatoes*
- *Jekyll & Hyde Together Again*
- *The Toxic Avenger*
- *Assault of the Party Nerds*
- *Earth Minus Zero*
- *The Legend of the Roller Blade Seven*
- *976-EVIL*
- *Cheerleaders' Wild Weekend*
- *DC Cab*
- *Class of Nuke 'Em High*
- *Lust in the Dust*
- *Once Bitten*
- *Porky's*
- *A Polish Vampire in Burbank*
- *Reform School Girls*

Not exactly a master class in filmmaking, but God, were they fun! The audience absolutely ate them up. We did show some pretty good movies, too, including John Hughes' *Sixteen Candles*, which gave us a shred of legitimate movie street cred. I also hosted a few horror films that were pretty good, including the original *Halloween* and *Creepshow*. Even Bill Maher was a guest on the show, because he had starred in a B-pic that I'll bet he wishes would be forgotten, 1989's *Cannibal Women in the Avocado Jungle of Death*. Netflix it and write him, please. He'll love it.

I think the lesson for me was that what matters is what people care about, what they love. Audiences don't necessarily fall in love with art, and just because something is silly and campy doesn't mean it's not good. It's easy to look down your nose at B-movies, Stephen King novels, or simple food like red beans and rice, but that's a mistake, because they'll be around long after today's *haute cuisine* and *cinema verité* are forgotten. Don't be a snob. Find what speaks to people—what gives them joy and pure pleasure—and then give them more, and you'll always be successful.

> **Shear Honesty:** *A lot of women hide their light because they self-censor. "I couldn't do that" is something I hear a lot. Yes, you could. You're assuming that someone won't let you, that you need permission. But here's the thing: if you're waiting for permission to break the rules and do something daring, you're going to be waiting all your life. Just do it. Nobody's watching (unless you're in a business like high finance, where everybody's watching), so figure out how you can do something different that thrills you and just make it happen. I've done that since I was twenty-two and it's made for an amazing life.*

As *USA: Up All Night* became better known and I became more famous, a young segment producer reached out to me. His name was Barry Poznick, and he thought outside the box. He was producing segments for talk shows that would be the forerunners of reality television, which he also went on to produce. Barry liked wild guests and was working with Joan Rivers and a myriad of other popular talk shows hosts. The more outlandish the guest, the better, and Barry found them. He liked sexy girls with an edge, the ones who would do anything to promote themselves. Enter Rhonda. He booked and rebooked the Barbi Twins, a set of Playboy favorites, twins who were so perfectly gorgeous that we were all convinced they were from another planet. He loved Anna Nicole

Smith. You get the picture. We became friends, and when he had a segment open on one of his many shows, he always thought of me. I even filled in for Vicki Lawrence when she was away having a salary dispute with CBS.

Barry and I became an odd couple, friends and kindred spirits. We got to know each other's Jewish parents and saw each other through the deaths of two of them. He was becoming more powerful in Hollywood, and I was becoming even better known from all my zany talk show appearances. I appeared as everything from a dating love expert to a bra expert (there's a bit of foreshadowing for you!). He booked a few of us consistently: Charo, Judy Tenuta, the Landers sisters, and me. The bigger the boobs and the personality, and, of course, the lower the necklines, the higher ratings soared.

I was constantly traveling between New York, Chicago, and Los Angeles, where these programs were all taped. I had no fear of any situation at this point. Barry and I even started collaborating on show ideas and pitching them to networks. One was called Bedtime with Rhonda. It was a play on USA: *Up All Night*, but instead of hosting movies, I would head up a wild talk show. It wasn't meant to be, but Barry went on to become one of the biggest moguls in reality TV arena and game shows, including *Are You Smarter than a Fifth Grader?* He's still who I call when I have an idea for a show, and I will bother him forevermore about the show that we still haven't done together.

(Update: just before I completed this book, Barry became head of unscripted programming for MGM Television Group. My fingers are crossed that my old friend's position will give me a chance to finally get that TV show I've always wanted. Stay tuned.)

The Bimbo's Revenge

What made UAN beloved more than anything else was my sexy, dumb-like-a-fox blonde Rhonda persona and my signature "UP...All Night!" delivery. Remember the TV ad I did for Shape Spa in New Orleans, with the tagline, "It's great to be in shape!"? I knew a good tagline could go a long way, and I wanted to have one for the show. My signature tagline and high-pitched delivery came to me when I was sitting in my kitchen with Tommy Lynch, who became the producer when Tim Conway Jr. left.

To emphasize that this was a character I was playing, we kept the references to me in third person, so it was always "Rhonda is happy to be with you." Rhonda also had a lot of naughty nicknames: "Your Bedtime Buddy," "Your Late-Night Lamb Chop," "Your Midnight Morsel," and so on. These were the parts of the show that stuck with viewers.

My breathy "UP"—and the fact that I did most of the show's interstitial (between movie segments) sketches in lingerie, changing into sexy new outfits throughout the films—kept my wonderful audience awake and watching. I changed costumes more often than Madonna, sometimes wearing three or four outrageous, revealing outfits in a single episode. That was the start of my earliest lingerie design ideas, and it was also when I started realizing how empowering intimate wear could be.

Here's what I mean: I had a production assistant named Stacy Hope Herman, who eventually worked her way up to great things in the industry. However, as the only girl on an all-male production crew, she wore flannel shirts and oversized pants, trying not to attract too much attention from the guys on the set. One day she brought me into the ladies' room and unbuttoned her baggy shirt:

under all those layers, she was wearing a push-up bra and garters! Sexy lingerie was her secret power, she told me. Just knowing she had something sexy on made her feel more confident, no matter what she wore on the outside. I was blown away!

Shear Honesty: *That moment planted a seed that would one day have me designing intimate wear of my own. I want all women to have that secret power, that confidence, even if it's just for themselves. Of course, I also worked with some wonderful designers who would let me use wardrobe pieces or buy outfits and lingerie at cost. I started to learn more about the design and manufacturing of apparel, all while sitting in my intimates, with my bubbly character and big hair. That was my start as a businesswoman, though I didn't know it.*

O.J., Kato, and Me

My character might have seemed ditzy, but if you listened closely, I was snarky, self-deprecating, and wittily observational. Playing a bimbo takes intelligence; Marilyn proved that. We also did a lot of topical humor in our sketches and bits, poking fun at the issues of the day. For instance, in 1994, we made fun of the O.J. Simpson trial, the most watched television of the 1990s.

Of course, there was nothing to laugh about in a tragic story of a fallen football hero and his wife and a waiter from a local restaurant being brutally murdered. No one could believe that an American hero like O.J. could have committed such a horrific crime—a gory scenario that played out like the horror films I showed on Friday nights. We were all glued to the trial of the century, one of the first to be televised gavel-to-gavel.

LEFT: *Kenny Ellis and me performing our mechanical doll routine at the famous Masquers Club in Hollywood. We were unstoppable twenty-somethings.*

RIGHT: *Taping an episode for UAN during Mardi Gras, circa 1993.*

LEFT: *Taken by Harry Langdon, my agents used this headshot to send out to casting directors and producers.*

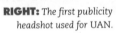

RIGHT: *The first publicity headshot used for UAN.*

RHONDA SHEAR
SAG/AFTRA

RIGHT: UAN always started and ended in the Rhonda bedroom. Guests would enter the Rhonda world, and anything could happen. This was a very typical look, circa 1994. Just look at that phone!

RIGHT: Hilary Schacter and me on the set of UAN. Hilary was an executive at USA when he and Steve Feder hired me to be the new host with Gilbert Gottfried. He later ended up moving to Los Angeles and produced the show for several years. We share some amazing memories and remain friends.

ABOVE: *Behind the scenes of a taping of UAN. Sometimes we were totally on location and sometimes complete shows were done in Hollywood on a sound stage.*

LEFT: *With Kato Kaelin on USA Network's B-Movie Awards. Gilbert Gottfried and I hosted, and Kato was a presenter. He starred in several of the B-films we presented.*

ABOVE: On the set of UAN with the famous Barbi twins, Shane and Sia. They appeared in Playboy many times.

LEFT: Toxie the Avenger scaling a building in New York City to scare me. Toxie, a Lloyd Kaufman film creation, was a regular on UAN and beloved by our fans. Pure camp!

ABOVE: *Caesars Palace welcoming me to the taping of a UAN special. As a standup comic, seeing my name on iconic billboards in Vegas was a dream come true.*

ABOVE: *Headlining the Improv Comedy Club in Las Vegas.*

BELOW: At a Golden Apple autograph signing with some of the most famous scream queens: Brinke Stevens, Linnea Quigley, Julie Strain, Monique Gabrielle, Michelle Bauer, and Joyce Mendel. They made regular appearances on UAN, and we aired many of their movies.

ABOVE: Performing standup at Caroline's Comedy Club in New York for the television show Caroline's Comedy Hour.

ABOVE: A stamp made for the Democratic Republic of the Congo, circa 2001.

ABOVE: *Publicity shot with Bob Hope for* The Starmakers. *Bob personally selected me during an open call with thousands of girls and began my career in Hollywood.*

LEFT: Bob Hope and me during the taping of our sketch for The Starmakers.

RIGHT: Working with George Burns on the set of Hour Magazine. I demonstrated the exercises George said would help people live to be 100 years old.

RIGHT: *Getting a kiss from Sammy Davis Jr. at the LA Press Club. We were at the roast of Muhammad Ali, and I sat on the dais with him and Howard Cosell, the famed sports journalist. I had the honor of presenting awards to all the attendees and Muhammad Ali.*

BELOW: *I shared an enviable kiss with Henry Winkler, the Fonz, on the Vaudeville episode of Happy Days with Donny Most looking on.*

RIGHT: *On the set of* Cheers *with Ted Danson. We had great chemistry.*

LEFT: *Wishing Hef a Happy New Year with a hug and a kiss at the Playboy Mansion. He was flanked by early blonde girlfriends.*

RIGHT: *On the set of* Wrestlemania X *with Burt Reynolds and Jennie Garth, famous for her role in* Beverly Hills, 90210.

ABOVE: *My favorite scene with Henry Winkler on Happy Days. I played a model, and he strutted his stuff for me.*

ABOVE: *With Gilbert Gottfried. He hosted UAN on Saturday nights, and I hosted on Friday nights. We worked together many times, and we're still friends today.*

LEFT: *On the set of Dukes of Hazzard with the Dukes. I originally had shorts and a tank top on, but Daisy Duke told the producers I looked too sexy. They took me back to wardrobe and dressed me down...way down with glasses. I played a used car salesperson.*

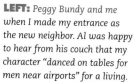

LEFT: *Peggy Bundy and me when I made my entrance as the new neighbor. Al was happy to hear from his couch that my character "danced on tables for men near airports" for a living.*

RIGHT: *Richard Simmons and me at the doll show at Javits Center in New York. We knew each other for years before, and he's also a New Orleanian.*

ABOVE: *With wild and crazy guy Steve Martin, "Weird Al" Yankovic, Judy Tenuta, and John Cleese at the American Comedy Awards.*

BELOW: *Chef Emeril Lagasse made his first TV appearance on UAN before his own show took off.*

BELOW: *Posing with Alan Thicke, after appearing on his game show Pictionary.*

RIGHT: Posing with Pamela Anderson before a celebrity baseball game at Dodger Stadium. We received a lot of attention that day.

BELOW: I had the honor of being roasted at the iconic New York Friars Club. Usually just men were allowed, but this was for a special taping of UAN. Some of the greats are in this photo: Harold Rand, Louise DuArt, Soupy Sales, Pat Cooper, Dick Capri, Jackie "The Joke Man" Martling, Bobby Kelton, and Scott Blakeman.

LEFT: *With my childhood idol, Barbara Eden from I Dream of Jeannie. Barbara was as beautiful on the outside as the inside, and I loved parodying her on UAN.*

RIGHT: *George Hamilton and me on set together. George played my love interest in a pilot, which was produced by Jeff Franklin of* Full House *and* Fuller House *fame.*

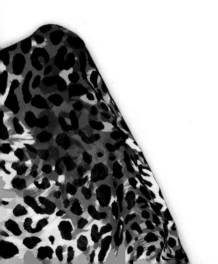

Why did we cover O.J. so much? Because I knew people who testified; Hollywood is a very small town. Also, the trial was all people were talking about. Everyone dashed home after work to watch Judge Lance Ito run his courtroom, and every network was talking about the case constantly. *UAN* was supposed to seem live and in real time, so we had to talk about the trial. This made for some memorable segments. One entire episode featured me in a white Ford Bronco, but instead of masks and mustaches, I was putting on makeup, Rhonda style.

We did nine months of shows devoted to the trial, so I feel qualified to give you my personal insight into what went on in 1994 and 1995. Brian "Kato" Kaelin was a longtime friend, a budding comedy actor with a career ready to explode. He was living in O.J.'s guest house, helping with the kids, running errands, whatever O.J. and Nicole needed help with, in exchange for a place to stay. The children even named the dog after him. He was also auditioning and saving money. Kato is a good, smart guy, but the press made him a joke because his testimony has been weak and contradictory.

I couldn't get away from the trial. My personal physician, Dr. Robert Huizenga ("Dr. H" on *The Biggest Loser*) ended up testifying. His partner treated O.J. in their Beverly Hills office, and Rob testified regarding O.J.'s general health and his arthritis. His nurse told me later that she had been at O.J.'s house collecting pubic hairs for court-ordered DNA testing (ewww!) when O.J. bolted out the back door and took off in the infamous white Bronco. Creepy. My dear friend Carol Connors, who co-wrote the Oscar-nominated theme from *Rocky* and is a Beverly Hills icon, also testified as a character witness.

I wanted Kato on *UAN* because he was funny, and I knew our ratings would soar. He was an old friend, so he agreed...after the network coughed up the $5,000 fee that his attorney insisted on. We showed a B-movie he'd been in a few years earlier, did our funny banter thing, and had a really good time. Ratings were through the roof. Mission accomplished.

We also leaked Kato's appearance to the press, and when we finished and opened the back door to leave, a barrage of photographers' flashes blinded us. Instant media circus. We granted one interview, to *Entertainment Tonight*. Of course, they asked Kato if he thought O.J. was guilty, and I thought he was going to faint. I saw his skin flush and break into goose bumps, but he kept his cool, stayed funny, and diverted the interviewer's attention. Still, I knew what he was thinking.

Years later, Kato said that he thought O.J. had killed Nicole and Ron Goldman, but at the time he was afraid for his own life, and I don't blame him. Who wouldn't be? O.J. was terrifying. After the trial, his career foundered, and he did mostly some reality TV and game shows. It was a shame. Fortunately, that was another relationship that I refused to let die, and things came full circle once again when Kato briefly partnered with my company on a clothing line.

That was a pattern that I repeated again and again in my career, before and after *UAN*: helping my friends. Entertainment is a tough racket, but so is business, law, or real estate. The point is, if you're not the person who needs the helping hand today, the time will come when you will be. Lend a hand if you're fortunate enough to be in a position to do so. I did whenever I could, and it's paid off in relationships that have lasted forty years in some cases...and still going.

FOURTH WALL BREAK!

I totally related to Kato. He did what it took to get in front of the camera. He could've gotten back into standup and gotten back the respect he had lost by being seen as the dumb blonde houseboy, but he didn't. For him, it was like the O.J. trial never ended. He never got out of that spotlight. I like Kato; he's smart and talented, but I feel like he bought into the lie that there's no such thing as bad publicity. There is. He still has his boyish good looks, and I think he would make the best game show host on the planet. But he needs to reinvent himself, and he's in the perfect business to do it. Best of all, he's still famous, so he could have a great career if he chose to. I hope his time comes soon.

Becoming an Icon

On UAN, we didn't just cover current events. We hosted all the major "scream queens" and promoted their projects. I did a show with Linnea Quigley, who starred in the immortal *Sorority Babes Slimeball Bowl-a-rama*. In 1992, I had Jason from the *Friday the 13th* movies on—hockey mask, machete, and all—and we did a fun bit where he tried to behead me while I, oblivious, read fan mail. I also got to do some terrific interviews. One of the first people was Stevie Nicks of Fleetwood Mac, and it turned out that *she* was a fan of *mine*. She did a wonderful impression of me, which was really cool.

In 1991, the show was sexy. In 1992, it got sexier. We changed producers every year, and every new producer had a different idea of what was right for the show. So every year I had to reinvent myself. I became "Your Bedtime Buddy." Shows usually opened with me lying on a bed in skimpy lingerie reading fan mail. After that, we would take our crew—and our celebrity guest, if we had one—out on the town in late-night Los Angeles. Most episodes would wrap up back on the set with the celebrity guest in bed with me.

Everything became about broad, slapsticky, wink-nudge sex appeal. I did an episode called "New York's Finest Bad Girls." I shared the sheets with Max Von Sydow, John McEnroe, Robert Altman, Lou Rawls, Sir Richard Branson, Liza Minnelli, Stephen Sondheim, Seth Rudetsky, Robin Leach, Alan Alda, Bill Maher (whom I dated), Don Johnson, Charlie Sheen, Sir Anthony Hopkins, Morgan Freeman, Helen Hunt, Demi Moore, "Weird Al" Yankovic, and even Bruce and Kris Jenner (when they were newlyweds, before Caitlyn was even a twinkle in Bruce's eye), and many more.

With all that exposure, I became a sexual icon and object of desire for an entire generation of adolescent boys. I'm sure I got many a young man through puberty. I'm proud of that. Even though we were told our ratings were split fifty-fifty between men and women, more men than women remember my name today.

It was fun, but it was also a shit-ton of hard work. We taped 450 shows. To put that in perspective, at the time, most sitcoms taped twenty-two episodes a season. So in eight years on UAN, I did the equivalent of twenty sitcom years. I did Top Ten countdowns as a parody of David Letterman. I interviewed hundreds of stars, from Barbara Walters to a young Paul Rudd. I look back at some of the shows on YouTube and it still blows me away that we were as good and funny as we were, working as fast as we did. It was hair-on-fire television, but it worked!

When we weren't on location, the set was jumping; we worked fifty weeks a year. This wasn't some cushy, thirteen-week sitcom schedule where you got months off at a time. Plus, it wasn't like I had to fill just one or two minutes. The network cut a lot of bad language and nudity from our movies for basic cable, so they were shorter. With films that had a lot of swearing and sex scenes, we might have to fill forty-five minutes to get to our four-hour run time. That meant doing long sketches, celebrity interviews, you name it. I put the "work" in working actress, hostess, and comedian.

Shear Honesty: *Don't sit around, sulking into a glass of wine, wondering when you're going to "make it." That's a mistake. You may have already made it and not realize it. So many of us think that one day, we'll "get there," but "there" isn't a place, an income, or a title. It's what gives your time meaning and lets you live a life that makes you happy. "Making it" for me had meant having my own sitcom, but in my second season on UAN, I realized that I had made it. I had my own show, was nationally known, had creative control, and was getting a decent paycheck. That it didn't look exactly like the image of making it I'd carried in my mind didn't diminish it. I'm glad I stopped long enough to figure that out so I could appreciate it. I hope you'll do the same.*

Anything Goes

But the freewheeling nature of the show gave me a lot of freedom, too. I wrote a lot of the shows myself. I learned all about what went on behind the cameras. I worked with amazing producers and directors, and many of the young people who worked on the show who started as young writers and production assistants went on to their own fame and glory. I love helping young people. I guess instead of producing my own offspring, I was meant to help others. It doesn't matter if it comes back to me; I love sharing what I've learned.

What else did we do over the years? God, what *didn't* we do? A sampling:

- We had the LA Rams cheerleaders as guests.

- We had porn icon Marilyn Chambers.

- We had every '80s scream queen you can think of: Sybil Danning, Michele Bauer, Brinke Stevens, Monique Gabrielle, and more.

- We hired a guy named Steve Schirripa, one of my favorites. He started as a doorman at the Improv at the Riviera Hotel in Las Vegas and went on to manage the Improv. My producers loved him and cast him as the quintessential greedy Vegas maître d'. We would bring him on in his tux to teach viewers things like how to wash a wig or make a sandwich. He had the perfect New York wise guy accent and was hysterical. Steve would go on to star as Bobby Baccalieri on *The Sopranos*.

- We gave Chef Emeril Lagasse his first airtime experience. We were friends from New Orleans, and he came on to teach "Rhonda" how to cook a Thanksgiving meal for a family of twelve. The family was a bunch of New York character actors, fighting and feuding while waiting for the dinner that I did not know how to cook. I kept spraying the scent of a cooking turkey into the air while Emeril prepared the meal. The cast and crew got to eat amazing food, and Emeril was a natural in his first TV gig.

- We covered Broadway premieres and movie red carpet events. I gained a lot of interviewing savvy from those shows, because I usually just threw myself at a star without knowing who he or she was. I interviewed a young Eazy-E, right after he won his first award—literally, straight out of Compton. We also caught some future superstars early in their careers, including Eddie Murphy and Robert Downey Jr.

- I put every standup comic I knew on the show. I loved giving all my friends screen time and showing video of their work. No actor objects to that.

USA Network was also associated with the World Wrestling Federation (WWF), so yep—I did wrestling. I became the darling of the WWF and was even in *Wrestlemania X: Ten Years in the Making*. I was the official timekeeper and did some sketches with my old friend Burt Reynolds. Donnie Wahlberg was the guest ring announcer and the show featured Vince McMahan and Jennie Garth. We covered Stone Cold Steve Austin, Lex Luger, Brett and Owen Hart, and Macho Man Randy Savage. We started a rumor that I was having a hot affair with wrestler Shawn Michaels and had a blast shooting the pictorial, which portrayed Shawn as being more vain than I was. Fun times!

Then there was working with Gilbert Gottfried. Everyone asks what that was like. Well, it was fantastic. Gilbert is a brilliant comic; his brain is amazing. But my God, is he dirty! I did his podcast, *Gilbert Gottfried's Amazing Colossal Podcast*, a couple of years ago and it was the filthiest thing I've ever done. I named some of the old comics who'd hit on me through the years, and Gil's indescribably dirty impressions of the likes of Red Buttons and Jackie Mason coming on to me had me in hysterics. That particular podcast was *quite* highly rated. We never could have gotten away with that sort of thing on *UAN!*

We also shot in New Orleans with my whole family—my sister Nona, my niece Brigitte, my brother Mel, my sister-in-law Briann, and my dear mom, Jennie. That was very special. Because I was known for my big hair, we gave my whole family big-haired wigs and shot at my childhood home. After that, we ventured out into the French Quarter and, of course, there was a parade going on, with floats. Talk about perfect!

In New Orleans, they have jazz funerals with bands and parties. When my time comes, I want a big-ass jazz funeral with a float and a parade! If I have to go out, I want to go out big and in style. As Mae West said (and I agree), "Too much of a good thing can be wonderful."

Shear Honesty: *Learn everything about what goes on in the business you want to be in. I didn't limit myself to acting and comedy; I wanted to know how to light a scene, why the cameras were placed in a certain location, how sound was recorded—everything. Do the same in whatever field you aspire to succeed in, because you never know what will help you. For example, as I built my company, I made a conscious effort to learn more about the international apparel business, from how clothing is made to the markets where raw materials are sold. What I learned ended up saving and making us money; we probably wouldn't be a $100 million company today without it. So learn. There's no useless knowledge. Someday, knowing how things get done behind the scenes could be the difference between getting the job and losing it.*

Me v. Howard Stern

UAN's popularity led to endless personal appearances, comedy headliner slots, co-hosting on radio and television shows, even business shows like Bloomberg and a lot of Fox News shows. But one of the most memorable bookings was on the *Howard Stern Show*. I did the show a couple of times as a guest because of the popularity and sex appeal of UAN and because *Playboy* had named me one of the sexiest stars of 1993. But my time with Howard Stern got really interesting because we ended up being talk show rivals.

I had landed a co-hosting gig on a Lifetime show called *Live from Queens*. The star was a gal named Sissy Biggers, a Martha Stewart type and former executive at NBC. She was my opposite but we had great chemistry; my sass and sand contrasted with her conservative character. I figured UAN was probably going to be ending for me in a couple of years, and I had fallen in love with the idea of working in a talk show format. So now I was flying back and forth between LA and New York to do both shows. I loved it. The show was dropped after a short run, but that's not the story.

In 1994, E! network's *Howard Stern Show* and *Live from Queens* were up against each other for a Cable Ace Award. So my producer and I decided to crash Howard's studio to get what we were sure would be an obnoxious, chauvinistic take on competing for an award against a Lifetime woman's talk show. It was a cold, snowy day in New York, and we got our cameras out and went for it. I dressed provocatively and slipped into my "Rhonda" character so I could get inside Howard's studio—and it worked.

It was great TV. Howard's cameras were on Sissy and me while we called from outside the building. Gary Dell'Abate, also known as "Baba Booey," put Howard on the speaker and I cooed, "Don't you want to meet Sissy Biggers? Her show is up against yours for an award." I knew that, eventually, he would let us in. His ego was too big, and the television was too good to pass up. Finally, he let us in, and Sissy presented him with a cake in keeping with her Martha Stewart persona. I figured we would last maybe two minutes. Sissy wasn't Howard's type. But I had to keep us in there—for Howard's show, but more importantly for our show. We needed to fill airtime.

FOURTH WALL BREAK!

The first time I went on Howard Stern's show, I went on as Rhonda from USA: Up All Night, and he was sarcastic but cool. He kept telling me how pretty I was, which I didn't hate. The next time, with Sissy, was more demeaning. But we went for it because we knew that if I was outrageous enough, we would get loads of fantastic TV coverage from E! It was loads of fun, even though I was wearing a skimpy outfit out in the snow.

As for what Howard is like, he's mostly like what you see on TV and when the mic is on. Howard is Howard; he's a huge star and he can be who he wants to be. There's not a big difference between Howard on air and Howard off the air, though he was always nice and professional to me. He's brilliant, and he's still doing his show all these years later, so he's obviously doing something right.

That's when I saw his tickle/bondage chair and dared him to put me in it. Howard's eyes lit up; into the chair I went. He tried his best to get me to laugh, taunting and teasing me the whole time. But I was still frozen from standing in the snow and I couldn't feel a thing! He was getting aggravated, and his long hair was hanging down in front of my face. All of a sudden, on impulse, I grabbed a strand of his hair in my teeth and yanked. Out it came by the roots! Howard screamed a few expletives and jumped back, and we were escorted out of the building with his camera and our camera following. It was great TV!

We edited the clip and it aired later that day: Howard Stern on *Live from Queens*. It was an instant classic, and E! and Lifetime showed it over and over again. You can't get away with that sort of ambush television anymore, but it was great fun and I was glad I'd had the chutzpah to instigate it.

Another episode that meant the world to me came when I was mock roasted at the New York Friars Club. If you're not familiar with the roast, it involves a bunch of comics honoring someone by getting them in a room with their drunken friends and then telling the filthiest jokes and stories imaginable. The Friars Club was a comedian's holy land, and I was roasted by some comedy legends: Soupy Sales, Freddie Roman (the original roastmaster), Jeffrey Ross (today's roastmaster), Louise Duart, Pat Cooper, Jackie "The Joke Man" Martling from the *Howard Stern Show*, Stewie Stone, Dick Capri, and the great Henny Youngman himself. It was Mr. Youngman's last appearance, and I got a picture and autograph. Pinch me!

I could go on for an entire book about everything we did. But I'll sum it up with this: few rules, great people, and fun, fun, fun. What more could you want from a job?

FOURTH WALL BREAK!

Howard Stern wasn't the most powerful, interesting person I met while doing my show. I also met three presidents. One day while filming in New York, my crew was walking through the lobby of The Plaza Hotel on Fifth Avenue. Walking in front of us was Donald Trump. He was a formidable presence, bigger than life, and walking with a couple of peers. This was his hotel and he fit right in. My Up All Night layout in Playboy had just come out, and I stopped him and said, "Hey Donald, just wanted to introduce myself. I love your hotel." Before I could get my name out, he replied, "I know who you are, Rhonda. I know your show and your layout is fabulous." Whatever anyone thinks of Donald Trump, he is smart. He was complimentary, not flirty, and very sweet.

I also met Gerald Ford when I was Queen of the Food Festival at the Washington Mardi Gras Ball. I also had the honor of meeting George H.W. Bush at a Washington event. There is something special about meeting the most powerful person in the free world.

Fans, Feet, and Fetishes

I did all of this for the fans, who were devoted...some more than others. For instance, we found out that people have a lot of sexual fetishes: pie-in-the-face fetishes, long-glove fetishes, foot-and-hosiery fetishes, you name it. Well, I had a lot of fans with foot fetishes. In production, we would pan the camera over my whole body and end at my feet, and before long I started getting letters from guys saying how much they loved my feet, shoes, ankles, and stockings. Men wrote letters asking me to dangle my shoes off my feet on camera, which I happily did. Who was I to deny a guy something that got him off?

My foot-fetish fans were my most devoted and best gift givers. They sent shoes, toe rings, and anklets, confessing that they wanted to suck my toes. So what the hell, we started playing to the foot fetish crowd! USA Network never had a clue. I started squishing food with my feet on camera, including an episode in November where I stomped all over a Thanksgiving dinner while the cameraman zoomed in for a close up. If you listened intently that night, you could probably hear foot fetishists having orgasms from coast to coast.

Foot-fetish magazines even approached me and asked me to shoot layouts. It was all harmless. The foot fetishists were very sweet and devoted, and sent shoes, teddy bears, and candy. Eventually, *Leg Show Magazine* asked me to do a foot layout. How could I resist? I went back to Harry Langdon and we did some racy photos—not nude, but boudoir-esque. I had done *Playboy* and was feeling great about myself at thirty-eight. My fans loved the layout, and I didn't mind the nice payday. The lesson: whether you are selling or putting on a show, always know your audience and acknowledge them, and they will love you for it!

FOURTH WALL BREAK!

Oh my God, the foot fetish thing was so bizarre, but also very sweet. I think of it as my own version of David Letterman's Top Ten Lists or Stupid Pet Tricks. Yes, it was pandering, but it was also silly, over-the-top physical comedy. I think everyone wants to smash grapes and make wine like Lucille Ball did in I Love Lucy. Thanksgiving dinner already looks mushy, so we made it mushier. We did a pie in the face on one episode, and Hilary Schacter couldn't wait to hit me in the face with a pie. That night, we actually had a crew pie fight off camera! How fun is that?

After that, I found out that there's a fetish for just about anything you can imagine...and probably some things you'd rather not imagine. I still have foot-fetish fans to this day; not a week goes by that I don't get an email from someone asking me to wiggle my toes. So you can age, but your feet stay young forever! It's harmless.

As my popularity grew, the number of letters from (mostly male) fans started growing so fast that I couldn't keep up with them. I wanted to answer all my fan mail, so I started a fan club, which my mother and sister ran for me. Fans paid a membership fee to get a newsletter, photo, and one of my "Go For the Gold" posters from 1984. I told my sister to keep all the money; if she could make a little profit, great. Well, there were so many fans that she was eventually able to buy a house with the money!

Most of the mail was innocent, sweet, and kind. I got a few marriage proposals. I got letters from men telling me that their wives or girlfriends (who, based on the pictures they sent, looked nothing like me) loved to dress like me. I got letters from guys thanking me for improving their love lives. I got shoes from my foot fans. I got a cashmere coat, a diamond ankle bracelet, and hundreds of teddy bears.

Other mail was decidedly weird. One day, in an envelope that my mom had the misfortune to open, we found pubic hair (yuck!). One fan sent me a brand new nine-millimeter pistol with the holster and ammunition, probably worth $1,000. I had a friend who works for the FBI check it out just so we could be sure the fan hadn't murdered someone with it. But it was clean, and in the letter that came with it, the fan said that he wanted me to be able to "protect myself from scary fans." Van has it today.

Another fan sent me a clit clip. Yes, you read that right. It was eighteen-carat gold and handmade, and looked kind of like a bobby pin with two chains on each side and a small gold ball hanging off of each chain. Apparently, when you clip this on your clitoris (which I had never spent much time with until I got this gift), the balls gently massage it as you walk. Well, I had to try that, and I can happily report that it was quite erotic. That's not the sort of thing you announce you're wearing, and only once did I wear it with a man: my husband. But it's kind of sexy knowing you are wearing something a little naughty like that.

(Years later, I was moving and my niece Brigitte and her friend Peter Crabbe (a standup comic and writer) were helping me pack my bedroom. Everything was packed until Peter noticed this shiny thing on the mattress, grabbed it, and exclaimed, "We have everything, except your one earring!" I fell over laughing and shouted, "That's not an earring!" That clit clip went flying across the room. We laugh about it on Facebook to this day.)

A really sweet fan moment came after a comedy show. I would sign autographs, and fans would wait patiently in line—often with *Playboys*—for me to sign. One night, a big, burly guy was confessing his devoted affection for me and my show. He had waited patiently and was the last person in line. He pulled up a chair next to me, leaned in, and said, "Do you mind signing this?" He was about six-foot-three, built like a football player, with a hairy chest. But when he opened his plaid flannel shirt, I saw a silky pink teddy. He quickly let me know he was not gay, but he enjoyed wearing women's intimate apparel under his clothes. It was adorable, and I signed his teddy, thankful for such an interesting career.

This period might be the best example of me following my fundamental philosophy, which is that the situation is what it is; you either control it or it controls you. Fans of UAN were going to turn me into a sex symbol; it was inevitable. I could choose to be offended by it (silly, since I had deliberately designed my Rhonda character that way) or I could play to it, have fun with it, and find ways that it would benefit my career and my life. If you throw the bait out there, it's dishonest to get upset when a fish grabs it. Put on your big girl panties and reel it in.

The End

In 1995, *UAN* moved to New York and everything changed. The producers gave me an ultimatum: either I would travel to New York to tape or they would replace me. So off I went. Then they figured out that it was cheaper to fly me out from LA and get four or five shows in the can than to relocate me. I got to keep living in Los Angeles, which made me happy.

However, I wasn't happy about having to work with Gilbert Gottfried's producer, Marty Byk. He started making me more like Gilbert and taking away the sex appeal. I would go out on the streets of New York wearing a clown suit or dressed as an ice cream cone or a car window washer. That was far from my character, but those were some of the smartest episodes we ever shot. Marty knew what he was doing.

The following year, I started working with producer/director Vida Pelletier, and she challenged me to do things I had always wanted to do. That meant one thing: my takes on the classic sitcom characters of the '50s and '60s. I impersonated Lucy from *I Love Lucy*, Alice from *The Honeymooners*, Jeannie from *I Dream of Jeannie*, Samantha from *Bewitched*, Mary Tyler Moore, Cher (with Bobby Kelton playing Sonny), Ginger from *Gilligan's Island*, and more. I easily morphed into most of them—Alice, Lucy, and Cher especially. I hadn't known that I had a talent for impressions, but I did. What fun it was!

Shear Honesty: *It's important to find a balance between standing firm and rolling with the motion of the ocean. You're not the only one with great ideas, and while you should fight for what you believe to be good, you should also be willing to accept when it's time to adapt because an idea's not panning out or somebody* *has a better one. My New York producers' ideas sent me in a new direction, but they were right. Some lingerie ideas that I've loved turned out to be terrible products, and I had to be willing to let them go. Sometimes, the mark of a successful, self-assured woman is the ability to admit a mistake without judgment. Let it go and get back in the saddle!*

UAN kept rolling along for two more years. For USA Network, we were the little cash machine that could. Our little show, which cost maybe $20,000 a week to produce, was bringing in huge profits because of the advertisers, allowing the network to fund hit original shows like *Silk Stalkings* and *La Femme Nikita*. You could say that original cable programming like *The Walking Dead* got its start with us. The network also loved crossovers between its shows and stars, so I appeared on *Weird Science* and *Silk Stalkings* and their stars appeared on *UAN*.

Alas, nothing that good can last forever. In 1997, Barry Diller bought the network, and by 1998, the president of USA knew his days were numbered. Everyone's days were. The new leadership didn't see the need for movie hosts; they would just show the movies. So at the end of the 1998 season, I got a call from Rod Perth, then president of USA network. He was as kind as he could be in letting me know that my show was done. I got six months more severance than I should have because Rod liked me and knew that I was always a team player. And that was that.

The end of *USA: Up All Night*'s long run was sad, but it was also liberating. I was in my early forties and it was time for something else. I was still working, doing standup and a lot of television. I found that was harder to get cast after *UAN*. The bimbo image was sticking. Unlike Cassandra Peterson, who played Elvira, I had used my own name. I appeared on lots of talk shows as the love and sex expert. But as far as other roles, it was, "No thanks, we'll call you."

Maybe if I'd stayed in LA, I'd still be working, getting the busty, lusty cougar movie roles that go to Jennifer Coolidge (Stifler's mom in *American Pie*). I feel like she stole my career, because I could have been up for all those parts. I would love to play a MILF, then a cougar, and then a cougar grandma! But I don't believe in regrets. Too many people spend their lives kicking themselves for the decisions they made ten or twenty or thirty years before, but that's foolish. We all make the best choices we can, based on who we are in the moment; it's easy to say, "If I'd only known then what I know now," but you didn't. You couldn't.

Nobody looks at a critical moment, when a relationship or a job might hang in the balance, and says, "You know, I think I'm going to make a decision here that will screw up my life for years." We do the best we can with what we have. Forgive yourself and move on.

I made the best calls I could during UAN, and I can't complain. I had an eight-year run on my own show. Not many actors can say that. I got a taste of what it was like to be a star. I had limos and even a few private jets taking me where I needed to go. I had paparazzi taking my picture and screaming my name when I went out to a red carpet event or when I left my hotel in New York. It was a cool, fun part of my life. I worked with incredible people and touched a lot of lives. When the show ended, I was ready to move on to something else...and somewhere else.

⤜ ON THE WAY TO TODAY ⤛

What did I get out of the USA: Up All Night years that fueled my rise in so many other areas of life? Slide under the covers and take a look...

- ☐ *The greats like Mel Brooks are great because they really care. Find something you can care about that much.*

- ☐ *If your work's not fun, you're doing it wrong.*

- ☐ *Get the inside scoop if you can. If no one else does it, that's their problem, not yours.*

- ☐ *People want to feel like someone is listening to or speaking for them. If that's you, they'll love you.*

- ☐ *Typecasting is a real thing. If you don't want to be associated with it, maybe you shouldn't do it. A reputation is hard to change.*

- ☐ *If someone gives you an inch, date a different guy! (Just kidding. If someone does give you an inch, take ten miles.)*

- ☐ *Follow the news and know what's going on in the world.*

- ☐ *If you're smart, you can use other people's egotism to your own advantage.*

- ☐ *When you work with fantastic people, work might be hard but it will always be rewarding.*

PART *Three*
FLORIDA YEARS

LESSON NINE
Love Has No Expiration Date

—— *In which our heroine dates a roster of Hollywood power players and millionaires, flirts dangerously with the casting couch, and reunites with her childhood sweetheart in the most romantic—and funniest—way possible.* ——

A young woman dating an older man is like feeding a parking meter. The man is wondering, "How much more money am I going to have to put into this thing?" while the woman's wondering, "How long before he expires?"

Buh-DUM-bum. Thank you, I'll be here through Thursday.

But seriously. *Men.* Can't live with 'em, can't stuff 'em in the trunk of your car—am I right? I've certainly had my share of adventures with men—some funny, some romantic, and some scary. But my experiences with men helped me discover a lot about myself and shaped who I am today, so I think it's only fair that I share them with you.

One obvious thing that we can get out of the way right now: *sex makes men stupid.* Look at all the powerful men, from Bill Clinton to Anthony Weiner, who have wrecked their reputations or careers because they couldn't keep it in their pants. In Hollywood, otherwise smart men seemed to think my sexy bimbo act was real. They probably figured that since I *looked* easy, I *was* easy. Far from it. I could close my legs faster than a hockey goalkeeper. But that didn't stop guys from trying, starting early on in my career.

When I started in Hollywood, the casting couch was still very much in service. It's still around today, although social media has made it a lot more dangerous for producers and other jerks to risk being accused of harassment. But plenty of pretty girls have slept their way into roles—or were promised roles or auditions in return for sex. But even at twenty-five, I knew that some questionable producers, directors, and agents would say anything to get a girl in bed, and I wasn't interested. I would flirt and flatter my way through any situation and then get the hell out as fast as I could.

Remember, back then the men controlled everything. Because feminism and years of work have turned women like Jodie Foster and Angelina Jolie into power players in their own right, women today can call the shots and refuse to put up with any shit. Back then, Hollywood was still a boy's club, with Bill Cosby as its president. An ego-bruised producer could ruin your career. You had to be careful.

Hot Seats

I was, and I still got hit on all the time by all kinds of men. One of the strangest was Wally George, a cadaverous, white-haired guy who was probably best known as Rebecca DeMornay's father. He did a bizarre Southern California talk show called *Hot Seat*, where he played a hyper-conservative reactionary blowhard, a proto-Rush Limbaugh. He had a cult following and his audiences would stand in line for hours to get a seat. Because they were mainly guys, Wally would book a lot of actresses playing various sexy roles. Inevitably they got thrown off by his bodyguards; that was part of his shtick.

His "guests" were made out to be immoral people at whom he would get angry: bakers of pornographic wedding cakes, Bible deniers, and so on. He asked me to be on his show, and I just wanted to be on camera, so I accepted. I wound up appearing on his show four times, always playing different characters, wearing crazy wigs, and having a ball. Once I was a call girl, and I played it to the hilt. I got thrown off every time. Some of those shows are still available on YouTube, and they're worth watching.

Hot Seat was great practice for many of my comedic characters to come. But off the set, Wally was very polite and asked me out. I accepted and got a great dinner out of it. He wrote me beautiful love letters and even proposed. He was harmless, but just a little too creepy.

Other encounters with Hollywood opportunists were a little more harrowing. Once, a modeling agency that represented *Playboy* models took me on as a client. They would send you out for general meetings where casting directors would meet with you—not for a specific project, but for "future possible work." In today's more sexual harassment–aware culture, that would raise more red flags than a Chinese New Year parade, but back then...well, you can imagine what went on.

This agency sent me to a meeting with Ray Stark, an old-time Hollywood bigwig who had produced *Funny Girl* and *Funny Lady*, in his bungalow on the Columbia back lot. I was very excited, but I was still very cautious about men. Stark flipped through my portfolio, and then he looked at me and said, "You know, you're a beautiful young lady, but you have to be willing to wallow in the dirt of Hollywood to get ahead." I sat stunned; I couldn't believe that line had just come out of his mouth. He must have said it hundreds of times before, and I guess some girls had wallowed. Not me. I heard my mom's voice ringing in my ear, saying, "Run!"

I giggled to break the tension. Then he said, "I really like you and I really want you to meet me at my home at Palm Springs for the weekend." At that, I thanked him, excused myself, and walked out. I was mortified. Maybe some women would have taken that leap, but not me. I called my agent, said, "You set me up," and fired her. That was the end of that relationship.

Another of the more memorable encounters was with basketball immortal Wilt Chamberlain, who I met at a party at Dorothy Hamill's house. As the evening went along, Wilt invited everyone to his fabulous pyramid-shaped home in the Hollywood Hills. The house was amazing, with an undulating pool that went from inside to outside the home. Then Wilt offered to give me a private tour, including the mirrored couch room that sat in the middle of the house. But the only way to get into the room was to crawl. So, at five-foot-four, I slithered in.

But when I turned around, I saw that not only had Wilt followed me into the room, he had decided to whip out his one-eyed monster. I've never seen anything else that big attached to a man, before or since. Remember, in the NBA they called him "Wilt the Stilt," and in his autobiography, he claimed to have slept with 20,000 women. With that redwood, he could have satisfied several women at a time!

I don't know what he thought he was going to do with me, but all I could do was laugh from shock. As it always does, laughing proved to be an effective libido killer. I slithered out as fast as I'd come in and asked Wilt to take me home, which he did. Whew, escaped another one. All I can think is that the pharmacies in

Beverly Hills must have made a lot of money on Monday mornings when Wilt was still with us.

The audacity of some showbiz types was appalling. A big-time agent, Mike Greenfield, who represented Linda Evans of *Dallas* fame, had the gall to call my mother and father and say, "Your daughter needs to sleep with me. If she sleeps with me, I'll represent her." Greenfield was a top agent, and if he handled me, it could have been huge for my future. But I couldn't even imagine doing that. My parents were mortified and furious.

FOURTH WALL BREAK!

*It wasn't shocking to have men make passes, but this was before sexual harassment became a thing, so they could get away with some awful behavior. It was sickening and disheartening, because some people would say I was asking for it by not dressing like a nun. Let me state it clearly for the record: **no woman, no matter how she is dressed, is ever, ever "asking" to be humiliated, degraded, attacked, or raped. Period.** I wasn't, that's for sure. I was proud of how I looked, and I didn't think I should have to dress in a tent to keep men from groping me. When I realized that sexual harassment existed whether I was in entertainment or running for office, if I didn't want to hide under a rock, I had to learn to deal with it.*

Then there were the producers who pursued me to the point where it got scary. One literally chased me around his desk and out to my car. Another, who had legitimate shows on the air, invited me to a five o'clock meeting with him at his offices at Universal Studios. But once we were in his private office, he tried to get me to do a love scene, telling me that I really had to "get into the scene" with him.

With a chill, I suddenly realized that the outer office was closed and there was no one else around; he had dragged the meeting out until everyone else had gone home. A wave of fear washed over me. I knew girls in Hollywood who had been raped, and I had no interest in joining their ranks. I stood up and said, "I have to go," and as I walked out, the halls were dark and empty. If he'd come after me, I don't know what I would have done. I vowed never to put myself in such a vulnerable position again.

After that, I got savvier. A few months later, I was doing a shoot for this photographer who told me that he wanted to take one last shot on a hill above the city. I wasn't about to put myself in harm's way again, so when he got in his car, I got in mine to follow. The area above the basin that forms most of LA is hills filled with winding, dead-end roads and the big open space of Griffith Park. That's where this photographer led me, going up, up, up as the sky was getting dark, dark, dark.

All I could think about was the Black Dahlia and the Manson murders; I was convinced this guy was going to slit my throat and dump my body in the hills. He kept leading me back into the dark until I finally broke out in a cold sweat and said to myself, "This does not feel right. Go down. Find streets that go down." I turned suddenly on a street that led back down to Sunset Boulevard and when I got back to lights and people, I was shaking. I never heard from that photographer again, and I knew my instincts were probably correct.

Shear Honesty: *Trust your instincts, especially when something seems too good to be true. The world is full of good people, but there are always a few who will try to manipulate you into giving them something you don't want to give up, whether it's sex or money or what have you. The test is simple: if someone's offering* *you exactly what you want and promising it will be easy, walk away. Nothing you want is ever easy. That's what makes finally getting it so sweet.*

Art Fisher

During this early era, I did have one notable romantic liaison that ended badly. In fact, it haunts me to this day. The man's name was Art Fisher. He was the director on an audition I went on during my first months in Hollywood. I was terribly green, and he cast Judy Landers instead of me, but I was the one he asked out.

Art was a genius. He directed variety shows like *Sonny and Cher* and *The Carol Burnett Show*, invented the green screen and lighting techniques that are still used today, and won an Emmy for directing. He was thirty-six, Jewish, drove a Harley, stood six-foot-three with long, curly hair, and was enchanting. He owned a big home in the Hollywood Hills. Strangely, there were two pairs of female eyes painted on the bottom of his pool and the side of the house, and he told me he had been looking for the girl whose eyes matched those eyes. It might've been a really creative line, but damned if they weren't just like my brown, almond-shaped eyes! It was all terribly romantic. Before long, I was in love and we were caught up in a whirlwind romance. Then one day, I found out that I was pregnant.

Art was thrilled and wanted to marry me right away, but I freaked out. I was only twenty-three with my whole life ahead of me; I didn't want a baby! I also knew that the weight gain that came with a pregnancy would put my career on hold at the very least. I didn't know what to do. Art was talented, creative, and like no other man I had ever met, and part of me wanted to marry him and live in the house with my eyes on the side. Another part of me wanted to run. There were also my parents to think about; if they found out, they would demand I come home.

Nature solved the problem: I lost the baby. I was sad but relieved. Art, however, was furious. We fought and broke up. But afterwards, he wrote me the most heartfelt, beautiful letters I've ever received. It took years before I could reread them without crying, and even longer to truly understand them. He really did love me. But he was a man and I was a child, and I never knew what he saw in me.

After we broke up, Art bought a helicopter. Boys and their toys, you know. One day, he took it up, crashed into a utility pole, and died instantly. I was devastated. I later found out that he'd had a rebound affair with his agent's secretary and she'd given birth to his son. Years later, she told me through tears that he would never have married her because he was still in love with me. That's a tragedy worthy of any Hollywood screenplay.

Free Agent

Then came 1989 and Bobby Kelton, and I stopped dating around for the most part. But when USA: *Up All Night* became a hit and I became better known, my dating options expanded. I still had Bobby as a shield, but now I was thinking long-term. Meanwhile my mother, who hated Bobby, was nagging me to break up with him. In her opinion, he would never be anything more than a road comic basking in the fading glory of his *Tonight Show* appearances—and to be honest, she was right.

I loved Bobby as a comic, loved that he was well-read and that he had the best vocabulary on the planet. I cared about him and he cared about me. But I wanted more out of life than he did. He confirmed this when he told me, "You will never live lower than what you have right now." That's not the kind of line to sweep a girl off her feet! We lived in a nice apartment in Beverly Hills, but I was ambitious. I wanted the world. I wanted to create and have adventures and be a star. He was content with gigging on cruise ships. We weren't compatible anymore. In 2000 we finally split up for good, and I was a free agent.

I wasn't sad; quite the opposite. I was in my forties, well-known, looking great, and could get a table anywhere, so it was fun to spread my wings. I had done my time at diners and cafes during my standup years, and now I wanted Spago. Well, I got it. I dated an eclectic array of guys. Some had potential, others were just for the fun of it, and some were excuses to get out, see and be seen. I dated a lot of famous, wealthy, and infamous men, some of whom went on to be huge in entertainment or business. I'm still good friends with many of them.

For instance, if you're old enough, you might remember Red Buttons, a comedian who was in lots of films and became famous for roasting other celebrities. Old-time male comedians tend to be naughty and horny, and Red was no exception. Once, I was at a house party, and Red pulled me aside (he had to be about 150 years old at the time) and said, "I can do things to you with my tongue that you can't even imagine." I didn't want to think about it, and I ran off to get another piece of cheesecake.

I went on a couple of dates with Donny Most, who played Ralph Malph on *Happy Days*. I went on a date with Larry King after appearing on *Larry King Live*. According to the tabloids, I had a fling with my pal Burt Reynolds; allegedly, we'd been caught having sex at a World Wrestling Federation event. It wasn't true, but Burt was in the middle of divorcing Loni Anderson and he was furious. He wanted to sue the tabloid, and I had to go on Joan Rivers's talk show, *Gossip! Gossip! Gossip!*, to refute the story.

Shear Honesty: *That experience taught me the power of PR, good and bad. I became a lot more careful about how I answered questions. Perception is reality, and we live in a society where, thanks to social media, people are very quick to judge you based on scarce or false information. Protect your reputation and brand. Be smart about what you post, tweet, and email, and remember that crafting a careful answer to a question takes about one-tenth as much time as damage control after the fact.*

I also dated Glenn Frey of the Eagles. He was debuting his first solo album, *No Fun Aloud*, and I auditioned for the lead in the music video for the song *The One You Love*. I got it and was ecstatic. I wound up dancing and making out all day (on camera) with Glenn while he sang in my ear. After the shoot wrapped, he asked me out, and of course I said yes.

I rarely went over to a guy's house, because that was asking for trouble. But Glenn wanted to cook for me and show me the finished video, so how could I say no? Well, it turned out to be a wonderful evening: champagne, amazing chicken, Glenn playing the piano and singing to me. He was also an incredible kisser. He wanted me to spend the night, but I declined.

He told me that all girls love shiny things, and I thought, "Is he bribing me with jewelry for sex?" No, thank God (because jewelry is my kryptonite and I might have buckled), but he did show me the biggest, shiniest mountain of cocaine I have ever seen. I didn't partake and he didn't push. I asked him why he enjoyed coke and he said that he liked to sustain the same high that he had while he was performing. Privately, I wondered how one could enjoy the highs if there were no lows.

We didn't date again, but Glenn cleaned himself up and went on to marry a lovely woman and have a beautiful family. He was a good guy, and I was happy for him. Years later, Van and I went to see Glenn in concert. It was a romantic, fabulous show, and I acted like a groupie. We sat in the front row and as he took his bow, I screamed "Hey Glenn!" He recognized me, shouted "Rhonda— Rhonda Shear?" and blew me a kiss from the stage. I swooned... and Van seethed with jealousy. Sadly, Glenn died in 2016, and the world is poorer for it.

FOURTH WALL BREAK!

I never did drugs, which I thought was normal because I also didn't drink. I was too afraid, and I was always a hypochondriac. I've always been afraid (and still am to this day) that someone will slip something into my drink, because I've seen it happen. I have to see the bartender make my drink and then put my hand over it. Back then, since I didn't drink I didn't know what getting high was, so I didn't know what I was missing. I was pretty square, but I was not judgmental. Nobody ever made me feel awkward or pushed drugs on me. But I always wondered, "Why do they need it?" I was in Hollywood, working in my dream job, so I was already high!

Serial Dater

I was a serial dater, but it was unnerving to accept gifts and favors from men. I'd built my career mostly through my own hard work, and I hated the idea that I could be dependent on anybody. But I can honestly say that none of the men I dated ever helped me in my career. I always wanted to make it on my own terms and not owe anyone anything, and I have. I'm proud of that.

Shear Honesty: *Advice and opportunities are one thing; handouts are another. I never got a role because a boyfriend pulled strings, made a call, or paid someone off, ever. It's fine to accept help based on your merits—getting a job because the HR director worked with you before and knows you're a champ—but accepting charity diminishes you and puts you in other people's debt. It's much better to make it on your own terms and owe no one.*

I dated Bill Daily from *I Dream of Jeanie*, who told me that he always brought a candelabrum on the road with him. I had a couple of dates with Soupy Sales. My "man that got away" date was Phil Alden Robinson, who wrote and directed *Field of Dreams*. I was flying to Orlando to tape a pilot, back when I was still terrified of flying. People were recognizing me from *USA: Up All Night*, which was embarrassing because I was having a panic attack from the claustrophobia.

I talked to a flight attendant who recognized me and moved me into an empty seat in first class. In the seat next to me was Phil, who had his nose deep into a book because he didn't want to talk to anyone. You know how it is: you're trying to have a peaceful flight and a chatterbox talks your ear off—especially if said chatterbox finds out you directed a classic movie. Well, Phil apparently found me charming, because he put down his book and we talked nonstop through the most enjoyable five-hour flight I'd ever had. I didn't know who he was until later in the flight, but I was immediately attracted to his wit and smarts. I was still with Bobby, but I went out with Phil and had a great time. But he flat-out told me—and rightfully so—that he wasn't going to continue seeing me while I was with Bobby.

I liked Phil a great deal, but he intimidated me. He was brilliant and erudite and lyrical. My friends all thought I should be with him. I met him at a club one evening, and while we were there he gently backed me against a wall and said, "I want to see you, but you need to be free." It was romantic and sweet. But I chickened out and stayed with Bobby, so I never knew what might have happened between us.

I didn't just date men in showbiz, either. I dated a guy who owned a shipping company. I dated a couple of doctors. I dated an adoption attorney and a real estate attorney. It was an interesting mix of men and I really enjoyed them, though I felt a little nutty at the time. I would have lunch with one guy and dinner with another.

Does that make me a slut? Who cares? I was having fun.

Leon and Ron

Few of my dates were serious, but there was one guy I was hoping would be "the one." Leon Schneider and I were born on the same day in the same year. He was classy, intelligent, and supportive of my comedy career. He was everything that I like, and I had deep feelings for him. But things with Leon didn't go anywhere. One night we were sitting in his car in front of my house, and I was saying sweet things to him until he turned to me and said, "Don't go there. You're too old."

That stopped me dead. "Too old for what?" I asked.

"I want kids."

I was floored. I said, "So do I, that's not a problem." But he was adamant. I was crushed. I thought I was in my prime, empowered, fit, and sexy, but I got a rude awakening about my age and how I was seen in Hollywood. It was awful and demoralizing.

It's not that different today. Sure, there are plenty of stars over forty who are smoking hot, from Julia Roberts to Cate Blanchett.

But how many of those gorgeous women would be stars if they tried to start their careers at forty or forty-five? *None of them.* For all its talk of women's empowerment, Hollywood is still a sucker for alabaster skin and a size zero ass. Directors and producers lose interest in us just when we're at our most interesting.

My story with Leon came full circle, though. I invited him to my New Orleans birthday bash, and he showed up looking dapper. During the evening, he blurted out to Van, "You've had her long enough. You can have her in Florida and I'll share her with you in California." I think he was only half kidding. Leon had married a couple of times since our days in LA, and the marriages hadn't worked out. He was lonely and regretful. I'd been there for him when his mom passed away. I'd met his family. He'd followed me to comedy gigs. There was something between us that he couldn't replace, even with all those young gals and their fresh ovaries. In a great irony, he never had children, which was sad. If there's a moral in there, I think it's that sometimes, what we want is right there... if we can just see it.

Shear Honesty: *Boy, is that a lesson! I feel bad for Leon even today, because he was so busy looking for the ideal (which doesn't exist) that he missed what was right in front of him. He was filled with regret, and that's the worst emotion in the world, because there's nothing you can do but live with it. Don't make that mistake. People are not ideals; they're people. Nobody will be perfect, but they don't have to be. They just have to be perfect for YOU.*

One of my most interesting suitors was Ron Perelman, owner of Revlon. Ron was brilliant, fascinating, and one of the country's richest bachelors. We went out a few times, and I even traveled with him on his yacht, the *Ultima II*, to the island of St. Barts. Being with Ron was always interesting; for instance, he had bodyguards. But even though his lifestyle seemed like a fairytale, I connected more with his dad than with I did with him.

Power is an aphrodisiac, and Ron had that. In New York, everyone knew him. It was fun to sit at the best table at the hard ticket restaurants. He was constantly surrounded by admirers and had several bodyguards close by. I liked Ron, but it wasn't meant to be. It was amazing to get a peek into that ultra-rich lifestyle, but it was never something I could have handled for long. Too many guards, too many people folding your toilet paper into little v's when you walked out of the bathroom. I always used to picture my personal belongings in someone else's closet, and I just didn't see my red rubber dress and boa working in an Upper East Side mansion. Ron was an amazing businessman, endlessly charitable, and a collector of fine art. I'm glad I had the experience to peak into his supercharged world, but I'm an old fashioned Southern girl. For all my love of material things, I need to feel like I can walk around my house naked. I would be lying if I said that kind of power wasn't intoxicating, but fortunately, it wasn't too intoxicating.

FOURTH WALL BREAK!

I'd been around a lot of rich people in my time in Hollywood. I'd been to mansions and been around wealth, but Ron's world was like nothing I'd ever experienced. He had guards because he was afraid he would be kidnapped and held for ransom. He didn't drive himself anywhere, and when he got out of a car, a bodyguard got out with him. It was surreal. Being part of that life was a fun fantasy, but in reality, I could never have seen myself living that life. I'm too down to earth at heart.

Childhood Sweethearts

However, all the rich and famous men I dated pale in comparison to my one true love, Van Fagan. In all the years between New Orleans childhood and our reunion and marriage, Van was in the back of my mind, the sweetheart I couldn't quite shake. Fortunately, fate brought us back together, but the full story starts a lot earlier, back in the Big Easy.

We met at Gregory Junior High when I was twelve and in the seventh grade; Van was in the eighth grade, but even at thirteen he was handsome. He went to every one of my dance recitals, mostly because he wanted to see me kick high in leotards. As far as I'm concerned, that was a normal, healthy reaction for a pre-teen boy, but back then I would have been irritated at him for not appreciating my perfect *tour jeté*.

We quickly became inseparable, but it wasn't what you think. We were kids together. We went through puberty together. We'd sit in the backyard of my house (so my mother could keep an eye on him), play in my mother's rock garden, and steal chaste kisses when we thought she couldn't see us. It was all very sweet.

Why did I marry Van so many years later, after we'd been apart for so long? This is why. We were in my backyard one day and I picked up a philodendron leaf from the ground and said, "If you love me, you'll eat half this leaf and keep the other half for the rest of your life." Without hesitation, Van grabbed the leaf and ate one half, but it turned out that that he was allergic to it and his throat started to close up! Fortunately, he was all right and I quickly forgot about the leaf. But years later, on our second date, he produced the torn, dried up other half of the leaf. Butterflies swooped in my tummy. Talk about romantic!

My mother adored Van and loved that he was the best-looking boy in school. But because we dated so intensely and had such deep feelings for each other, she put the fear of God into both of us. She let him know that he was not allowed to put his hand above my knee, and that under no circumstances was he allowed into my bedroom. She scared the shit out of Van. Even when we were married, when Mom was in her eighties, he was scared of her. Probably a good idea.

We did make a cute couple, him with his Beatle haircut and me with my bikini bod. Van was my first real boyfriend, and we went steady throughout most of high school. We had a deep love for each other, so when it came to drama, we could have given Romeo and Juliet a run for their money. Every summer, his family would put him on a train for Lafayette, Louisiana, where he had family. We *pined* for each other, and one summer, we begged and pleaded until Van's family let him spend the summer with my family in New Orleans.

In retrospect, it wasn't a smart move, letting two teenagers who were madly in love stay one bedroom apart. Van roomed with my brother Fred, and the intervening wall barely contained our screaming hormones. You could have cut the sexual tension with a knife. However, we were very well behaved. There was plenty of fondling and what was known then as "heavy petting," but that was all. Later on, when I was fifteen or sixteen, he finally took my virginity, but I have no regrets.

Shear Honesty: *Don't settle. Please. If you're swooning over all this teenage passion and think it's romantic and wonderful that Van and I ended up married, you're right. But imagine if I had gotten complacent and stayed with Bobby? I would never have known what I was missing, but part of me would have* *died. Great loves are rare; if you have one in your life, don't give up on it and do whatever you must to try and make it work. If it doesn't, it will still be an adventure, and you can go forward without regrets.*

Green-Eyed Monster

The downside to all this teen passion was that we were both insanely jealous and would fight like cats and dogs. My physical development, dancing, and outgoing personality made me very popular, so Van was always getting in fights with boys who flirted with me. He even got his perfect nose broken over me, and it's still adorably crooked to this day.

Van would get furious and possessive even if I talked to other boys on the phone. At my age, my mother didn't want me to be exclusive; she wanted me to date around. But Van was having none of it. One day, he called the house and I had gone for a ride with another guy, Nicky Gristina. In our community, guys were either "frats" (respectable guys who typically belonged to school fraternities) or "hoods" (disreputable guys from the wrong side of the tracks who got in fights and drag raced). Nicky was a "hood;" Van was a "frat." Nicky wore his hair in kind of a pompadour and drag raced a Mercury Cyclone with flames painted on the rear end. He wasn't a bad boy, but he had the bad boy look, and Van hated him. However, I was intrigued with Nicky and his gang.

When Van saw that I was out with Nicky, he flipped out and broke up with me on the spot. (Nicky's name still gets Van's back up to this day; I like to torture him with it.) We also fought about his fraternity. In New Orleans, high school fraternities and sororities were a big deal, and Van's fraternity, TKO, named me their little sister but didn't make me their sweetheart. A competitive fraternity, SPO, made me sweetheart. We had a screaming match because he didn't fight for me to be named TKO sweetheart. Love is not only blind but stupid.

Another time, Van saw me driving around New Orleans with my parents. I was in the back seat with a friend of my cousin, a young guy who was getting ready for medical school. It was completely innocent, but Van saw us driving down Canal Street, stopped his car in the middle of the street—blocking traffic—got out, ran to my father's car, and pounded on the hood, crying and screaming.

Drama? Oh yeah, we had drama, right here in River City. I do believe if we could have gotten married at that age, we would have, and it would have been a disaster. Because I, your angelic narrator, a Southern lady of sweet and refined disposition, had my moments of jealous rage, too. Even when Van and I were going steady, I still didn't completely trust him. He would walk home after school and more than once I followed him home in my car to make sure he didn't go to another girl's house. Once, when he spotted me driving with my mom, he said, "Why didn't you just pick me up? I had to walk miles!"

In tenth grade, I was terribly jealous that while I was in one Spanish class, Van was in a different one with two girls I knew had the hots for him. I was horrible at Spanish and would use any excuse to get out of class, so I got a bathroom pass and walked past his classroom—only to see one of those hussies rubbing the back of his neck, and Van not stopping it from happening! I saw red, and we broke up again for a while.

Obviously, Van and I didn't end up together then, which was just as well. We were too volatile and emotional, and things were changing for both of us. I wanted a career in showbiz; he wanted to get out of the city and away from its drug scene. So we drifted apart. But we ended up back together, and his passion made it happen.

Reaching Out

In 2001 I was seeing a guy named Mitch Cohen, a director and a producer who looked like a young Richard Gere. We had a hot, heavy three-month relationship, but what Mitch was really doing was pulling me out of my idle years with Bobby. He said, "Rhonda, you can't live off your laurels. You've got to make calls to every single person you know in this industry and make things happen." He would come over and we'd work the phones together, trying to breathe life back into my dormant career.

That's what we were doing one October day, me at my computer and him on the other side of the table on the phone, when I got a message from Van through Classmates.com. I had been searching for some old girlfriends, but I was also looking for Van because... well, because that spark for your first love never really goes out. I couldn't find him, but the site alerted him that I had been searching for him, so he joined and emailed me.

I hadn't followed Van a lot through the years, but I knew that he'd gotten married, had kids, and moved away from New Orleans. That was about it. That day, he sent me a long email that brought me up to date: he was living in Lafayette, was divorced, and was running his own software company for the oil industry (he's always had a terrific head for business). He sent me his home phone number, pager number, and office number, and said he would love to get reacquainted.

There I was, sitting across from Mitch, who had no idea, and my heart was a little bit aflutter. *Oh my God, my first love just emailed me!* I joined Classmates.com and emailed Van back: "Where have you been? I've been waiting for you." He cut right to the chase in his reply: "I'm not married anymore, and I'd love to catch up." Deep breath.

I gave him my phone number and three minutes later, he called me. So now I was on the phone right in front of Mitch, but I didn't really think anything was going to come of it. This was someone I hadn't seen in a quarter-century; what could possibly happen? We chatted and flirted some more, and then I said, "You should come out and see me."

Pause. "I'll be on a plane tomorrow."

I hung up the phone, turned to Mitch, and said, "I think I just invited my first boyfriend to come out and see me." He dismissed it out of hand. In his mind, there was no way I would have any interest in anything with a guy from my past who lived in Louisiana, was probably fat and bald by now, and shopped at the Piggly Wiggly. He reminded me that I lived in Beverly Hills and was a celebrity. "Everybody wants to reach out to their first love," he said, "but it's stupid."

I resented his big-city snobbery, but I also thought he was probably right. I *was* living in Beverly Hills, sitting across from this sexy producer-director, sort of famous and dating millionaires and lawyers from Manhattan. I didn't want Van coming out and messing up whatever it was I had going on—especially the fling I had going with Mitch. So I emailed him back and found out that he had already made plane reservations! He wasn't kidding around.

I told him that something had come up. He wrote back, "I'm sure something came up, just like old times." I had always talked to other boys even when Van and I were going steady. Then he wrote me an email that said I was missing out on meeting the sexiest man alive, and even if we just became friends, it would be a wonderful thing to reconnect. For some reason, that message did it for me. Van had seen me on television over all these years so he knew what I looked like, but I had no idea what he looked like. But his confidence really piqued my curiosity.

Shear Honesty: *Juggling multiple relationships isn't just exhausting; it also takes a lot of time—time you could be using to run your business, train for your marathon, or write your novel. Dating's supposed to be fun, not work. If your romantic life feels like a job, simplify it. It's okay to take a break from searching for your soul mate and just have a good time.*

Butterflies

For the next three months, Van and I talked and he played this little teasing game with me. I kept saying, "Why don't you come see me in New York?" because I was going to New York pretty regularly to work a comedy club or two. I figured that if Van met me there, I could keep him and my LA life separate. But he saw right through me.

"I know your game," he said one day. "You don't want me coming to LA because you've got something going on there." Busted. We went back and forth for a couple of months—an email here, an email there, and he was as charming and funny as ever. Then one day I told him that I was planning to go to New Orleans to see my mother for Christmas and I suggested that we get together there. He thought that was a great idea, and we agreed that we would work out the timing. But we never made definite plans.

Then, at the airport just before I boarded my flight to New

Orleans, I had a blowup with Mitch. On the flight, I had an empty, mad, sad feeling, and as soon as I got to New Orleans, I decided to call Van. Why not? Mitch and I weren't engaged and I wasn't going to spend the holidays alone. Plus, I was powerfully curious about what it would be like to see my first love, the boy who stole my virginity, and if he was still as sexy as I remembered. This could be fun!

I talked with Van, and he was going to spend Christmas Day with his kids, but he promised to drive down to New Orleans to meet me on December 27. The day came and I was filled with nervous excitement. Then he pulled up to my mom's home in his candy apple red, four-door Ford F250 crew cab. I had been picked up in limos, Rolls-Royces, Ferraris, and Mercedes-Benzes, but never a truck. That was hot. Then I saw him, dressed all in black, as I rounded the corner from the back of my mom's house. My heart actually skipped a beat. Sparks flew as soon as our eyes met. He held out his hand, and he had brought me a single yellow rose.

Oh my God.

FOURTH WALL BREAK!

After spending all those years in Hollywood and with millionaires, here comes this guy who's cooking the fish he caught in the house he built, and it was a total turn-on. We were both strong people, and we both needed to be with a strong person. Van and I had walked all over people who weren't as strong as we were. Sometimes, we clash, but every marriage has give-and-take and moments where you have to pick your battles. I like knowing that Van is strong and I can depend on him. But he doesn't cater to me. I fend for myself and I take care of him just as much as he takes care of me. We can also be pretty spur-of-the-moment and take chances that a lot of people our age won't. If we weren't spontaneous, we wouldn't have gotten married and we wouldn't have started our business.

He wasn't bald, and he wasn't fat, and he sure as hell didn't look like he shopped at Piggly Wiggly. He was so handsome, just like I remembered him. He was forty-seven and I was forty-six. Off we went in his truck, and I was all a-flutter. I had dated producers, directors, moguls, actors, rock stars, lawyers, doctors, and billionaires, but this was the first time I had butterflies in my stomach. I was already planning how I would get him into bed just to mess with him for breaking my heart when we were kids. I was in terrific shape and in fine dating form, and I knew how to toy with a man. I was very flirty, and after we had a couple of small dirty martinis at Arnaud's, I grabbed him and kissed him hard. He was shy and flabbergasted, but the kiss was still magical.

We went to a Saints playoff game the next day, but we never watched the game. We were totally absorbed with each other. After the game, I suggested checking into a trendy hotel in the Quarter; I wanted to strip for him and show him what he had been missing for all these years. We got our hotel room, and when I did my strip tease, we were both so overcome with emotion that we couldn't even have sex! It was adorable.

Van and I spent fifteen incredibly romantic days together in New Orleans, and on the fifth day he took me to a restaurant we had frequented as kids, Tony Angello's. Mr. Tony knew everyone and was famous for his "feed me" menu. You didn't even have to look at a menu; Mr. Tony would just bring you his mouth-watering specials (he passed away in 2015, a courtly host to the end). All of a sudden, during dinner, Van got down on one knee in the middle of the restaurant and proposed.

I had been proposed to before, but I knew in my heart of hearts that this was it. He was the one, the soul mate, the old shoe, mine for the rest of our lives. Plus, he was still alive after eating the philodendron leaf, which was definitely a sign. I said yes, and on New Year's Eve we made love for the first time in decades upstairs in my mother's second-floor bedroom—while my mother sat downstairs, oblivious. We felt like teenagers again. It was a sweet, hot, whirlwind romance...a whirlwind more than thirty years in the making.

Man's Man

Now we were engaged, but we hadn't made any plans and things remained volatile. I had been planning to go back to LA for a while, but my cousin Margo told Van, "If you let her get on that plane and go back to all those suitors in LA, the wedding won't happen. Don't let her go, or go with her." She was right.

Van had plans to drive back to Lafayette to see his kids and come back to New Orleans to ring in 2002 with me. So I stayed, and after making love to me, Van left. He always spent New Year's Eve with his kids lighting bonfires and things like that, so he went back to do that, which was sweet. However, all I knew was that he'd proposed, taken me to bed, and then disappeared, leaving me waiting all day in bed in my PJs for his return. I was not a happy woman.

A day later, he came back to New Orleans and brought me a little piece of jewelry—*guilt jewelry*—to apologize for standing me up. Then he asked me to come to Lafayette and meet his kids, Thomas and Emily. So the next day, off we went to Lafayette. We went to his house, and I settled in for one of the most romantic nights I've ever enjoyed.

He had lit candles everywhere in the house, which he had built himself. He had laid kindling in the fireplace, and when we needed more, he would go outside and chop it. He cooked me fish that he had caught. He was completely different from any man I had ever met in Los Angeles, a man's man: rugged, good with his hands, and tough. I was used to pretty, immaculately dressed directors and lawyers who were comfortable ordering in French off a menu and thought any problem could be solved with a gold AMEX card, but who wouldn't last five minutes if their Benz broke down in the Louisiana bayou. Van was something else entirely. I was overwhelmed. He was the opposite of anyone I'd ever known.

The next morning, he introduced me to Thomas and Emily and told them we were engaged. Later in the day, I found out that he had gotten in touch with the county courthouse. Louisiana has a 72-hour waiting period to get married, which I suppose is to allow hotheaded young kids to recant proposals offered in the afterglow of orgasm. But Van and I weren't kids and we knew what we were doing, so he got the county to push our marriage license through the same day, and we eloped that afternoon.

But nothing's ever easy. As we were heading to the courthouse, I got a call from Bobby Kelton. He was so sweet and I started crying, wondering, "Am I doing the right thing?" I hadn't thought this through. I was caught up in the romance of being with my first love on this crazy fling. Van, bless him, said, "Rhonda, you don't have to do this." But I had waited twenty-five years for Van, and I wasn't going to screw it up. I hung up the phone and said, "No, we're doing this." My mind was made up. I don't know what gave me the courage to do it, but I felt like it was right.

Shear Honesty: *The unknown is scary. Making a radical life decision is scary. Hell, marriage is scary! That doesn't make any of them bad. Humans are naturally resistant to change; that's why we settle and get complacent and then look up and go, "Huh, where did those twenty years go?" Don't let the natural fear of change stop you from making big decisions. Butterflies are normal; so are doubts. But if you're sure, if you've done the math, if the relationship is strong and has weathered tough times and you're still in love, then go for it.*

We stopped at a store called Service Merchandise on the way to the courthouse and picked up wedding bands. Now, I was brought up Jewish by heritage, though we didn't go to temple. I had dated Jewish guys my whole life; Van was one of the few who wasn't a Jew. So I was delighted when we got to the courthouse and the clerk said, "Okay, Judge Rubin is going to marry you."

I thought, "This is awesome! How are we getting a Jewish judge in Lafayette, Louisiana? This is meant to be!" Then we went into the judge's chambers, and in walked Judge Rubin...a black guy with an Afro! It was so absurd that I still laugh.

We were married in that room by our black, Jewish judge, with a portrait of Martin Luther King Jr. on the wall. One of our witnesses shot a few photos, and Judge Rubin never got Van's name right. His middle name is Aubrey, and he called him "Aubrey Van" the entire time. But it was legit and we were finally on the books as husband and wife.

Making it Work

Life wasn't a storybook after that, of course. I have always been a city girl: New Orleans followed by Los Angeles, with generous helpings of New York. I love streetscapes, taxicabs, restaurants that are open late, and art galleries. I am *not* a country girl. But there I was, living in Lafayette, population 100,000...but much smaller than that in practice. It was Green Acres, and I was Eva Gabor.

In a small city like that, everybody knew everybody, so I was an instant outsider. Second, the area is extremely conservative, so I became a scorned woman. None of the women in town would talk to me because I had appeared in *Playboy*. I guess I was a hussy or a harlot or whatever ridiculous term they used to describe sexually liberated women. They would invite Van to social events but not me. But even without the toxic social scene, the adjustment would have been hard.

Calling where Van lived "the sticks" would have been a compliment. The first sound I heard on my first night there was, "Mooooo." The countryside was so flat that you could hear farm animals that lived miles away. I heard roosters when I woke up in the morning and thought, "What the fuck?" It was so foreign to me. I was used to breakfasts at Canter's Deli on Fairfax and shopping on Rodeo Drive. Van was a little bit country, and I was definitely a little bit rock and roll.

But we made it work. I was still doing some television appearances and headlining comedy clubs on the road every other weekend. Three months after we eloped, we had a gorgeous ceremony at the Omni Royal Orleans for 150 close friends and family. I had always wanted to marry in the Grand Ballroom of the Royal Orleans, and my mom wanted me to have a traditional wedding, so she was thrilled. Even though we had eloped, we treated the ceremony like it was a true wedding: bridesmaids, an officiant, family, gowns, dinner, band, and dancing. We even had a second line parade!

I picked out a custom-made Richard Tyler gown, simple but flattering. My mother wanted me to stand out, so she picked out some less-than-flattering bridesmaid gowns, too. My bridesmaids weren't pleased, but they went along with it. My sister, niece, and brothers were in the wedding, and Emily, Thomas, and Van's brother, Vernon, were part of the ceremony as well. My mother and Van's parents were still with us, and we were thrilled that they could all experience this magical moment. The wedding was perfect. Even though we were already legally married, when I walked towards my true love my knees were shaking. We spoke the vows that we had written, and even with all my experience as a standup and live performer, I got emotional and nervous. I was a real bride.

Today, we have a dream life that's no less romantic than those days when we were mooning over each other as teens back in New Orleans. We have a gorgeous home—my Barbie Dream House, I call it. We have a thriving business that lets us be creative, give back to the community, and travel. We cook together, plan together, care for our dogs together, and just are together.

When it comes to love and Van, I am a hopeless romantic. How could I not be? We loved each other desperately when we were kids. Out of all the men I dated, went steady with, or even had a tête-à-tête with, he was my true love. When I kidded with him on the phone and said, "I've been waiting for you," the first time we spoke after all those years, it was true. I never had a burning desire to marry any of the men I dated in my previous life. But he was the man I'd wanted to be with for my whole life. I talked about him for years, even on television appearances. I thought about him. And even though I tease him that we missed each other's hottest physical years, it feels like we were never apart. True love has no age limit and no expiration date. Grab it when you can.

Our relationship has withstood some major issues. We lost three of our parents while we were married. We hit rock bottom financially. We've had arguments and falling outs with family members, and then kissed and made up. We moved from California to Florida. Through it all, Van has made me feel safe. He was the missing piece of my puzzle. He is my lover, friend, confidant, audience, handyman, goof off, business partner, competitor in the kitchen, and best cheerleader. At the end of the day, it's Van and me. He's still the devastatingly handsome schoolboy I knew way back when. That's true love.

ON THE WAY TO TODAY

What did my roundabout trip back to true love teach me?

- ☐ You always have the right to say no.

- ☐ Value yourself enough not to tolerate bullshit or disrespect.

- ☐ Wealth means nothing without character.

- ☐ You're not arm candy. If a guy doesn't appreciate you for your brains and depth, find another guy.

- ☐ Situational awareness: if you don't know him well, know where all the exits are located.

- ☐ Beware of complacency.

- ☐ Your ability to have babies not does define your worth.

- ☐ Young equals foolish. Don't make decisions at twenty that you can't take back.

- ☐ If you can't stop thinking about someone, there's a reason.

- ☐ The right person won't just put up with your tribulations. He'll share them with you.

- ☐ The right person isn't the one who makes you FEEL better, but the one who MAKES you better.

LESSON TEN

Building Something Is Always Harder Than You Expect...But Worth It

—— *In which our heroine relocates, hocks her rocks, becomes a home shopping phenomenon, builds a company, makes it possible for women of all sizes to feel gorgeous, and shows the world that she's no "bimbopreneur."* ——

*T*rue love is glorious, but it doesn't pay the bills. After Van and I married, we were going with the flow, not planning too far ahead. We hadn't given much thought to how we would combine households, where we would live, or how we would make a living. Van owned a business in Lafayette, so I downsized my apartment in Beverly Hills and moved into his house. We didn't know what to do next.

We did know that our financial problems were growing worse. I had $70,000 in credit card debt. Before we wed I told Van about my financial woes, and he melted my heart when he told me that after we married, my debts would become his and he would take care of me. I loved hearing that. I didn't need to be taken care of, but his chivalry meant the world to me. We were a team, husband and wife for the long run, and we would climb this mountain together.

> **Shear Honesty:** *Money matters in a relationship. Don't ever let anyone tell you otherwise. Money woes break couples up all the time. The three main reasons: one partner makes more than the other, one partner spends more than the other, or one partner hides accounts from the other. Also, one of the biggest reasons businesses fail: divorce. Assets get split up and the company can't survive. Be smart. Be open about finances with your significant other. If you own a business, sign a prenup before you get married. If the other person complains that it's not romantic, make it a deal-breaker. Taking care of the unromantic details now lets you enjoy love and romance—not stress, conflict, and heartache—later.*

Well, we underestimated the challenges. Van had started a successful software company, but things were falling apart there, too. A few months before our wedding, he had sold equity in the company to get more operating capital. However, in taking on new partners, he lost his controlling interest. He was also under financial pressure from his divorce and child support. After we were married, Van ended up paying most of the expenses for Thomas and Emily. Donna, his ex-wife, had left Van during a midlife crisis and clearly wanted to enjoy her freedom while Van picked up the tab.

Meanwhile, Van's relationship with his new partners was deteriorating. Finally, they bought Van out and just like that, the company he had built was gone. All the stress led to our first real fight. I stomped off the back porch of his house and started running, until I heard him scream, "Stop!" It wasn't a theatrical "Stop!" from a romantic comedy; he really meant it. Apparently, I was headed straight for a closed cesspool. I had been trying for a dramatic gesture that would have worked in Beverly Hills, but I couldn't get away with that out in the country, not unless I wanted to end up immortalized in a honky-tonk song called "The Night Rhonda Drowned in the Cesspool."

Hocking My Jewelry

Van started looking for a job, and before long he got one with a software company in Dallas. Hallelujah! A big city again! We moved and downsized again, since half my stuff was still in Los Angeles. For some reason, I craved a foothold in Beverly Hills, even though the rent was crazy. It was a link to my old life and the career I hoped to keep alive.

We were in Dallas for eight months, and I liked it. Unfortunately, the software company wouldn't let Van do things his way, so he quit. We relocated to San Diego, but Van could never find a job there. He was in his forties and commanded a salary that most software companies weren't willing to pay when they could find a twenty-three-year-old kid out of San Diego State who would work twice the hours for half the money. It was 2002 and now we were out of luck.

I took a deep breath, and told Van to go hock my substantial jewelry. This was a big, BIG sacrifice for me. As I've already mentioned, I have carried on a torrid, lifelong love affair with all things sparkly. Ever since a boy named Dudley threw a costume jewelry ring on my desk in the seventh grade and asked me to go steady, I've been smitten with things made of gold, platinum, and precious gems. A little sparkle just makes you feel good.

Boys have been giving me jewelry my whole life, and I still have almost all of it, including Van's promise ring from when we dated. He also carved me a wooden ring in the eighth grade, and I treasure that more than any diamond. I still marvel at how he carved this perfect circle with engraving that read, "Rhonda & Van."

My passion for jewelry is so intense that twice I've been thrown out of important places. In 1996 I visited the Tower of London, where I was so awed by the Crown Jewels that I was nearly sent to the tower. Tourists were confined to a conveyor belt that circled the precious items, including diamonds the size of baseballs. Yours truly tried to duck under the rope for another ride and I was immediately escorted from the building.

Then, in 2015, on a visit to Italy, I saw the Vatican Jewels. The sign said "No Photographs," but can you blame a girl for trying to sneak a picture on her iPhone? Yes, if you're the Vatican authorities, who invited me to make my way to the main corridor. The point is, I love jewelry, so giving Van permission to hock my favorite pieces was like asking him to sell one of my kidneys. Losing the kidney probably would have been less painful.

Van got the name of a shop on Beverly Drive. Honey, we were down and out in Beverly Hills, hocking jewelry in the 90210! This girl doesn't go bargain basement even when she's broke. Anyway, after years of collecting and receiving gifts from fans and suitors, I had some *gorgeous* pieces: a five-carat diamond ring, a 26-carat diamond bracelet, a 27-carat necklace, a Rolex, and a lot more. That day, Van pawned three pieces worth at least $300,000 and got $30,000 for them. You never get close to full value. But it was our last resort.

Afterward, we felt like shit, but the worst was the 30 percent interest rate. We would have to renew the contract and pay the interest regularly or I would lose my jewels. The day Van hocked them, he said, "I will get it all back for you." Don't cry; the story has a happy ending. Van kept paying the interest and renewing the contract, and when we got back on our feet about eight months later, he got it all back for me. It was like a family reunion! More importantly, Van and I had faith in each other. We knew we could survive and flourish together.

Shear Honesty: *You're going to have to sacrifice. The world doesn't surrender wealth or happiness without a fight; you have to expect bumps and setbacks. Sometimes, to deal with them, you'll have to give something up. I gave up my jewelry so we'd have more time to figure out our next move. You might have to give up cable TV, a friendship, a cherished belief, or something else meaningful. If you can't, then ask yourself what's really important. I decided that my marriage was more important than my bling.* **What you have is only worth what you're willing to give up to keep it.** *Choose wisely.*

HSN

How did we get the money to bail my jewelry out of prison? Patience, honey, I'm getting there. We moved back to LA, using the money from the jewelry to live on for a while. The turning point came later in 2003. We were living in my Beverly Hills apartment and wondering what to do next when I ran into a friend who was in the swimsuit business. She told me how she would go on HSN to sell her products. Now she was moving her business to QVC, but she wanted to manufacture products that I would go on HSN to sell for her. That never panned out, but that was my introduction to the lucrative world of direct TV sales. The intimate apparel business on HSN was small but growing.

HSN launched in 1982 as the Home Shopping Club, hosted by an industry legend named Bob Circosta. Bob became famous in the sales world in 1977, when an advertiser on the radio station he worked for ran out of money and paid the station in can openers. Bob went on air and sold the can openers for $9.99 each and the home shopping industry had its origin story. Today, HSN has sales totaling around $2.5 billion a year. I have to mention that it might never have grown to that point without the brilliance of former CEO Mindy Grossman, who's now CEO of Weight Watchers. Mindy is a hero of mine, a woman who inspires and empowers other women around the world with her leadership and vision. She's been on the *Forbes* "The World's Most Powerful Women" list multiple times, and I'm proud to call her a friend.

Anyway, my friend told me that I should contact HSN about selling intimates for them. I knew that HSN was big and that the most successful brands were the ones with representatives who could charm a television audience. I could certainly do that! I reached out to HSN, and luck was with us. The network was looking for a celebrity, and my friend's departure had left them with no vendors in intimate apparel. I was widely known, and they knew I could handle myself on camera, so they decided to give me a try.

Now we needed a product to sell. Time to risk everything on a throw of the dice. Pooling what cash we had left, Van and I went to wholesalers in downtown LA and bought product from other people's lines and relabeled them with our label, which is legal. Neither of us knew anything about the apparel business, so I picked things that I needed for my ever-changing bod. I figured if I needed it, other women probably would need it, too. HSN's first purchase from Shear Enterprises, LLC was about 6,400 panties, bras, and camisoles. We packed them ourselves and shipped them to HSN in Florida. They gave us an airdate in 2003, and we sold out in ten minutes. Those ten minutes changed our lives!

FOURTH WALL BREAK!

The first time I was on HSN was to sell a line of dolls for Madame Alexander, and I didn't take it seriously. For my first appearance with my own clothing line, I thought I was doing a comedy set. I was writing jokes about the camera being a "crotch cam" and that sort of thing. But I quickly realized that you don't do that on HSN. I'd always been funny on the air, but this was its own thing and you had to sell. I had to be myself and be funny being myself, but I had to sell. I could happily retire from HSN, but when I'm on I get into it and enjoy the different hosts. At the end of the day, I have 700,000 dedicated customers who have watched me through the years, and I owe it to them to bring my best. The interesting thing is that I've been doing HSN for fourteen years— the longest steady gig in front of a camera that I've ever had!

In the next few months, we would get a crash course in the apparel business. But at that time, all I cared about was being back on TV. It was my old life; I was a performer again! I had fun with it: cracking jokes, asking the hostess things like, "Where's the crotch cam?" and having a ball. Basically, I was doing standup. It turned out that was *exactly* the right thing to do. Charismatic hosts sell product on HSN. Meanwhile, while I was hamming it up, Van was in the green room counting how much money we were making, which he had to do because finance is really not my calling. The final verdict: we cleared $11,000 in ten minutes.

I couldn't believe it could be that easy. I'm a comic, and for someone to tell me I can be on television, tell jokes and stories, have a great time *and* make thousands of dollars in minutes—*that's* what I want to be doing!

I think we had such success because I *wasn't* selling. I've never sold anything but myself, so I'm genuine and transparent. I use my comedic sense and become one of the girls. On HSN, they want you to make money while you're on air, and every minute that you're telling a joke, you're not selling. So I would make jokes and tell stories but work selling into them, and it turned out that I had a knack for making people like me. I also relished being live and working without a net. The comic in me loved those moments when an arm fell off a mannequin—which *did* happen. I would turn it into a joke that put everybody on the floor. The comic in me loved that while other personalities were afraid of being live, I savored it.

I don't write my presentation down like so many do; it comes from my heart. I love to kid with my ladies and talk about body parts and crotches and bras and gussets. I'm 100 percent real, and I believe in my product. Viewers can tell if you care, and I do. And because I'm a comic, I will push the boundaries of taste as far as I can without crossing the line. Other actors and comics have tried to sell on live TV and failed because they need a script. But being a comic is all about being in the moment. If a joke flops, you try something else. If a heckler gives you a great piece of material, you improvise. Joan Rivers was brilliant at it. It's a unique skill, and my years of doing sketches and improv with Kenny, standup with Bobby, and working on TV had been the perfect classroom.

Shear Honesty: *Most people hate to be sold. You do; I do. We don't like when somebody is in our face feeding us cheesy "I have to talk to my sales manager" bullshit. I'm great at selling because I don't sell. I engage. I entertain. I relate. I care about the women who are watching and that comes through. An old marketing maxim says, "We do business with people we like." It's true. Don't sell. Care. Connect. Give people much more than they expect.*

Solve a problem and do it with confidence. Your audience or your customers will like you, respect you, and in the end, they'll buy from you. Works every time.

A Brand Is Born

After our initial appearance, the HSN buyer asked when we could come back. Not thinking, I chirped, "Next week!" Van kicked me under the table: we didn't have any product to sell. But I didn't care; I just wanted to be on TV again. Silly as it sounds, in the back of my mind I thought maybe some director would see me burning up the set on HSN and cast me in a movie. Know what? In all the years I've worked with HSN, I've never gotten a phone call from a producer saying, "Rhonda! Baby! I saw you on TV selling brassieres and you simply *must* come and star in my movie with Brad Pitt!" Still, it was television and I was *over the moon.*

But Van knows business, and he knew that we needed product. If the speed with which we'd sold out was any indication, we needed a *lot* of product. Van understood the business end of this immediately. That's why we've been such a perfect team. It didn't matter what he had sold before; the principles were always the same: we needed capital to purchase inventory and a brand to promote.

We used the money we'd made from my first appearance to buy more product, and when I went back on HSN, we doubled our profits from the first show. We did the same thing again and on my third appearance we quadrupled the first show. The next thing you know, we had been on HSN for a year and increased our profits *ten thousand percent* over the first show. We were a runaway success! We were HSN stars and we had a brand. But we needed more than that.

Though we were selling a ton, we were living hand to mouth. We used every dollar we made to buy more product to sell on the next show. We had no capital to invest, knew nothing about the apparel business, and nobody was supporting us. We tried reaching out to investors who might get us the capital we needed to build a company, but they all wanted to own everything. Then a guy I'd dated—a very smart businessman—told Van, "If somebody offers you something that sounds too good to be true, it usually is. I know it's rough for you guys, but keep doing it on your own."

That was good advice, because to this day we own 100 percent of the company and do things our way. We don't have any debt; we paid cash for our building. That gives us a lot more freedom to do things our way and focus on quality.

Shear Honesty: *I was lucky to have Van, because he's a businessman and I was a comedian. You might not be so lucky, so even if you're not planning on starting a business, learn the basics of business. Learn how companies build brands, get capital, market their products, determine their expenses, and set their prices. Those essentials will help you, no matter what you do in life.*

Also, take the same advice we took, and keep what you build. Unless you have no choice, don't go looking for venture capital or angel investors. You'll wind up losing control of what you've built, compromising your values, and hating what you used to love. Work hard, do great work, and the results will come.

Leaving Los Angeles

With HSN demanding that I be on air as often as possible, we started to look at making our own product rather than buying someone else's and putting my name on it. That, like everything else, takes money, which we didn't have. In business terms, we were profitable but illiquid. Next, we looked at "factoring" companies, which advance you cash based on your accounts receivable. In theory, that would give us operating capital, but the factoring companies all wanted a huge cut of our revenues, which Van wouldn't even consider.

Van is great with numbers, and he worked hard to build relationships that made sense for us. For instance, after years of not having a bank behind us, now we have a big credit line. But back then we couldn't find a bank that would work with us. We also had to find factories that would work with our little company, and that was hard, because the minimum number of pieces you can order in the intimate apparel business is sky-high; we didn't need 50,000 corsets. It's the same old story for anyone starting out: nobody believes in you until you make it happen. Those original manufacturers who believed in us are still with us, because they were good to us from Day One, when we were paying up front and didn't have anything to fall back on.

After that first year, we had gone from zero to building something sustainable. We were still based in Los Angeles, so we upgraded to a really nice apartment in Beverly Hills. But then we started thinking we should spend more time in Florida, where HSN is based, because they might use us more. At that time, they would fly me in overnight, I would sell product, and then I would fly home. Our business grew that way. But it was tiring, we were spending a lot of time in Florida, and the flights were tough on our dog, Chicky, so we rented an apartment in St. Petersburg and stayed there for six months.

However, paying six months' rent in Florida and the rent on our place in LA got old fast. We downsized again—this time, to a really small apartment. I wasn't mentally ready to give up Los Angeles yet. By now, the situation had become ridiculous: living in an apartment in Florida, stuff in storage in Los Angeles, the rest of our stuff still in Lafayette. We soon realized that this was not sustainable. It was time to look for a house in St. Pete. We found a place, rented with an option to buy, finally bought, and I gave up my foothold in Los Angeles. We adopted a second dog, and we were Floridians. We've been living there since early 2005.

FOURTH WALL BREAK!

In the beginning, it was completely mortifying to be in Florida. I know how that sounds, but that's how I felt. I didn't want to give up my 310 area code, especially since I lived in Beverly Hills. I was as much an LA snob as you get with people who are snobs about living in Manhattan. There's no place else in the world. For years, I would say, "I'm from Los Angeles," even when I wasn't living there. Florida was unlike anything I expected. The zoning here is strange, so you might see a trailer park next to a mansion next to a doctor's office. I'd look at the homes and think, "Yuck." But living here got into my blood, just like living in LA did. Now I can't imagine living anywhere else.

Falling in Love with Helping Women

Meanwhile, I was learning the business side and Van was being the pragmatic businessman. I wanted success right away, but like my standup comedy career, which took years to build, it takes years to build a successful business and brand. I had to learn about my customers inside and out. I had to learn about textiles, importing, financing, buyers, designing, fit and quality control, labeling, and distribution. I had to learn some of the business basics that were second nature to Van. It was a lot. But there is nothing more satisfying than growing a business from the ground up, especially when you're doing it with your soul mate.

We made mistakes, but the business kept on growing. Before long, I began working with manufacturers and designing based on my own needs. We started as a shapewear company, selling what used to be called girdles. *Girdle* is a dirty word to any woman. We'll suffer for a pair of Christian Louboutins, but do you really want to rearrange your liver and spleen for a wasp waist? I don't. So I started designing based on what felt good on me and made me look my best.

I was edging closer to fifty, and even though I was slender, some mornings I would wake up with—surprise!—a new body part, or a part in a new location. A glob here, a waggle there, and I had to invent items that would help smooth me out comfortably. I knew if they worked for me and my hypochondriac self, they would work for most women. My hunch was right. Customers loved that I wasn't designing for emaciated waifs with thigh gaps but for real women. I also wanted to create a brand for *everyone*. Even when I was a size four, I was curvy and had trouble fitting into things right off the rack. Not good enough; I wanted all women to feel beautiful.

I created a size range that went from a petite XS to a woman's 4X. That's reality, folks. Not every woman is tiny, but every woman deserves to feel gorgeous and sexy. Beauty comes in all shapes and sizes; that's my mantra. Women feel the most vulnerable undressing or trying on bras and panties in a department store under harsh lights. I wanted them to feel comfortable shopping from home, knowing they were getting quality items that would fit and feel magical on their skin—items they could try on in complete privacy, crafted by someone who truly cared about them.

I also designed with my past in mind, inspired by pageant garments and Hollywood costuming. I had learned a lot about the art of illusion and camouflage from years in front of the camera and by befriending costume designers and makeup artists. It was clear: my years in Hollywood and on the runway had been training for my ultimate career—helping women feel better about themselves and their bodies. And since I spent most of my 450 *USA: Up All Night* shows prancing around in lingerie, it was clear that I was meant to be in this industry. I've gone from working *in* lingerie to working *on* lingerie!

As the months and years went on, I loved the industry more and more. It was a surprisingly easy transition from comedian and actress to intimate apparel designer. I reinvented myself without trying. Everyone wants to know what our business plan was. Business plan? It was two things: *survival* and *love*. I don't recommend it to all entrepreneurs, but we played the cards we were dealt and made it work. Van and I were building something wonderful using our strengths: my creativity and marketing skills, and his patient and detailed head for business and finance.

I was falling in love with helping women, and they were loving our company right back. On HSN, I was getting live, on-air testimonials from crying women who told me they weren't able to wear a bra because of the pain it caused them, or that they'd had double mastectomies and my undergarments were the first ones that were soft enough to wear. I got a lot of funny, honest calls.

I thought I could never love anything more than the sound of an audience's laughter, but now I was helping women around the world, and it made my heart glow. This was my ultimate calling. I even had a nun call live on air and tell me she had all the other nuns in the convent wearing my matching Pin-Up Bra and Panty Set. I laughed so hard at that one. You can't get a higher testimonial than that!

Another customer called in one night and said, "Hi, Rhonda, I just have to tell you I love your Ahh Bra and it's just the most comfortable bra I've ever worn. I have all my girlfriends wearing them, my sister loves them, and my mother, who recently passed, even requested that we bury her in her Ahh Bra because she loved it so much!" I did my best not to laugh on air (this was live) and told the caller that I was honored to have brought her mother comfort.

I love getting calls from customers. Women still call in all the time talking about body parts and sharing their names for their "girls" (Thelma & Louise was one), names for muffin tops (one said, "I call it my bear claw, because I don't eat muffins"), and generally being as real with me as if we were a couple of bottles of wine into girl's night, not on live TV with millions watching. It's wonderful.

Shear Honesty: *If there's a better high than having your work change someone's life, they haven't invented it yet. That is the BEST thing about what I do. Use that as a compass for your own ventures. Is what you're doing helping someone else? Could what you aspire to do make the world a little brighter? Even if you're on a life path where you're not helping people directly, you can still volunteer or give of yourself in some way. Helping out is the gift that gives back. It fills you up and makes hard work seem a lot easier. Try it. If you're already doing it, brava.*

The Ahh Bra

I mentioned the Ahh Bra, didn't I? That's foreshadowing. As sales grew, I tried to stay ahead of the curve (no pun intended). I wanted to work with the latest textiles, the newest underwire, the best padding. I became intrigued with yarns that were a combination of nylon and spandex and could be knitted on Italian machines called Santonis, which were derived from hosiery machines but could handle heavier yarns that could create a "four-way stretch." With that yarn, those machines could knit garments on a single continuous cylinder to create a product called "seamless." There are literally no seams on such garments, so there's nothing to dig into the skin or leave marks like elastic or underwire. Those garments would change our company and our lives.

Seamless was in its early stages, but I worked with our Canadian factory first on an arm shaper and then on a bra. I was on air talking about the bra, and I said, "It's like 'Ahhhhhhh...' you won't even know you're wearing a bra." The name stuck, and that's how the Ahh Bra, the most popular bra in the world, was born!

It was Ahh-some, and after that, everything became about the Ahh Lifestyle. Finding your Ahh moment. Being yourself and being comfortable. Even though we've sold more than fifteen thousand different items, that bra came to define our business. It changed the industry, because women started demanding comfort—bras that conformed to their bodies instead of their bodies having to conform to the shape of the bra. Go figure (pun intended)!

I also learned that 90 percent of women don't know their accurate bra size, and every company has its own specs and guidelines anyway. Most gals stick with the size from the first time they were fitted for a proper bra at the age of fourteen, but things change. Things move. As we age and put on a few pounds, the girls get fuller. I became fascinated with bras. For example, did you know that a regular underwire bra is sewn together from more than 100 pieces? I didn't, but I do now. The Ahh Bra is one continuous piece of fabric. I myself can't fathom life without it, and more than 35 million other women worldwide feel the same way.

This was the bra that won awards. This was the bra that made me an entrepreneur and not a "bimbopreneur." I started getting asked to speak in front of business groups and clubs. It felt great, and I only wished that my parents had been there to see their daughter become an award-winning businesswoman.

Then Van said, "Why not do an infomercial just for the bra?" Great idea. We found a reputable, honest company in Canada that would do a deal with us and we produced the first Ahh Bra infomercial on a small budget in our own boutique in St. Petersburg. We all pitched in: writing the script, decorating the set, and finding models and people—friends, employees, family members, random passersby—willing to try the bra and give us honest on-air testimonials. Halfway through the shoot, we put on a runway-style show to show the versatility of the Ahh Bra as a fashion piece. The crew filmed me in the dressing room "getting real" with real women about their bra sizes, what they hated about traditional bras, and what made the Ahh Bra so comfortable and unique. It was TV gold.

The infomercial tested really well and we realized we were onto something. We ramped up production and started selling the Ahh Bra internationally. Our partnership with our Canadian producers flourished, with Shear Enterprises, LLC providing the product while they bought the airtime and handled the placement. Everybody made money. For a while ours was the number-one infomercial in the world, and to date we've sold more than 40 million bras in thirty-four countries.

FOURTH WALL BREAK!

When I found out about the first bra knockoffs, I felt violated. I never saw anything like that coming, because I didn't know the industry and didn't think it would happen. All of a sudden someone is not only copying your work but copying the set you use on TV and even using your product to sell theirs. I was so angry and I couldn't figure out why we couldn't sue. With the Writers Guild or Screen Actors Guild, you have the power to sue. But there was no recourse. None.

At this big New York lingerie show, we got an idea of how brazen these people are. Van and this guy, Keith Marciani, who runs a big infomercial company, had lunch. His company was selling the Genie Bra, a total knockoff of the Ahh Bra, and before lunch he turned to Van and said, "Are you packing?" Meaning, was Van carrying a gun. These are the kind of people we were fighting. At that lunch, Marciani said, "I sleep well at night. I knock people off every day, but the only thing I'm missing is Rhonda. I could make you rich." Thanks, but we're already rich. Those people are why we never did another infomercial.

Knockoffs

Unfortunately, I was about to discover that apparel is a brutal business. If you have a successful product, unscrupulous players will copy it before you can blink. Before too long, knockoffs and new "comfort" bras were popping up in every major intimate apparel line. Imitation is flattery up to a point, but I took those first few knockoffs personally. The Ahh Bra was my baby (I was a proud "bra-ma"), so you can imagine how much it infuriated me that a bunch of slick copycats were copying my bra with record speed.

There wasn't anything we could do. It's hard to patent a popular piece of apparel. Other designers changed the trim or used a different yarn, and bam! They had a piece of our pie. Sleazy overseas companies came out of the woodwork with cheaper versions of our products because that's part of their business model. They copied our marketing, created infomercial sets that looked like ours, and even hired similar models. I was furious but powerless. In LA, if someone steals your script or idea, you're protected by the Writer's Guild, but not in the fashion industry.

Before we knew it, knockoffs were popping up all over the world. It was a game of Whack-a-Mole: go after one knockoff and ten more pop up somewhere else. My team went to the Canton Fair, a huge fair in China for all kinds of products, and found hundreds of booths saying they sold The Original, Authentic Ahh Bra. It became a phenomenon in the industry, and now that seamless fabric is sold everywhere.

At the end of the day, I've had to let go of my anger over the copycats, knowing that my customer is always getting the original and best from me. Nothing can replace a customer's trust, and while we could have sold many more Ahh Bras if we had used cheaper yarns, dyes, or trims (like the other guys do), I'm confident in our product's integrity, and we've gained a loyal following of Ahh-mazing customers because of it.

Shear Honesty: *If you're doing something well, somebody will try to copy it. It sucks, but that's life. In the face of piracy, you have three options. First, you can seek bloody vengeance, which* *is satisfying but potentially messy. Second, you can curl into a ball and let them get away with it. Third, you can prepare for it. Copyright, patent, or trademark what you can. Go public with a website or articles so everyone will know you were first. Have a great lawyer ready to write cease-and-desist letters. And if you're in a business like mine, where preventing piracy is almost impossible, plan on it and get past it. The good thing about being a creative, original thinker is that no matter what, the copycats will always be a step behind you.*

Branching Out

So that's how Rhonda Shear Intimates and Shear Enterprises, LLC became an industry leader. Today, we have more than twenty employees, and we're one of the fastest-growing woman-owned companies in the country, with about 1,200 percent growth in the last three years. We sell more than 5,000 different items on air on HSN, in boutiques, and at large online retailers like HerRoom, Amazon, and Zulily. The business has changed since we started in 2003, and we've worked hard to stay ahead of the curve by offering value, variety, and in-depth information on our own site and through retailers selling our products. We're at $100 million in annual sales, and that's exciting.

I'm proud of our company, where we've come from, and where we're going. I adore designing and seeing my creations come to life, but the icing on the cake is when the customer loves what I have designed. I get chills when a customer says that a product changed her life and the way she feels about herself.

Creating a brand is personal for me. Each product has to stand for what I believe in before I'll put my name on it. Each has to have an identifiable look and feel that will appeal to our customers. Bras and shapewear are still our mainstays, and I make sure that old-fashioned Hollywood glamour shines through all my designs. I take otherwise basic-looking silhouettes and knit in jacquards, add feminine details like lace, or create beautiful color stories in my multipack items to make my line mine. I'm proud of the fun and flirty retro feel we combine with the latest in intimate apparel technology and cutting-edge fabrication. Fun, flirty, and feminine is what the Rhonda Shear brand is about.

We're also always trying new things, because you can't be static in any business. Innovation and creativity win. We've branched into loungewear, camisoles, pajamas, and nightgowns. We've launched a perfume on HSN: Shear Desire, with Playmate Alana Campos as my signature model. I felt she captured the essence of the notes: playful, sensual, mysterious, captivating. We worked with a top New York perfumer from scent to bottle design. It's really exciting to launch something as personal as a fragrance and have other women love it.

How's this for Hollywood fun? We're launching a sexy line of intimates called Up All Night! I always joke that I sell "lingerie with a purpose." I've yet to meet a woman who didn't like having a few sexy pieces in her lingerie drawer. It's also hard to find sexy, sassy lingerie in fuller sizes (that bias against real women again), so the Up All Night line goes from small to 3X. Sexy comes in all shapes and sizes.

Designing for Real Women

For decades the intimate apparel industry was run almost exclusively by men. That must be why most products are designed for fantasy women named Victoria. But I'm a real woman designing for real women. You achieve success by knowing who your customers are and letting them know that you understand them. Real women sometimes need clothing that smooths this, lifts that, keeps them cool when a hot flash hits, or supports the girls without underwire (just call me the Wizard of Ahhs).

These are the things women want, the things we need, and the things we can't find in the junior section. We have curves—some we want to minimize and some we want to flaunt. I know that, because that's me. In any creative line of work, you're faced with the same question: create for myself or create for my audience? I'm a firm believer that you create what lights you up, because you can't read people's minds. The best art doesn't come from a focus group, but from the vision of the artist. Create your passion, and if you're in touch with your audience, that passion will speak to them.

When Van and I started out of our bedroom office in Beverly Hills, we were the designers, buyers, accounting, shipping, packing, labeling, you name it. If you are going to build a business, you have to do it all. We still do that. It sets an example, because everyone sees that you are not too important to do every job. But now we work side by side with our incredible team. We want each of our employees to feel valued. That's what leadership is, and it's how small companies like ours can do such a large volume of business. We surround ourselves with people who have the drive, skill, and heart to get things done, we work just as hard as they do, and we love every minute of it.

HSN is still our biggest customer. I average about ten hours of airtime a month, and we make about 40 percent of our sales on the network. I love being able to go on air and explain each product in detail to my customers. That can't happen in a brick and mortar store. Nothing beats a designer talking about a product that she created, and I love connecting with my customers.

Shear Honesty: *If you're a woman (and most readers of this book probably are), and you're not wearing things that make you feel beautiful and confident, why not? Try it; it really does make a difference in how you carry yourself. Remember my production assistant from USA: Up All Night who wore sexy stuff under her schlumpy outerwear? She did it because she wanted to remember that even when she was treated like one of the guys, she wasn't. She was special. Look, life's tough. You need every edge you can get. If that means wearing something sexy and flattering that makes you feel va-va-voom, what can it hurt? That little swagger might be the difference between no and yes!*

Pinch Me

That's how my little company came to be. We've managed to thrive in a cutthroat business, and while we deal with challenges every single day, the good is very good. We've won a lot of awards:

- *Inc.* 5000 List of "Fastest Growing Companies" 2013

- *Tampa Bay Business Journal*'s "Tampa Bay 100" 2013

- Ernst & Young Retail and Consumer Products Category, Florida Entrepreneur of the Year 2012

- Women President's Organization Third Fastest Growing Women-Owned Business 2012, Sponsored by American Express

- Enterprising Women of the Year 2012 ($25 million+

category)

- Best Product Award at HSN 2012 for the Ahh Bra

- *Gulf Coast Business Review* Entrepreneur of the Year 2012

- *Tampa Bay Business Journal's* Businesswoman of the Year 2012

- *Entrepreneur* Women in Business Stevie Award Silver 2012

- Most Innovative Company of the Year Stevie Award Bronze 2012

FOURTH WALL BREAK!

Winning the Ernst & Young Award was unbelievable. Mindy Grossman, who runs HSN, nominated me. You go through a judging process and they interview you and you go to a dinner. It was like Miss Louisiana, only I didn't have to wear a bikini! I was up for Entrepreneur of the Year, and I won, but only I got recognized, not Van, became my name is on the company. But he was wonderful, of course; we both knew we'd built the company together. In my speech, I ad-libbed and said, "I never thought of myself as an entrepreneur. Maybe a bimbopreneur." That stuck, and it opened other doors, got me lots of speeches, and other awards. It was also a great year for the business; people wanted to buy us. I felt so validated. I still go in and visit my awards from time to time. It's all very special because we built the company, and our lives, from nothing.

That success has given Van and me the chance to get involved with charities and become part of the St. Petersburg business community. It's let me advocate for other women entrepreneurs who are just starting out, teaching them to be resilient and take risks. Van and I agree that if something is worth a try, we go for it. You never know what will be the next big thing, and you'll never find out if you don't take a risk.

Risk is a part of the game, just like in comedy, when you walk out on a stage in front of hundreds of people hoping your jokes will land. Sometimes, ideas surprise you. You create something that you're sure will kick ass, and it flops. You try something you figure will flop, and it sells out. Sometimes, you roll the dice, and if things don't work out, you try again. Once you've gone out on a limb once and survived, you always know you can do it again.

But apart from helping women feel great about themselves, the most satisfying part of this business ride is that nobody thought I could do it. I was supposedly just a dumb, blonde ex-actress. But while I've playfully called myself a "bimbopreneur," I'm nobody's fool. There are a lot of versions of Rhonda Shear, just like there are a lot of versions of you. We can be anything we set our minds to, and if you choose to reinvent yourself, you don't need anyone's approval. You just need them to get out of the way.

Stereotypes were made to be broken. I've never had any interest in a cookie-cutter lifestyle. I sure as hell haven't lived one. No matter what happens, I believe in myself. I know that I can roll with the punches and come out a winner.

It's Ahh-mazing.

⮌ ON THE WAY TO TODAY ⮌

What did your faithful servant pick up from my trek into the jungles of design, apparel, retail, and home shopping? Let's see…

- ☐ Love's grand, but money's important.

- ☐ Sometimes, it's okay to just survive until the stars align.

- ☐ There's always another option. Don't give up.

- ☐ You can survive anything as long as you have trust.

- ☐ If you can't give something up, you don't own it. It owns you.

- ☐ Debt stinks. Pay it off.

- ☐ Opportunity can come from the strangest places.

- ☐ The answer is always "Yes, I can do that." Then, pee yourself in private and figure it out.

- ☐ Always choose quality. Let the other guy be the cheap commodity.

- ☐ Know your audience, their aspirations, and their pain.

- ☐ Keep ownership of what you build.

- ☐ When you find people who will be loyal to you when you're just starting out, stay loyal to them after you make it.

- ☐ In hiring, character means more than experience. You can train people with great character to move mountains.

- ☐ Don't sell. Connect.

LESSON ELEVEN
Women Should Feel Great About Being Women

—— *In which our heroine finds what she cares about, helps women with breast cancer, makes stomachs beautiful again, gives hope to abused young girls, dances with the stars, and finds her place as a philanthropist.* ——

My life today is so rich that I can't help but give back to others, and the group I care most about helping is women. Now, when you think of an advocate for women, I'm probably not the first person who comes to mind. I've spent a good part of my life conforming to a lot of female stereotypes. I was a beauty queen. In Hollywood, I was often cast as the designated jiggle who would walk into the set with her hair teased and her cleavage popping. These days, I like to play up my shopping, my Barbie doll mansion, and my bling. But before you dismiss me as an aging, clueless ex-beauty queen obsessed with her toys, listen up.

Aging? Sure. Everybody's doing it, and as they say, it beats the alternative. Anyway, I wouldn't want to go back in time. I've loved every stage of my life. But clueless? Not on your life. I was a child when I started in the world of pageants, but by my early twenties

I was making conscious decisions about the direction of my life. Sure, I played up my physical attributes, but I did it with a goal in mind. Hollywood used me for my smile and my boobs, but I used Hollywood right back and got it all: the career, the fella, the notoriety, the business, the wealth, and the satisfaction.

As my life has changed from that of a serial dater and comedian to a married, successful entrepreneur, my perspective on what's important has changed as well. I've come to understand something: *I've always been a feminist.* My life has always been about doing what I wanted to do despite other people dismissing me and telling me I couldn't do it. According to the powers that be (mostly men), I was too young to run for office. I was too sexy to be a success in standup. I was too inexperienced to be a successful businesswoman.

They were all wrong.

What none of them ever saw was that I've always been extremely focused, not looking right or left of the target. I was never lazy. I never rested on my laurels. I never cared about what the competition was doing, and I still don't. I've fed off the doubts and proved that being beautiful, sexy, and funny has nothing to do with being business-savvy, determined, and capable.

That understanding, along with my financial success and influence, has changed me from an "accidental feminist" into a real one. I love giving back to my community and helping women. I've been asked to be a keynote speaker at many events, especially events targeting women entrepreneurs. I enjoy sharing the details of my journey and the wisdom I've picked up along the way. Plus, not many speakers can nail a punchline like I can or share stories about getting lucky at the Playboy Mansion.

I'm privileged to be at a place in my life where I get to give back, and nothing gives me more joy than making a difference in the lives of other women.

Double Standard

What I do is important, because despite all the progress women have made, society still calculates a woman's value based mostly on her looks. That's why I had a small amount shaved off my nose. I don't regret it, because I knew it would give me an edge in getting the roles I wanted. But should it have been necessary at all?

As I've already said, I'm not opposed to cosmetic enhancement if it makes you look and feel better about yourself. But the real question is, why is there a double standard of beauty for men and women? Why aren't men subjected to the same standards? Why are men in Hollywood allowed to age, but women aren't? Why was Jack Nicholson (sixty) an acceptable boyfriend for Helen Hunt (thirty-four) in As Good As It Gets? Those are questions worth asking.

If I had a young daughter today, I would be worried. Society's view of women as sexual beings first means we're always potential targets of sexual violence. Like it or not, that's the truth. I'm always reminding the girls who work for me to be careful. I'm always super careful and aware of my surroundings, and I don't take chances. I don't think women should be paranoid, but there are a lot of dangerous people out there who don't care if you're old or young. Many women don't know how to handle a dangerous situation, and if something does happen, they don't know who to talk to or what to do.

I can't stress this enough for a woman of any age and any size: learn how to defend yourself. Contact organizations like T.A.K.E. Defense about classes. You'll learn the right self-defense mindset, situational awareness, simple moves to disable an attacker long enough so you can escape, and why you don't need to be a black belt in anything in order to protect yourself. If you have daughters, take them and teach them.

> **Shear Honesty:** *Self-defense isn't so much about the ability to kick ass (no matter what the movies show, a 120-pound woman is not going to take out a 210-pound man, no matter how much training she has) but the confidence not to let anyone mess with you. If threatened, will you curl into a ball or say, "You are NOT going to do this to me!" and fight back? It's about refusing to be a victim.*

Giving Women Their Bodies Back

One of the other women's issues that's near and dear to my heart found me rather than me finding it: breast cancer. Once the Ahh Bra became big, we were flooded with testimonials from breast cancer survivors saying things like, "Oh my God, this bra is amazing! I just had breast cancer and it's the only thing I can put next to my skin because it's so irritated." I've heard story after story like that since the bra became a bestseller.

One woman who called into HSN told me she'd had a mastectomy and breast reconstruction but was so sore after her surgery that she couldn't dress or leave the house. "I could not wear anything, and I had to wear something," she said. "I couldn't put things up over my head, but I could pull your bra over my hips and get it on. If I wasn't for you, I couldn't go to work or be seen in public." She said I had literally saved her life. You can't imagine how good that makes me feel.

FOURTH WALL BREAK!

The testimonials are incredible because they're real. These are not actresses. They're real women calling in, and they have funny names for their boobs, bellies, and butts, and they just want to be heard. Some call me in tears because they've lost weight and wearing these products makes them feel so good. I heard from one policewoman who said she liked to wear the Ahh Bra under her bulletproof vest! It was kind of like getting laughs from a standup crowd, only better. When you can make a difference in people's lives, that's cool.

It hasn't just been cancer survivors, either. We've gotten a steady stream of testimonials from other women thanking us for helping them get their bodies back. They wanted to feel like their body was their own again after having a baby, and after putting on our shapewear they felt like they had their old figures back. Women who've had breast augmentation have told us that the bra was the only thing that was comfortable because they couldn't wear underwire. Women have said that our products helped them keep better posture, get through their workday without pain, and more.

When those stories got out, the American Cancer Society came calling and I was glad to help. First, it was donating bras to local breast cancer survivors. That's a big deal, because specialized bras for wearing after breast cancer can be expensive. But there's more to it than that. When you take away a woman's breast—or worse, both breasts—you take away part of her womanhood. Some women take it better than others, but when you cut off a breast, their confidence often disappears. I've heard about women who said, "Take them off, I don't care," and others who mourn like they've had a death in the family.

Any surgical alteration can be disfiguring to a woman who's sensitive about her body image. One girlfriend who had a lumpectomy told me that because one breast is smaller than the other now, she's terribly ashamed. So I made bras where you can pad one side and not the other. It's definitely an advantage to be a woman doing this, because I get it. I understand what it's like to place such importance on your body, especially the girls.

D Cups

Back in the 1980s, I had my boobs done for the same reason I had my nose done: for myself. I had a C cup but didn't love the shape of my breasts when I was braless, and we're talking the time when the braless, unbound look was in. I was losing parts that were going to girls with bigger, shapelier busts, so I went to Dr. Steven Hoefflin. What Dr. Kamer was to faces, Steven was to boobs.

I loved my new girls. They looked amazing. Dr. Hoefflin took me from a small C to a nice D cup. The shape was superb, I fit in with all the jiggle girls of the '80s, and I immediately felt more confident at auditions. Years later, when I posed for *Playboy*, none of the editors could believe that I'd had a bit of enhancement. There was no scar and they were soft, not shaped like softballs.

Today, I'm a triple D, which is good because my customers know that I can relate to being large-busted. But sometimes I wish that I was a C-cup again. If I'd known I would grow two more D-cups around those original Ds, I might have done things differently. I'm convinced that Dr. Hoefflin added fertilizer when he did the augmentation.

I've always loved my boobs regardless of their size, and I know how important it is for women to feel beautiful and feminine. Breast cancer may be a sensitive topic for some—I know women who can talk about the subject all day long while others won't even say the "C word"— like it's catching—but I have learned so much about it through my customers that I knew I had to do whatever I could to help.

Shear Honesty: *In her essay "In Jerusalem," the great author Susan Sontag once wrote, "Whatever is happening, something else is always going on." That means that no matter what you might think you see on the surface, you never know what someone is going through, so don't judge. I had no idea there were women who felt so disfigured by breast cancer surgery that they wouldn't leave the house. But you listen, you empathize, and you learn that yours isn't the only experience. That's how you start helping.*

Not Going without a Fight

The other topic close to my heart is women and body image. In our culture, it's still pretty messed up. Look at how crazy the media goes when a magazine runs a photo spread of a model who hasn't been Photoshopped, or uses a "plus size" model who's still thinner than 80 percent of the women on the street. Look at the social media feeds of girls who proudly starve themselves down to shadows. Talk about warped perceptions of beauty!

Women have been doing strange things to conform to society's expectations of beauty for a long time. When I was growing up, girls would stuff their bras with Kleenex (one of our funnier family stories revolved around one of my brother's dates, who jumped into our pool only to have the toilet paper stuffed into her swimsuit top come floating up to the surface).

I grew up in the era of the pre-Madonna cone bra. Remember

that? The cup was shaped like an ice cream cone. Who in hell has breasts shaped like that? Many a woman has excused herself to the bathroom at a party, taken off a bra or piece of shapewear that was supposed to twist her body into sex kitten form, and tossed that thing into a garbage can. Women should not have to suffer to look our best.

I also hate this idea that women's bodies shouldn't change with time. They do. When I hit fifty, fifty hit back. Seemingly overnight, I woke up with pit cleavage and muffin tops, and my muffin tops turned into wedding cakes. Where was this extra body stuff coming from? Had the tooth fairy turned into the evil body fairy in the middle of the night? Bitch.

Women over forty have been dealt a rotten hand in our culture. We're in our prime as far as our careers, wisdom, earning power, and political influence. We finally have our shit together in relationships and life in general. We're probably at our sexual peak and hot as Hades. But as soon as our butts get an inch wider or we show a hint of cellulite, we're passed over for the promotion or the part or ditched for a younger girlfriend. It's not fair. It's not right. And I'm not letting women go down without a fight.

My company is all about helping women feel better about their bodies no matter what their bodies are like. We're all beautiful in so many ways that have nothing to do with washboard abs: our intelligence, compassion, sense of humor, sexiness, and the depth of life experience that a twenty-five-year-old Hooters waitress with pneumatic boobs just can't have.

I want women to feel good about their shape. A lot of women hate their stomachs. It's childbirth; the stomach never quite goes back to the way it was. I never had kids, but with age and menopause, my stomach wants to do its own thing. I hear complaints all the time about body parts with minds of their own, so I've designed products that help women feel proud of their stomachs, butts, and breasts—feel beautiful. I think feeling beautiful is a human right.

Shear Honesty: *Look, your body is going to change. Them's the breaks, ladies. If you don't favor shapewear, there are two things you can do. First, take care of yourself. It's amazing what an exercise program and a great diet can do to stave off the wobbles and wiggles while keeping you lean and fit. Women in their fifties and sixties today are hotter than ever, and it's because they do CrossFit and run triathlons and do other crazy stuff that keeps them in prime shape. Second, live. No matter what, you're going to get wrinkles and age spots and crepey skin on your arms. Turn those signs of aging into signs of a life lived fully: travel, start a company, produce a play, build a house, have a torrid affair with a guy half your age. The marks of aging are a map. Make yours a map of someplace exotic.*

PACE

I also donate bras to battered women's shelters and to an organization called PACE. PACE is a regional education program that takes in girls who end up in the juvenile justice system, get thrown out of school, leave home because of abuse, or come from a family that's been wrecked by divorce, drugs, or violence. You would not believe the stories. These girls act out not because they're bad kids but because they have horrifying home situations.

PACE puts them in classes, and while they can't graduate from PACE, the organization keeps them on track with their studies so they're not behind when they're ready to go back to regular high school. They even give each girl a personal guidance counselor who talks to them, advises them, and makes them feel cared about—sometimes, she's the first adult in their lives who's actually listened to them and held them accountable. They even send them home with food if they're hungry.

Some of these girls are so traumatized that it's amazing they're alive. One girl wouldn't talk at all, until finally it came out that a neighbor was raping her. PACE sent her to a doctor, and they found out that she had cervical cancer from an HPV infection. She was treated successfully, the neighbor was arrested, and she was finally able to talk about the horrors that she'd been living. PACE saved her in three ways.

I'm honored to supply PACE with undergarments. One of the ways they reward the girls for doing well in their studies is by having them do a fashion show. Or they might let the girls rummage through the PACE clothes closets and pick out one or two beautiful things to keep. My eyes were opened when I talked with a girl who said, "I want to thank you. I got one of your bras out of the closet, and my mother and I share it." That brought tears to my eyes. Having nice undergarments should *not* be a luxury.

I told that young lady, "From now on, you will have beautiful undergarments that are yours alone." Every Christmas, every girl at our local PACE Center for Girls receives brand new underwear from Shear Enterprises, LLC. I love PACE because they do amazing work, and they're in the community so I can see the results. I've met some terrific young ladies from the program who not only finished their studies and graduated from high school but went on to college as well. It's thrilling to be a small part of that.

I'm on the board of the heart disease awareness nonprofit Go Red for Women, which means a lot to me because my father died of a heart attack at sixty-nine and my brother had open-heart surgery about three years ago. I have the genes for heart disease, a silent killer of women, so working to raise awareness is something I care about a great deal.

The Florida Holocaust Museum in St. Petersburg asked me to do a fundraising voice-over for their "learning trunk" program. They send these trunks free to any school that asks for them, from eighth to twelfth grade. The trunks contain age-appropriate lessons about the Holocaust, with hands-on tools and artifacts that the students can use and learn about. It's really neat. The trunks are free but the shipping isn't, so I was happy to record that voice-over and help them reach their fundraising goal so they could teach kids about hate and genocide.

Shear Honesty: *We think of heart disease as something that kills men, but did you know that after menopause, women have a higher risk of heart attack? It's true. Plus, our symptoms aren't the same as men's, so women tend to overlook a heart attack until it's too late. Get yourself checked out. It's easy. Simple bloodwork, a blood pressure cuff, and you'll have a clear idea of your risks and what you can do to reduce them. Learn more at goredforwomen.org.*

Fighting Abuse

I also do a lot to benefit abused women. In 2013, I did *Dancing with the Stars* for Hands Across the Bay, a nonprofit run by my girlfriend Julie Weintraub, and that was a blast. They treated it like the real *Dancing with the Stars*; I had to train for three months. I was a dancer for years and you don't ever lose the chops completely, but it was still a lot of work. In the end I got to wear a fabulous red dress with fringe and sparkles, carry a white feather boa, and shimmy on stage with my fantastic partner, Alberto. And we won!

FOURTH WALL BREAK!

Dancing with the Stars was a blast because I was a dancer when I was young and hadn't danced on a stage in years. Plus, I wasn't in the kind of shape I was in years before, so it helped me improve there. Once I got my groove on, that dancer's mentality came back and even though I was up against younger dancers, I won Best Female Dancer. It's not easy; partner dancing is really hard. I like to lead; I'm not a great follower, which will surprise no one, least of all Van.

Hands Across the Bay picks four charities a year to benefit, and they're almost always for battered and abused women. Last year, I got to meet a marvelous young dancer who's now a big part of the charity. I noticed that one side of her face drooped a little bit, and later I found out that when she broke up with her college boyfriend, he called her a few months later and said he wanted to come over and say goodbye.

When she met him in front of her mother's house, he pulled out a knife and stabbed her more than twenty times, severing nerves in her face and neck. She survived, and now she's this amazing advocate for abused women, so beautiful and brave. Meanwhile, the son of a bitch who attacked her went to prison, hopefully for the rest of his life. I'm proud to be part of any organization that includes courageous women like her.

My company sends undergarments to another organization that helps the victims of domestic violence feel better about their bodies so they have the confidence to go on job interviews. That's the first step to independence for a lot of abused women. It can take so little to change a person's life.

Blessed

Barely a day goes by that I don't have the chance to help a woman feel better or live better. I'm deeply blessed to be able to do that. I get so much more out of it than I give. The thank-yous are humbling and rewarding. In fact, my love of charity and helping gets me in trouble sometimes, because it takes me away from running my business. In the last year, I've had to back off a little. But if I had time to do more, I would.

I just tell everyone the same thing: "I'm here, and if you need it and I can provide it, you've got it." A few years back, I decorated my house as a winter wonderland for Christmas and opened it up as a fundraiser for Florida Orchestra. People paid $25 to walk through my house, if you can believe that! We had a live Santa, a sexy Mrs. Claus singing at the piano, a giant live teddy bear, and a Nutcracker (my awesome friend Chuck, who's also the best realtor in town) greeting donors as they walked through.

I love all of it. I love being involved and helping. In a close-knit city like St. Pete, I can be hands-on and really make a difference. I'm privileged to have the financial resources and celebrity to make things happen.

I've never faced the challenges some women face. I haven't had cancer, thank God. I've never had someone beat the shit out of me and kick me out of my house. But I have had hard times. I've hit the financial rock bottom and been in some scary situations with men, so I know about fear and desperation. I know about being judged by your looks and kicked to the curb when you no longer fit the ideal of youth and beauty. That's why it's so important to me to help women. After all, we're all in this together.

∽ ON THE WAY TO TODAY ∽

What have cancer survivors, abuse survivors, body-shamed women, tough young girls, and my own female employees taught me about being a woman? A lot...

- ☐ *When you feel bad, give. Help someone.*
- ☐ *Don't be afraid, but don't be reckless, either.*
- ☐ *Men are not the arbiters of any woman's worth.*
- ☐ *Beauty norms are not only unrealistic but unhealthy. Don't feel pressure to conform to them.*
- ☐ *Sometimes, people just need someone to listen and tell them they're not alone.*
- ☐ *Often, all it takes to make someone's life better is for someone else to care a little.*
- ☐ *What's inconsequential for you might be everything to somebody else. Perspective.*
- ☐ *We're much stronger than we realize. We're survivors.*
- ☐ *Speak up if you suspect a woman is in trouble, because she might be afraid to.*
- ☐ *Success comes with a responsibility to give back.*
- ☐ *We're all in this together.*

EPILOGUE

*A*nd that's it. Well, not really. I could go on and on with more stories if I wanted to. Heck, just looking for material for this book led me to my old diaries from my Hollywood days, and they reminded me of so many things: the time Loretta Lynn sang "Happy Birthday" to me, the time I escorted the great Sir Lawrence Olivier off the stage at the Emmys, and the time I talked makeup in the green room with one of my idols, Joan Collins. The point is, I've had an amazing life, and I've been proud to share it with you.

The funny thing is, until I did this book I didn't realize what a feminist I've been my whole life. Maybe that's because I was always typecast as every anti-feminist stereotype: the bimbo, the sexy neighbor, the sexy bimbo, you name it. But I learned that if you use it right and keep your wits about you, sex appeal and beauty can become power. So I played the game and played it well, and now I get to decide how I play.

You've probably heard of the book *The Secret*. It's basically about putting your goals out there and seeing them come to pass before they do. That's something I have been doing my whole life, long before that book came out. I have always visualized where I wanted to be and what I wanted to accomplish, whether it was winning a pageant, getting an acting gig, landing a joke, or completing a sale. I saw the end result in my mind and put it out there for the universe to work on. But I didn't stop there. I also put in the work. I trained. I prepared. I believed in myself.

If anything, my life is a testament to the power of positive thinking. Seeing the glass half full, not half empty. A winner is never a quitter, and a quitter is never a winner. Corny as those sayings may be (and I heard them for years from my father and pageant officials) they work. But this is my favorite: *luck favors the prepared.* There is only one way to make luck: work your butt off. Of course, you don't see how true this is while you're going through things. I didn't; nobody does. Instead, every tiny obstacle and temporary setback is the end of the world. If I had a dollar for every tear I shed over a loss or a rejection, I would be retired. But you learn from every loss. Your skin grows thicker. You become more focused and look only at your end goal.

I've learned from my years as an actress, comedian, and entrepreneur that being yourself is the ultimate secret weapon. In my life today, I've considered going into politics (I'm thinking about a run for the St. Petersburg city council, so stay tuned) and reviving my career in comedy, which remains my first love. I'm always pushing the boundaries of my business and using it in any way I can to help women feel better about themselves and live better lives. I've written this book, which will lead to who knows what?

The point is, nobody thought I could do the things I did when I set out to do them—until I did them. That's the way of things: nobody, not even the people closest to you, will completely believe you can do what you say you'll do until you're standing in front of then with the award, the diploma, or the big check. Don't wait for other people's validation. Find out what you're hungry for, clear a path toward it, and don't ever let anyone tell you that you can't get there.

The last piece of advice I want to give you is this: have goals, but don't be blinded by them. Be open to other opportunities that you didn't plan for, because while life might throw you curveballs, sometimes they'll be terrific curveballs. For example, I wanted my own sitcom more than anything, but I wasn't so single-minded about it that when USA: *Up All Night* came along that I didn't give it a shot. That one decision changed my life. When the chance to appear on HSN turned into a once-in-a-lifetime shot at starting a business, I went for it, along with Van. It didn't matter that I didn't know the apparel business or that I was still halfway in Los Angeles; I had an open mind, and that decision, too, changed everything.

I love my life. I love the richness and fun of my past and the people from that past who are still with me. I love my present life with Van, living in my beautiful house, spending time with my wonderful friends, and growing my company. I love my future, because I don't know what it holds. Maybe I'll travel. Maybe I'll marry Chuck. Maybe I'll start a second company, launch a charity, go back on the road as a comedian, or run for governor. I have no idea what will happen, but I know this: I *always* land on my feet. With perfect, sparkly toenails, of course.

There's no magic to what I've done, ladies. Confidence is the main ingredient for a successful life. You have what it takes, even if you don't realize it. So much of life is having the faith to show up and try. You can win the job, the gig, the person of your dreams. I did it when all the odds were against me.

Mindy Grossman paid me the nicest compliment at a birthday party she threw for me. She said, "All women love you, young and old alike. You transcend age." I think that's because I love myself, and that gives girls and women permission to love themselves. And that's my last word: *love yourself*. You are amazing, and if nobody else knows it yet, show them what they've been missing. Maybe you won't be a beauty queen, but you can have a beautiful life.

 *From the keeper of the sizzle kiss,*

it's Rhonda, UP...all night!

Nighty night!